Monetary Policy, Interest Rate Rules, and the Term Structure of Interest Rates

STUDIEN ZU INTERNATIONALEN WIRTSCHAFTSBEZIEHUNGEN

Herausgegeben von Prof. Dr. Michael Frenkel

Band 8

PETER LANG
Frankfurt am Main · Berlin · Bern · Bruxelles · New York · Oxford · Wien

Ralf Fendel

Monetary Policy, Interest Rate Rules, and the Term Structure of Interest Rates

Theoretical Considerations and Empirical Implications

PETER LANG
Europäischer Verlag der Wissenschaften

Bibliographic Information published by the Deutsche Nationalbibliothek
The Deutsche Nationalbibliothek lists this publication in the Deutsche Nationalbibliografie; detailed bibliographic data is available in the internet at <http://www.d-nb.de>.

ISSN 1618-503X
ISBN-10: 3-631-55894-5
ISBN-13: 978-3-631-55894-2
US-ISBN 0-8204-8738-4

Printed in Germany 1 2 3 4 5 7

www.peterlang.de

For Elena and Fabiana

Preface

The subsequent piece of work has been accepted as my habilitation thesis at the WHU – Otto Beisheim School of Management (Vallendar) in June 2006. Without the persistent support of many colleagues and good friends this project could have hardly been accomplished. In the first place I would like to express my sincere thanks to Professor Michael Frenkel. For many years I have not only benefited from his professional competence but also from our amicable relationship.

I am also much obligated to my actual and former colleagues at the Department of Economics at the WHU. In particular, these are Dr. Katja Funke, Isabell Koske, Kerstin Frank, Irene Delzer, Christoph Swonke, Dr. Günter Schmidt, Jan-Christoph Rülke, and PD Dr. Georg Stadtmann. All of them have contributed significantly to this work. A special thank is directed to Professor Jürgen Weigand who agreed to act as the second assessor for my habilitation thesis.

Additionally, I profited from professional advice from many colleagues outside the WHU. Among them are Professor Georg von Fürstenberg, Professor Jordi Galí, and Professor Matthew Canzoneri. A special thank is devoted to the members of the Deutsche Bundesbank Research Department, where I spent six productive months in 2004. Among them are Sandra Eickmeier, Dr. Heinz Hermann, and Dr. Karsten Ruth.

Without the constant support of my family over the course of the last years it would not have been possible to master the habilitation. A deep thank has to be devoted to my parents who always believed in me and my work. Finally, I would like to thank the two most important persons in my life for their understanding and their energetic backing during good and bad times: "mille grazie" to my wife Elena and my daughter Fabiana.

Ralf Fendel — Sulzbach (Taunus), October 2006

Content

List of Figures

List of Tables

Introduction and Overview

During the past decade, various issues of stabilization policy have returned to the macroeconomic research agenda. This process has been stimulated by the development of a new model generation that combines elements of real business cycle theory with new Keynesian economics of nominal rigidities. Within this new research agenda, monetary policy has gained renewed interest of academics. In particular, the formulation and the empirical testing of interest rate rules to guide and to describe central bank behavior is currently a main part of macroeconomic research activities. This study is intended to provide a critical analysis of the main findings that this research has put forth so far, and to contribute to the ongoing research. With respect to the latter, the contribution of this study mainly lies in the inclusion of the term structure of interest rates into the theoretical and empirical research on interest rate rules.

The study is divided into two parts. Part I consists of chapters 1 through 3. It intends to contribute to the ongoing research program and also presents a structured overview of this research. Taken together, all three chapters of part I provide an extensive critical analysis of the status quo in macroeconomic research on stabilization policy. Individually, each of the first three chapters can be seen as condensed review of a particular field within the comprehensive research program.

Chapter 1 gives a general introduction to the new directions in stabilization policies that are commonly summarized as the "new neoclassical synthesis". The chapter highlights the main findings and policy implications of the "new neoclassical synthesis". The appendix to chapter 1 provides a formal description of the baseline model of the "new neoclassical synthesis". This model belongs to the class of dynamic general equilibrium models and is, thus, not immediately suitable for policy analysis. Therefore, chapter 1 also demonstrates how this large-scale model can be reduced to a more convenient model that consists of only three equations. The condensed model is often refereed to as the "new IS/LM model" and is becoming increasingly popular in policy analyses.

Within the research program characterized in chapter 1, monetary policy has found a renewed interest. No matter which scales and which particular focus the models under consideration have, monetary policy is normally formulated as a monetary policy rule within that model. For instance, the "new IS/LM model" contains an interest rate rule as one of its three equations. Chapter 2, therefore, provides a closer look at monetary policy rules and their theoretical foundation such as the derivation of interest rate rules. It also contains a proposal for a classification scheme in order to categorize monetary policy rules for the subsequent analyses and discusses their applicability for monetary policy in practice. The appendices to this chapter contain analytical details for the derivation of a welfare criterion of the central bank and an optimal interest rate rule based on this welfare criterion as well as an analytical analysis of the determinacy of interest rate rules within dynamic rational expectation models like the "new IS/LM model".

Chapter 3 is closely connected to chapter 2 and focuses on the empirical analysis of monetary policy rules. It discusses econometric issues of the estimation of interest rate rules and also provides estimates of monetary policy rules in the form of interest rate rules which serve as benchmarks for subsequent empirical analyses. Here – like in all empirical analyses presented in the different chapters – the focus is on the monetary policy of the Deutsche Bundesbank during the period before the creation of the European Monetary Union and on the monetary policy of the European Central Bank afterwards. Particularly, the estimates for the later represent a new contribution to the existing literature, since hardly any estimates for the ECB have so far been presented.

Part II of the study combines the theory and the empirical evidence of interest rate rules with the term structure of interest rates. It comprises chapters 4 through 6. Whereas part I focuses on the critical analysis of the research, part II mainly contains new and original research results. Chapter 4 extents the optimizing model for an optimal interest rate rule discussed in chapter 2 and explicitly contains arguments of the term structure of interest rates. The optimal rule in the presence of term structure effects can directly be compared to the one derived in chapter 2. Chapter 4 also discusses the more general consequences of term structure effects for the conduct of monetary policy.

Chapter 5 picks up the issue of the information content of the term structure for monetary policy and broadens the scope of the empirical analysis of chapter 3 by accounting for term structure effects in the estimation of interest rate rules for the Deutsche Bundesbank and the European Central Bank. It is shown that the information content of the term structure significantly enters the empirical reaction functions and, thus, validates the theoretical arguments from the analysis of chapter 4. Such estimations have so far not yet been presented in the literature.

Chapter 6 presents a new approach for estimating monetary policy rules together with term structure effects. It combines the research on interest rate rules with affine term structure models which represent a popular tool in the finance literature. In doing so, an estimation procedure for interest rate rules based on the Kalman filter approach consistent with the absence of arbitrage in financial markets is developed and presented. The appendices to this chapter also provide technical details of the estimation procedure.

Part I: Monetary Policy and Interest Rate Rules

Chapter 1

The New Neoclassical Synthesis and the New Directions in Stabilization Policies: An Overview

1.1 Introduction

An understanding of business cycles and the optimal policy response to their occurrence still lies at the heart of macroeconomic research. Starting with the contributions of John Maynard Keynes, we have witnessed an ongoing intellectual debate on these issues. Despite the knowledge macroeconomists have gained in both empirical and theoretical work, we still lack a clear understanding of the driving forces of business cycles, and thus continue the search for an appropriate policy response.

Recently, a new class of models suggested a new approach to business cycle theory. Goodfriend and King (1997) labeled this class of models the "new neoclassical synthesis" (NNS), whereas other authors prefer to label the fresh impetus the "new Keynesian models" (Galí, 2002). The first title may be an overstatement and some economists dislike it for this reason (Blanchard, 1997). Nevertheless, it indicates one crucial characteristic of the new class of models, which apparently merge two formerly opposing schools of thought. Historically, the first synthesis goes back to Paul A. Samuelson and John R. Hicks who, among other economists in the 1960s, developed and presented the (original) *Neoclassical Synthesis*.

The NNS combines crucial elements of the *New Classical Theory*, especially of the *Real Business Cycle Theory* (RBC theory), with those of the *New Keynesian Macroeconomics* (NKM). On the one hand, the new models build on the principles of intertemporal optimization and rational expectations adopted from the RBC theory, while on the other hand they utilize the central elements of the NKM, namely imperfect competition, and the dynamic price and wage rigidities caused by costly price and wage adjustments. Arguing that the main merit of the new class of models lies in combining these two distinct types of models, which still seemed irreconcilable just a decade ago, the term 'new neoclassical synthesis' will be adopted throughout this chapter, but nevertheless a critical discussion of its value added is presented.[1]

Opposing the 'old synthesis', the NNS contains elements that lead to very different policy implications, especially with respect to the conduct of monetary

[1] This chapter is the extended version of Fendel (2004a).

policy. However, this new line of research is still evolving, and final assessment of its value added remains arduous. Nevertheless, it has already found its way through the academics into the central banks, and is thus likely to influence the thinking of monetary authorities sooner or later.[2]

This chapter aims at providing a critical analysis of the new class of models without elaborating on all its complexities.[3] To this end, the chapter has the following structure: section 2 presents the main features of the new class of models, to some extent separated according to their respective schools of thought; section 3 highlights the transmission mechanisms in the new class of models; section 4 revisits the Phillips curve debate in the light of the new approach; section 5 discusses the policy implications; section 6 presents a small-scale model that has become the new 'workhorse model'; and, finally, section 7 concludes by identifying the main issues for future research.

1.2 Foundations of the New Neoclassical Synthesis

In order to understand why the new class of models has been labeled 'new neoclassical synthesis', it is useful to review the two main classes of business cycle theories that preceded the new paradigm while at the same time displaying crucial ingredients for the NNS. These theories are the Real Business Cycle Theory and the New Keynesian Macroeconomics. For the sake of brevity, this chapter will refer only to their core elements, although the reader should be aware that there is an extensive literature contributing to both approaches.[4]

1.2.1 *The contribution of the Real Business Cycle Theory*

Consideration of the intertemporal optimization of households and firms with respect to their decisions on consumption, labor supply, and investment and labor demand, can be seen as the most crucial and, indeed, innovative element of

[2] In several central banks and other institutions there is currently an ongoing effort to integrate crucial elements of the NNS into their macroeconomic models. See, for example, Smets and Wouters (2002) for the European Central Bank and Bayoumi (2004) for the new General Equilibrium Model (GEM) of the IMF.

[3] An excellent reference for the formal and analytical aspects of the NNS models is Canzoneri, Cumby and Diba (2002a).
More technical details can also be found in Galí (2002) and in Appendix A to this chapter. Woodford (2003) presents a comprehensive treatment of the ongoing research.

[4] For a broader presentation of the main classes of business cycle theories see Arnold (2002). Appendix A to this chapter presents a complete analytical description of the technical details of the model that is sketched out subsequently.

the RBC theory. Actually, economists had long been aware that intertemporal substitution effects lie at the heart of macroeconomics, but had not integrated them into macroeconomic models. Together with (by the time of the formulation of RBC models already standard) intra-temporal optimization, the element of intertemporal optimization was integrated into general equilibrium business cycle models with flexible prices and perfect competition determining market clearing prices and quantities.[5]

Generally speaking, all RBC models yield at least two intertemporal optimality conditions. The first is the well known Euler equation governing the intertemporal path of consumption, the second is a relation governing the allocation of labor, which depends on the expected time path of wages. Due to flexible prices and wages, business cycles are interpreted as equilibrium phenomena with no involuntary unemployment.[6] Rather, households and firms respond optimally to shocks with voluntary variations in labor and, hence, production, their response being driven by substitution and wealth effects. This characteristic reflects the quest for a solid microfoundation of macroeconomic models expressed in the form of marginal conditions which govern the behavior of agents.[7]

Shocks to productivity are regarded as the main driving force behind the substitution and wealth effects, and thus constitute the main reason for the cyclical behavior of output and employment. This also means that the supply side is regarded as the crucial part of the economy when it comes to explaining business cycles. The approach takes into account that productivity shocks measured by the Solow residual exert two distinct effects. First, they change output given any amount of input, and second they may change the amount of inputs: in fact, bringing about changes in the intertemporal wage and interest rate structure, they work through the first order marginal conditions. In this context, productivity shocks have to be distinguished according to their degree of persistence: while permanent productivity shocks do not cause any substitution effects, temporary shocks certainly do.

Fiscal shocks also play an important role in the RBC models. For example, variations in income taxes have effects on economic activity due to their

[5] See, for example, Cooley (1995) for a representative sampling of the RBC literature.

[6] However, this is not the case in all RBC models: see, e.g., the search unemployment models by Andolfatto (1996) and Merz (1995).

[7] However, a note of caution should be added here. To be borne in mind is the criticism levelled at this approach emerging from the 1960s debate on capital theory underlying those models including questioning many elements: the inverse relationship between real wage and employment, the formulation of an aggregate production function and U-shaped cost curves (i.e., the convexity of production sets). This criticism would consider the microfoundation of the models under consideration as far from solid. For more explicit illustration see Sylos Labini (1988).

influence on the first order marginal conditions which, in turn, trigger substitution effects. Imagine, for example, a tax τ on labor income and the following production function in labor (N) and capital (K): $Y_t = Z_t F(N_t, K_t)$, with Y_t being total production and Z_t being a technology parameter. Then, given a perfectly competitive labor market, the after-tax real wage rate (w) at time *t* can be expressed as

$$(1.1) \qquad \frac{W_t}{P_t} = w_t = (1-\tau) Z_t \frac{\partial F(N_t, K_t)}{\partial N_t},$$

where W_t represents the nominal wage rate and P_t the aggregate price level. Thus, from the point of view of the marginal return of labor, the tax resembles the productivity parameter. In RBC models, an increase in the tax rate has practically the same consequences as a negative technology shock (McGrattan, 1994).[8]

Despite the integration of intertemporal aspects, the RBC models also introduced some 'technical advances' into macroeconomics. RBC researchers constructed models in which alternative policies can be compared on the basis of measures of utility benefits and costs rather than *ad hoc* objectives.[9] The models also allow for an analysis of the effects of policy changes and other shocks in the dynamic stochastic context of a fully specified system as required by the logic of rational expectations. The theoretical RBC models also come closer into line with the current methodology of empirical research. In particular, the numerical solutions obtained with the RBC models are directly comparable to the impulse response functions derived from VAR analyses.

The monetary neutrality built into the RBC models precludes a meaningful analysis of monetary policies, while the close correlation of money and output over the business cycle is mainly explained by endogenous variations in money supply. This leaves the RBC models somewhat incomplete for the purpose of analyzing monetary policy and, therefore, rather unattractive for policy support.

---

[8] However, there remains a difference. While a negative technology shock results in a fall in both real wages and the real interest rate, an increase in the wage tax reduces labor supply, increases the capital intensity and, hence, results in a fall of real wages and an increase of the real interest rate.

[9] However, one could also argue that while this means some technical advances in the analysis, there is also a step backwards since it implies a mono-dimensional notion of the economic agent.

1.2.2 *The Contribution of New Keynesian Macroeconomics*

The *New Keynesian Macroeconomics* provide a competing explanation for the existence of business cycles based on nominal rigidities and market imperfections compatible with rational expectations. While early contributions focused on the role of rigid wages, the more recent literature assumes price rigidities in the goods markets. This shift in emphasis also led to an increased interest in monopolistic price setting power in the goods markets.[10]

In a prototype NKM model, monopolistic firms are specialized in the production of one particular differentiated consumption good, c(j). All differentiated goods together form a composite consumption good, C, according to the CES function

$$(1.2) \qquad C_t = \left[\int_0^1 c_t(j)^{\frac{\theta-1}{\theta}} dj\right]^{\frac{\theta}{\theta-1}},$$

where $\theta > 1$ is the constant elasticity of substitution between different goods.[11] It also measures the degree of monopolistic power of individual firms. Intratemporal allocation of consumption by households leads to the demand function that each firm faces:

$$(1.3) \qquad c_t(j) = \left(\frac{p_t(j)}{P_t}\right)^{-\theta} \cdot C_t,$$

where $p_t(j)$ is the price of an individual consumption good and P_t is the aggregate price level defined as the minimum expenditure for one unit of the composite consumption good given individual prices:

$$(1.4) \qquad P_t = \left(\int_0^1 p_t(j)^{1-\theta} dj\right)^{\frac{1}{1-\theta}}.$$

Monopolistic firms set profit maximizing prices with a constant mark-up over nominal marginal costs, ψ_t. The size of the mark-up is given by the conventional formula and depends on the degree of monopolistic power a firm has:

---

[10] This redirection of research activities can be partly explained by the fact that rigid wages alone might be unable to explain business cycles if competition is not perfect. If, in this case, mark-ups were flexible enough, prices would be also flexible enough to restore equilibrium.

[11] The number of firms (and, thus, goods) is normalized to one.

(1.5) $$p_t(j) = \frac{\theta}{\theta - 1} \cdot \psi_t .$$

The most crucial assumption in the NKM is price stickiness, whose extent and precise form varies across models. In the simplest formulation, prices are fixed for just one period for all firms, which enables researchers to find a closed-form solution for the model. However, this formulation is empirically unsatisfactory since it leads to discrete jumps in the price level rather than observed gradual adjustment. The alternative is dynamic formulation, and the NKM literature shows two popular approaches.[12] The first – staggered price setting due to deterministic contracts (Taylor, 1980) – was originally developed for labor contracts, and postulates that firms and workers set a fixed wage over a contract length of, say, J periods. Wage bargains are assumed to be staggered through time with $1/J$ of the contracts set each period, which means that only a $1/J$ fraction of all wage rates is considered flexible. Since rational agents know that they will lack the ability to adjust wages over the life of the contract, the contracts are forward-looking in the sense that expected price developments will be priced in. The same reasoning applies if price stickiness is modeled instead of wage rigidity. Expected changes in marginal costs are taken into account in the pricing decision.

In contrast to the Taylor contracts, Calvo (1983) assumes that for each firm the possibility to adjust prices optimally arrives stochastically. Again, this leads to forward-looking pricing decisions on the part of firms, since they recognize that the chosen price will be constant for a stochastically determined period. Notwithstanding the stochastic nature of the pricing process, it leads to a very neat aggregate formulation of the overall price level which makes the Calvo pricing mechanism somewhat superior to the Taylor-pricing mechanism from the purely modeling point of view. In the end, both mechanisms lead to a slow adjustment of the overall price level which is much more in line with the empirical evidence than the (synchronized) static formulation of one-period price stickiness for all firms. However, this comes at the price of rather complex model dynamics that can only be established by calibrated simulation exercises rather than closed form solutions.

The fact that prices in the NKM models exceed marginal costs helps to rationalize the assumption that at least in the short run (defined as the duration of complete wage and price adjustment) aggregate output is determined by demand. Otherwise a firm would have no incentive to step up output at a given

[12] See Taylor (1999a) for a comprehensive treatment of price and wage setting behavior in macroeconomic models.

price when faced with an expansion in demand.[13] This makes the demand side of the economy the crucial driving force for business cycle fluctuations. By the same token, monetary policy has real effects in the short run.

1.2.3 *The Unifying Characteristics of the New Neoclassical Synthesis*

Intertemporal utility functions, originally introduced by RBC researchers, lie at the heart of the NNS models. By adopting them within a stochastic general equilibrium framework, an explicitly utility-based welfare analysis can be performed for alternative policies.[14] Despite varying parameters in the presence of different models, the utility functions always have at least two standard arguments: consumption and leisure (or the disutility of work as its negative representation). Whether real money balances are also incorporated depends on how money is introduced into a particular model. If no cash-in-advance constraint is modeled, money is an additional argument in the utility function due to the transaction services it provides.[15]

Together with an intertemporal budget constraint and a solvency condition, the utility function establishes a well-defined optimization problem for the individual household. It has to chose (1) the allocation of its consumption over time (i.e., bond holdings)[16], (2) its work effort[17], (3) its real money balances and – depending on the formulation of the model – (4) investment in physical capital if a variable capital stock is included into the model.[18] These choices constitute (up to) four optimality conditions. First, the allocation of consumption is governed by the Euler consumption equation which relates the change in consumption to the real interest rate and the household's preferences. Second, the work effort and, hence, production is determined by a marginal condition that equates the marginal disutility of work to marginal utility of the extra

[13] However, there is a limit up to which firms are willing to expand output, because marginal costs may not be constant. This limit, often ignored in the models, is known as 'participation constraint'. If taken seriously, it would poses some technical difficulties since it leads to discontinuities that are hard to handle (Canzoneri, Cumby and Diba, 2002a).

[14] This chapter focuses on closed economy models, although one important area of research are open economy models. For these approaches see, for example, Gertler, Gilchrist and Natalucci (2001), and Clarida, Galí and Gertler (2001 and 2002).

[15] An alternative formulation would be a 'shopping time technology' or a 'cash-in-advance constraint'. See, for example, King and Wolman (1996) and Cooley and Hansen (1989) for such formulations.

[16] The intratemporal allocation of the consumption expenditure among the differentiated consumption goods resulting from the static optimization problem is already given by equation (1.3).

[17] In some simple formulations consumers and producers are merged to a 'yeoman farmer'.

[18] For the sake of brevity the model in Appendix A abstracts from capital.

revenue available for consumption. Real money balances are pinned down by the third marginal condition that leaves the household indifferent between consuming a unit of the composite consumption good in the current period and holding the equivalent amount of money in order to raise utility-providing cash balances and to use the funds for consumption in the future. The fourth marginal condition (if capital is taken into account) leads to a no-arbitrage-condition.

The production side of the economy is modeled by firms that produce the differentiated goods by employing labor and capital. The technology is described by a production function whose productivity parameter is subject to stochastic shocks. As described before, firms possess monopolistic power and set prices above marginal costs. Let μ ($=\theta/[\theta-1]$) denote the markup; then the first-order condition leads to optimal labor demand (i.e., the value marginal product of labor is equated to the nominal wage rate, W) as[19]

$$W_t = \frac{P_t}{\mu_t} Z_t \frac{\partial F(N_t, K_t)}{\partial N_t}. \tag{1.6}$$

After dividing both sides of equation (1.6) by the price level, the real wage can be expressed as

$$w_t = \frac{1}{\mu_t} Z_t \frac{\partial F(N_t, K_t)}{\partial N_t}. \tag{1.7}$$

The market-clearing condition ensures that production equals demand in each period. While, in the short run, prices are fixed and production is driven by demand following the New Keynesian avenues, the long-run equilibrium is characterized by optimal prices and the corresponding natural level of economic activity.[20]

If price stickiness takes the form of staggered price setting, the economy described above is generally characterized by four distortions that justify economic policy interventions (Galí, 2002). The first distortion results from money holding. Private agents allocate part of their wealth to non-interest rate bearing monetary assets, which means that private opportunity costs of holding money coexist with zero social costs of producing money. This generates a

[19] Note that the monopolist has to lower prices in order to increase its sales due to the negative sloped aggregate demand function (1.3). This makes the marginal revenue less than the current price by an amount driven by the monopoly power (which determines the size of μ).

[20] This paragraph will only deal with staggered price setting and will briefly discuss sticky wages at a later stage. As can be shown, the coexistence of staggered price and wage setting has crucial implications for monetary policy.

monetary distortion, which could be eliminated by a zero nominal interest rate. This recommendation is the well-known Friedman rule.

The second distortion is reflected in the first-order condition (1.7) and results from the existence of monopolistic power. Prices are, on average, above marginal costs so that the marginal rate of substitution between consumption and leisure (i.e., the real wage) differs from the corresponding marginal rate of transformation (i.e., the marginal product of labor). This *average markup* distortion makes output too low compared to the social optimum (Blanchard and Kiyotaki, 1987). Note that the two distortions described so far are also at work in the case of full price flexibility: they are not related to the presence of nominal rigidities. Consequently, in order to work out the crucial new elements, this chapter follows the NKM literature and assumes that a comprehensive government subsidy financed in a non-distorting way takes care of both so that we can ignore them.[21]

This leaves us with two remaining distortions that are directly related to the price stickiness and the staggered nature of price adjustment. The third distortion, called *dynamic markup distortion*, is caused by the inability of a fraction of firms to adjust prices instantly, which leads to persistent deviations of the markups from their frictionless (constant) level given in equation (1.5). Variations in marginal costs in the presence of sticky prices lead to an endogenous fluctuation in the markups and, thus, let the static markup distortion discussed before switch to a dynamic one. From equation (1.7) we see that variations in μ, in principle, have the same consequence for the first order principles as variations in tax rates in equation (1.1).

The fourth distortion stems from the lack of synchronization in price adjustment after a shock (i.e., the staggered price setting) and the implied coexistence of different prices until the very last firm has the opportunity to adjust prices. This means that different quantities are produced (and consumed) for goods that enter the consumer preferences symmetrically and have a marginal rate of transformation of one-to-one. This *relative price distortion* gives rise to inefficiency in the allocation of resources within the economy. The latter two distortions have their origin in the presence of sticky prices and present a source of the non-neutrality of money within the NNS framework (Goodfriend and King, 1997).

If the assumption of sticky prices is replaced by flexible prices all firms are able to adjust prices optimally each period, taking the path of aggregate variables as given. The assumption of an isoelastic demand implies that they choose a markup given in equation (1.5). The markup will be the same across firms and constant over time. This implies that the real marginal costs (ψ/P), i.e.,

[21] See Canzoneri, Cumby and Diba (2002a) for its implementation.

the inverse of the markup, are also constant. All other variables (i.e., consumption, production, work effort and the real interest rate) are then also at their natural level. This equilibrium allocation under flexible prices coincides with the efficient allocation, i.e., the one that would be obtained under flexible prices, with no distortionary taxes and perfect labor competition. Under flexible prices, the equilibrium values of all real variables are independent of monetary policy, so that the classical dichotomy holds. This model version resembles the various versions of a pure, albeit non-competitive, RBC model (Goodfriend and King, 1997, p. 279).

Under fixed prices, firms do not adjust their prices optimally each period and, thus, real marginal costs and markup are no longer constant. After a shock, there is a gap between the actual markup and the desired (equilibrium) markup. Consequently, real marginal costs also deviate from their steady state level. Equation (1.7) already showed that a variation of the markup influences economic activity through the first-order condition. Imagine a monetary expansion which translates into higher demand and rising nominal marginal costs. In this situation, the inability of some firms to increase their output prices leads to an increase in the average real marginal costs and, thus, to a decline in the average markup.[22] Through the first-order condition (1.7), this leads to higher production. Production deviates from its (natural) flexible price level, i.e., an output gap opens.[23] Hence, monetary policy does have real effects. But in sharp contrast to the traditional Keynesian view it works through the channels of RBC models. Thus, Keynesian-style fluctuations originating in nominal rigidities are explained within the RBC logic.

However, it is not only the dynamic markup distortion that leads to real effects of monetary policy that can be explained within the RBC logic. Also the relative price distortion does. In order to explain this in a rather heuristic way, we first express potential output Y^*, neglecting any demand restrictions, as the aggregate over the production of differentiated goods $y(j)$ (see Yun, 1996, p. 355):

---

[22] To be more precise, two measures of the markup have to be distinguished: the *average markup* and the *marginal markup*. As suggested above, the average markup plays a prominent role in the transmission of monetary policy. At any point in time, though, a subset of firms have the possibility to adjust their prices and set a new markup level, which is the marginal markup. For a detailed analysis of the cyclical behavior of marginal costs see Rotemberg and Woodford (1999).

[23] Since the models present transitory departures of output from its potential level and, subsequently, give attention to the adjustment of prices and inflation expectations as the process through with actual output adjusts toward potential, some authors describe the new style of models as 'neomonetarist' (see Kimball, 1995). This, again, seems to justify the use of the term 'new neoclassical synthesis' since both schools of thought seem to identify themselves with the new class of models.

(1.8) $$Y_t^* = \int_0^1 y_t(j)dj.$$

This coincides with the flexible price (natural) level of output. However, we know that, under fixed prices, production is determined by demand according to expression (1.3). Market clearing also implies $C_t = Y_t$, so that equation (1.3) becomes

(1.9) $$y_t(j) = \left(\frac{p_t(j)}{P_t}\right)^{-\theta} \cdot Y_t .$$

Substitution equation (1.9) into equation (1.8) yields after rearranging:

(1.10) $$Y_t = \frac{1}{\int_0^1 \left(\frac{p_t(j)}{P_t}\right)^{-\theta} dj} \cdot Y_t^* .$$

Expression (1.10) highlights that the relative price distortion works like the variation in total factor productivity within RBC models (Goodfriend and King, 1997, p. 259). Unless the relative price is equal to unity, which is the flexible price equilibrium level due to the high degree of symmetry within the model, actual output deviates from its natural level and an output gap is produced. Again, money is not neutral.

1.3 The Transmission of Shocks

The presence of sticky prices has additional implications for the response of the economy to non-monetary shocks, over and above that of being the source of the non-neutrality of money. The exact dynamics following a specific shock depend on the parameterization of the NNS models. As mentioned above, once a dynamic price and wage setting behavior is taken into account, no closed-form solutions can be obtained. Rather, the models have to be calibrated and choices need to be made for the elasticities of intra- and intertemporal substitution, as also of labor supply, money demand, and so on. Instead of presenting one specific calibration, this section prefers to highlight the 'core dynamics' that seem to be present across a wide range of parameter sets. It will first focus on a monetary shock and subsequently on a technology shock.

As pointed out above, money is not neutral and works through the mark-up mechanism in the NNS framework. Standard calibrations lead to surprisingly large values of output fluctuations that can even surpass observed US postwar experience. Additionally, the effects are fairly persistent, especially if the Calvo mechanism of stochastic price adjustment is modeled. For example, Galí (2002) reports a half life of the output response to a one-standard deviation money supply shock of 3.2 quarters with a Calvo pricing mechanism that implies an average price duration of only 4 quarters. With a deterministic adjustment in prices it is more difficult to generate significant effects of money on output beyond the duration of prices (Chari, Kehoe and McGrattan, 2000).

An interesting feature that points to the difference between the NNS and former models of non-neutral money is the presence of a liquidity effect, i.e., a declining nominal interest rate after an increase in money. Across some calibration ranges (but not all) in the NNS models, a monetary expansion raises the nominal interest rate. Thus, some of the NNS models fail to predict the existence of a liquidity effect (for example, Galí, 2002), but this does not prevent monetary policy from transmitting its effects through an interest rate channel. In this case, monetary policy works through a decline in the *ex ante* real interest rate and, thus, through the intertemporal allocation of consumption via the Euler condition.[24] Actually, the absence of a liquidity effect is at odds with the empirical evidence but it does reveal the fact that the transmission channels at work in the NNS are very different from those of the traditional Keynesian models.

Exogenous variations in technology have been claimed to be the main source of the observed cyclical behavior of output by the proponents of RBC models. According to the traditional, flexible price, perfectly competitive RBC models, positive technology shocks lead to positive output and employment effects, so the question that naturally arises at this point is what the consequences of technology shocks are within the NNS models. Recently, some authors have mentioned a surprising aspect of the interaction between sticky prices and technology shocks within the NNS framework (e.g., Galí, 1999). A favorable technology shock is likely to induce a short-run decline in employment, as long as the response of monetary policy falls short of full accommodation. Again, this result is not necessarily the outcome of the technology shock in this model but holds for a large subset of parameter values.

In order to see the intuition behind this result, let us take the case of a positive technology shock and assume that monetary policy does not react. All firms experience a decline in their marginal costs, but only a fraction are able to react with lower prices. Accordingly, the aggregate price level will fall and

[24] See Christiano, Eichenbaum and Evans (1997) for more probing discussion of the lack of the liquidity effect and alternative mechanisms to restore it.

demand will rise, but less than proportionally to the increase in productivity due to the staggered price adjustment. Depending on the relative size of the partial effects this may bring about a decline in employment, since more output can be produced with less input after the productivity increase. This is clearly at odds with the implications of the standard RBC model, which predicts a strong co-movement in productivity, output and employment.

The contrast in the two models' prediction for the relation between employment and technology shocks has clear, testable implications, and it leads to the question as to what the empirical evidence tells us about the correlation between productivity and employment. However, an empirical examination of the correlation between productivity shocks and employment is no easy task. The Solow residual used by RBC researchers is not a good measure of productivity changes since it is biased in several dimensions. Hall (1988b), for example, starts from a production technology with fixed costs that is consistent with monopolistic competition and demonstrates that a Solow decomposition leads to the consequence that the Solow residual varies with the business cycle even if there is no productivity shock. Measurement errors and labor hoarding are other reasons that disprove the Solow residual as a reliable indicator for technology shocks.

Basu, Fernald and Kimball (2004) construct a measure of aggregate technology by controlling for possible non-technological effects in the aggregate Solow residual: increasing returns, imperfect competition, varying utilization of capital and labor, and aggregation effects. Their corrected technology residual shows a variability over time that is only about one-third of the Solow residual variability. In addition, although the Solow residual is strongly pro-cyclical, technology fluctuations tend to be counter-cyclical contemporaneously; they have a significantly negative correlation with inputs and a near-zero correlation with output. According to the authors' analysis, technology improvements lead to a reduction in employment within the year, but eventually to an increase, with a lag of up to two years.

Recently, researchers have tried to identify technology shocks within structural vector auto-regression (VAR) analyses. Within these studies, the main challenge is the formulation of identifying assumptions that rely on relatively few *a-priori* restrictions. One approach, for example, is to assume that technology shocks are the only source of disturbances that affect the level of labor productivity in the long run (Galí, 1999; Altig et al., 2002). The existing VAR literature on the influence of technology shocks on employment is rather mixed, and the issue is so far not solved. Galí (1999) claims that in response to a positive technology shock, labor productivity rises by more than output, while employment shows a persistent decline.[25]

By contrast, Altig et al. (2002) who use the same methodology as Galí (1999) find that a positive technology shock drives up hours worked, investment and output. According to their analysis, the difference to the literature asserting the negative correlation between productivity and employment comes from an omitted variable bias and an over-differencing of employment data, constituting a flaw in this literature.[26] However, both studies derive the same result, namely that technology shocks account for only a small fraction of the business cycle fluctuations (so that technological shocks cannot have been the major source of business cycle fluctuation as claimed by RBC proponents).[27]

1.4 Revisiting the Phillips Curve

The Phillips curve debate has always been at the heart of the discussion of business cycle theories. Competing theories have regularly been reduced to their Phillips curve implications. Not surprisingly, the NNS also has some crucial implications for the Phillips curve that differ from those of former theories. They can be derived in an intuitive way within the model framework set out above.[28] To begin with the similarities, the 'new' Phillips curve consists of the two elementary terms that are also present in the traditional Phillips curve. The first is an inflation term, the second a measure of economic activity, but their precise functional form and their meaning differ.

The inflation term of the new Phillips curve is forward looking. This forward-looking nature of inflation is inherent in the NNS models. Prices are set by firms that are constraint in the frequency with which they can re-set the prices of their goods. Today all firms able to re-set their prices recognize this constraint, and it is optimal for them to take into account their expectations regarding future costs and demand conditions. Since the change in the aggregate

[25] See Francis and Ramey (2001) who support Galí's analysis. However, Shea (1998) finds a decline in labor as a long run response, while it rises in the short run. It should also been mentioned here that Shapiro and Watson (1988) uncovered this result a decade before, but it went unnoticed (see Figures 2 and 5 in their paper).

[26] The possibility of over-differencing the employment data arises from the stationarity issue in time series econometrics. While Galí (1999) works with first differences due to non-stationarity in levels, Altig et al. (2002) use levels in hours worked. The latter authors also include more explanatory variables in their analysis.

[27] However, the debate still seems unresolved. See also Galí (2004), Uhlig (2004) and Christiano, Vigfusson and Eichenbaum (2004).

[28] For its exact analytical derivation see Appendix A to this chapter.

price level results from individual pricing decisions, inflation must have a forward-looking component.

As already mentioned above, the average markup is of crucial importance for the cyclical behavior of the economy. Variations in the average markup also imply variations in real marginal costs and, by equation (1.5), the desired equilibrium markup is accompanied by an equilibrium level of the real marginal costs (mc*). Once the firm has the opportunity to re-set prices, it will apply the desired markup. Price changes are therefore a function of the gap between the actual markup and the desired equilibrium markup. Thus, they are also a function of the gap between actual real marginal costs (mc_t) and the equilibrium level of real marginal costs defined as $\varphi_t = mc_t - mc^*$.

In sum, the inflation dynamic can be expressed as

$$\pi_t = \beta E_t \pi_{t+1} + \kappa \varphi_t, \tag{1.11}$$

where E_t is the expectation operator, β is a discount factor and the parameter $\kappa > 0$ is a function of the probability of a price change within the Calvo pricing mechanism. Additionally, it is possible to derive a stable relationship between the deviation of real marginal costs from its equilibrium level and the output gap $\hat{y}$, defined as the log deviation of output from its equilibrium level:

$$\varphi_t = \gamma \cdot \hat{y}_t, \tag{1.12}$$

where the parameter $\gamma > 0$ is a function of the model's parameter, e.g. the intertemporal elasticity of substitution. Combining equations (1.11) and (1.12), the new Phillips curve is conventionally expressed as

$$\pi_t = \beta E_t \pi_{t+1} + \tilde{\kappa} \hat{y}_t + u_t, \tag{1.13}$$

with $\tilde{\kappa}_t > 0$, and the shock term u_t is referred to as a 'cost push', capturing deviations from the relation (1.12).[29] By contrast, the traditional expectation-augmented Phillips curve has the following functional form:[30]

[29] A note on the parameter ß is called for. This parameter stems from the fact that price setters discount the future in their forward-looking pricing decision from which the new Phillips curve is derived. However, this discounting of the future introduces a long-run trade-off between inflation and output. In order to avoid this undesirable feature, this parameter is often fixed to unity, which is identical to the assumption that price-setters do not discount the future. See Appendix A for a formal presentation of this issue.

[30] However, Mankiw and Reis (2002) recently showed how the traditional Phillips curve can be derived under totally different assumptions. The authors assume sticky information instead of sticky prices, and the essence of their model is that information about macroeconomic

(1.14) $$\pi_t = E_{t-1}\pi_t + \chi\hat{y}_t + \nu_t,$$

where often static expectations of the form $E_{t-1}\pi_t = \pi_{t-1}$ are imposed. Neglecting the differences in the parameters $\chi > 0$ and $\tilde{\kappa}$ in equations (1.13) and (1.14), the crucial difference between the two Phillips curves is the degree of their forward-looking nature.[31]

In the traditional Phillips curve, past inflation counts in determination of current inflation and current inflation is positively related to current output. In other words, output leads inflation. This property stands in sharp contrast to the implication of the new Phillips curve. In order to illustrate this, equation (1.13) is iterated forward to get:

(1.15) $$\pi_t = E_t\left\{\sum_{k=0}^{\infty}\beta^k\left(\kappa\hat{y}_{t+k} + u_{t+k}\right)\right\}.$$

Expression (1.15) indicates that past inflation is not a relevant factor for current inflation. Furthermore, inflation is positively correlated with future output and expected cost pushes.[32] What this boils down to is that inflation leads output. The reason for this forward-looking nature of inflation is quite intuitive. With staggered price setting, the pricing decisions that generate the behavior of the aggregate price level are based on current and anticipated developments of marginal costs, which are in principle unrelated to past inflation (Galí, 2002).

Currently the empirical validity of the new Phillips curve is being debated in the literature. A number of authors argue that the new Phillips curve may theoretically be very appealing, but it cannot account for some features in the data that are well explained by the traditional Phillips curve. For example, the cross-correlation between inflation and de-trended output suggests that output leads inflation (Fuhrer and Moore, 1995). Not surprisingly, estimations of hybrid Phillips curves that contain lagged and leading inflation terms generally find a (sometimes totally) dominant influence of lagged inflation on current

---

conditions diffuses slowly through the economy. The model combines elements of Calvo's (1983) model of random price adjustment with elements of the Lucas (1973) model of imperfect information. In some ways, the dynamic response in the sticky information model resembles Phillips curves with backward-looking expectations.

[31] It has to be mentioned here, that this form of the new Phillips curve can only be derived with the Calvo pricing mechanism as presented in Appendix A. Using the Taylor pricing mechanism instead would yield additional lagged inflation terms which then would lead to a hybrid form of the Phillips curve with forward and backward-looking inflation terms present at the same time.

[32] The cost-push term vanishes if we assume a zero mean. However, some authors introduce a serial correlation of this disturbances term (e.g., Clarida, Galí and Gertler, 1999).

inflation (e.g., Fuhrer 1997), which again argues in favor of the traditional Phillips curve.

More recently, a number of authors have challenged this view (Galí and Gertler, 1999; Gali, Gertler and López-Salido, 2001) arguing that such results cannot be taken as evidence against the new Phillips curve, because de-trended output, no matter which method for de-trending is applied, is not a correct proxy for the output gap in the NNS models. This, according to the authors, this is a potential source of misleading results. In the NNS, the output gap has a very precise meaning being the deviation of output from its equilibrium level in the absence of nominal rigidities. Traditional output gap measures that are based on de-trended output might be a poor proxy in this sense.[33]

To overcome this problem, the above-mentioned authors estimate equation (1.11) as a test for the validity of the forward-looking nature of inflation instead, which means that condition (1.12) is no longer required to hold. The difficulty is to find a proxy for real marginal costs. Here, it proves favorable that, under certain assumptions about technology and price setting behavior, real marginal costs are proportional to labor income shares. The findings of such alternative tests – based on data for the US and the euro area – have so far been interpreted as reasonably encouraging for the new Phillips curve (Galí, 2002). In particular, parameter estimates imply an average price duration of one year for a firm, which is consistent with survey data (Taylor, 1999a). However, future empirical work will have to clarify the issue.

1.5 Monetary Policy Implications in Brief

The NNS models have crucial implications for the conduct of stabilization policies. Because nearly all models are based on Ricardian equivalence, the emphasis clearly lies on issues of monetary policy.[34] Optimal monetary policy in the NNS framework requires stabilization of production at its natural level that would emerge under full price flexibility. Interestingly, for a range of NNS models, no trade-off between output and price stabilization appears. Full stabilization of output is exactly guaranteed when the price level is fully

[33] There are several alternatives to measure the trend. Among them are (1) linear or quadratic time trends, (2) a Hodrick-Presscott filtering and (3) estimates of potential output.

[34] Research on fiscal policy in the context of the NNS models has only recently received more attention. See, for example, Linnemann und Schabert (2003) for the analysis of fiscal policy within the new neoclassical synthesis as well as Beetsma and Jensen (2002), Canzoneri, Cumby and Diba (2005) for the interaction of fiscal and monetary policy within a monetary union.

stabilized, i.e., in the presence of zero inflation. In contrast to conventional wisdom, this seems to be a somewhat provocative result.

The exact nature of monetary policy is defined by the presence of the (dynamic) distortions that were described above. The underlying logic is quite simple: since prices cannot react flexibly enough to restore the optimal allocation immediately following a shock, monetary policy should instead react in a way as to discourage firms from resetting their prices at all. This policy requires to fully counteract demand disturbances and to perfectly accommodate technology shocks (see Clarida, Galí and Gertler, 1999, pp. 1674ff).

In these models monetary policy is often expressed in terms of monetary policy rules which are the main focus of the subsequent chapters. These rules can either be exogenous or endogenous (optimal). Optimal rules are based on the minimization of a quadratic loss function that is expressed as the weighted sum of the variance of inflation and the output gap (and possibly additional arguments).[35] Such a loss function represents the quadratic (second-order Taylor series) approximation to the level of (expected) utility of the representative household in the rational expectation equilibrium associated with a given policy. Thus, there is a direct relation between the goals of monetary policy and the utility function of a representative household that lies at the heart of NNS model. This makes the households' utility a natural normative measure of monetary policy. In this sense, the approach to optimal monetary policy resembles models of the public finance literature. The reformulation of the utility function into a quadratic loss function is convenient for mainly two reasons. First, the nature of optimal monetary policy can be addressed within in a linear-quadratic optimal control problem that has been extensively studied. Second, the results are comparable with those of the traditional literature on monetary policy evaluation, which almost always assumes such linear-quadratic loss functions.[36]

In the following, the specific example of a technology shock should illustrate the design of the optimal monetary policy. Following a technological improvement, all firms face a decline in their marginal costs, but only a fraction is able to adjust prices and set the optimal markup instantly. We have already seen that this can lead to a decline in production and employment. A demand expansion caused by an accommodating monetary policy can offset this effect. It would stabilize the price level and the level of output at the same time.

The general logic of the monetary policy response can be understood in light of the RBC tradition. If a technology shocks hits the economy, it is optimal to redirect production into the present. In a standard RBC model, flexible prices would automatically create this effect, but here, due to rigidities, this is not possible. This is where monetary policy comes in. However, the ideal result of a

[35] An alternative approach would be the modeling of so-called Ramsey policies.

[36] See chapter 2 for a extended presentation and discussion of optimal monetary policy rules.

full stabilization can only hold if technology shocks are not sector specific. If the monetary authorities instead face sector specific technology shocks, even in the theoretical framework the full stabilization is not possible anymore (Canzoneri, Cumby and Diba, 2002a). Moreover, once we allow for the coexistence of staggered prices and wages, monetary policy is also not able anymore to achieve the optimal allocation that would occur under completely flexible prices and wages. Instead, the model exhibits a tradeoff in stabilizing the output gap, price inflation, and wage inflation (Erceg, Henderson and Levin, 2000). The optimal policy has to strike a balance between the stabilization of these three variables.[37]

In order to be able to replicate the flexible price solution in response to a technology shock, the monetary authorities need to know the degree of persistence of a particular shock. This puts high informational requirements on monetary policy such as they are hardly satisfied in reality. Researchers have consequently asked whether the sheer volume of informational requirements for design of an optimal policy response makes practical use of response functions irrelevant. In addition to the problem of observing and responding (contemporaneously) to different shocks, the theoretical literature identifies a second problem in terms of optimal policy rules, known as the 'robustness of monetary policy rules'. It has been shown by simulation exercises that specific forms of optimal rules are not robust to changes in some of the models' characteristics. If the monetary policy authorities work with a specific model and an optimal response function based on this model, the outcome might well prove poor if reality is better described by an alternative model. Thus, given model uncertainty, dependence on optimal response functions could well turn out to be truly hazardous.

Research on monetary policy rules has reacted to these problems. It has been shown that so-called simple interest rate rules (such as the well-known Taylor rule) that suggest that the central bank adjusts the interest rate in response to variations in inflation and the output gap generally provide a good approximation for the optimal rule, in terms of relatively small welfare losses compared to the optimal loss over a wide range of structural models. This explains the present attractiveness of the Taylor rule and other relative simple monetary policy rules.[38]

Proponents of the NNS favor a monetary policy strategy of inflation targeting with a target rate of inflation near zero (King and Wolman, 1996), which follows from the forward-looking nature of the price setting behavior. If agents expect stable prices in the future, markups and, hence, production are also stabilized. However, strict inflation targeting in the sense that monetary

[37] See Appendix A to this chapter for the analytical derivation of this claim.
[38] Again, the reader is referred to chapter 2 of this study where interest rate rules are discussed in more detail.

policy should adjust immediately to reach the inflation target is often found not to be the optimal strategy, flexible inflation targeting with a smooth adjustment over a longer time horizon being often preferred instead.[39]

The major challenge to monetary policy comes with the occurrence of cost-push shocks as defined previously in the context of the new Phillips curve. To the extent that such cost-push inflation is present, a short-run trade-off between inflation and output occurs (Clarida, Galí and Gertler, 1999). Stabilizing inflation by contracting demand would lead to a fall in output, while stabilizing output would mean leaving aggregate demand unchanged, but would lead to inflation. Here it is the preferences of the central bank, i.e. its inflation aversion, that determine the outcome within this trade-off.

1.6 The "New Consensus Model"

In order to achieve status as the new paradigm, the NNS framework needed to be unified in a workhorse model that proved easier to communicate than the rather complex models discussed above. This section outlines the so-called "new consensus model" (Meyer, 2001), which has become the widely accepted workhorse for macroeconomic policy analysis. The new consensus model can be interpreted as the successor of the traditional IS-LM framework, and in fact is often labeled "optimizing IS-LM model" since it is built up from a microfoundation or, alternatively, "expectational IS-LM model", because the new framework is modified to include expectational terms in the behavioural equations and because it is analyzed using rational expectations (see McCallum and Nelson, 1999a and 1999b).

The new consensus model can be summarized in three equations: an aggregate demand equation, the forward-looking Phillips curve and an equation determining monetary policy.[40] The aggregate demand equation is a forward-looking IS equation where the current real output gap $\hat{y}_t$ depends on its expected future level, the real interest $\hat{r}_t$ and a shock term x_t:[41]

$$(1.16) \qquad \hat{y}_t = E_t\hat{y}_{t+1} - \frac{1}{\sigma}\hat{r}_t + x_t,$$

---

[39] See Clarida, Galí and Gertler (1999) and Goodfriend (2002) for an in-depth analysis of the conduct of monetary policy in the presence of the NNS.

[40] An excellent introduction is King (2000).

[41] Nominal and real interest rates are linked by the Fisher equation, which makes the nominal interest rate equal to the sum of real interest rate and expected inflation.

Equation (1.16) is obtained by log-linearizing the consumption Euler equation after imposing the restriction that consumption equals output minus government spending (see Appendix A of this chapter for the derivation)

The expectational Phillips curve which relates current inflation to expected future inflation, the output gap and a supply shock has already been discussed in section 1.4. For convenience equation (1.13) is restated here:

$$(1.17) \qquad \pi_t = \beta E_t \pi_{t+1} + \tilde{\kappa}\hat{y}_t + u_t.$$

To close the model, it is necessary to specify the monetary equilibrium condition. As already mentioned, it has become very popular to specify an interest rate rule which specifies the nominal interest rate as the operating instrument of monetary policy.[42] Mostly a Taylor-type rule is formulated which relates the nominal interest rate i_t to the output gap and the difference between inflation and the central bank's inflation target π^*:

$$(1.18) \qquad i_t = \bar{i} + \gamma_\pi \cdot (\pi_t - \pi^*) + \gamma_y \cdot \hat{y}_t,$$

where $\bar{i}$ represents the equilibrium nominal interest rate, and γ_π and γ_y are the reaction coefficients with respect to deviations of inflation and output from their desired levels.[43] Under such a rule, the quantity of money is endogenously demand-determined at the nominal interest rate set by the central bank. For this purpose, a money demand function could additionally be specified, but since the

[42] The term 'operating target' would be closer to the use of the short-term interest rate. For example, the Fed does not manipulate its instrument in a literally direct fashion but rather conduct open-market operations only once a day (normally around 10:30 – 10:45 a.m.) with quantities chosen so as to manage a market-influenced interest rate that lies in some rather narrow band. Thus, the end-of-day or daily average value of the Federal funds rate can depart from the open-market desk's 'target value' by 20-30 basis points on any given day. Within the Euro system the short-term interest rate, typically represented by the EONIA ('European overnight index average'), moves close to the minimum bid rate of the main refinancing operation. However, for simplicity it is assumed throughout the study that the monetary authorities can set the short-term rate one for one.

[43] The interest rate rule in equation (1.18) abstracts from any lacked values of the nominal interest rate which would indicate some interest rate smoothing behavior as well as from any expectational terms which would state that the central bank reacts to expected inflation instead of actual inflation. The reaction coefficient with respect to inflation has to be greater than one in order to ensure stability. This is known as the *Taylor principle*. All these issues will be extensively discussed in subsequent chapters of this study.

quantity of money is not relevant for the determination of macroeconomic activity, models are often formulated without introducing money at all.[44]

Compared to the traditional IS-LM model, there are at least three innovations worth mentioning (Meyer, 2001). First, whereas the traditional IS-LM model assumes either prices or output to be fixed, the consensus model allows for both sticky prices in the short run and full price flexibility in the long run. Second, the consensus model replaces the LM equation which formerly described money market equilibrium by the policy rule. Modeling the process of interest rate adjustment by the central bank is much closer to the actual central bank policy observed in reality than treating the money supply as the relevant instrument. Third, the probably most important innovation is the explicit treatment of forward-looking economic behavior. If, additionally, adjustment costs or 'rule-of-thumb' consumers are modeled, the consensus model allows for both forward-looking elements and lagged adjustment.

Such a 'hybrid' model can be conveniently justified as follows (see Svensson, 1999). First, we need to assume that β equals unity in the Phillips curve function which we already justified above. Second, we assume adjustment costs that lead $E_t\{\pi_{t+1}\}$ to be replaced by $(1-\alpha_\pi)E_t\{\pi_{t+1}\}+ \alpha_\pi\pi_{t-1}$ in the Phillips Curve. Third, by the same token we replace $E_t\{y_{t+1}\}$ by $(1-\alpha_y)E_t\{y_{t+1}\}+ \alpha_y y_{t-1}$ in the IS curve, where $0<\alpha_\pi<1$ and $0<\alpha_y<1$:

$$\pi_t = (1-\alpha_\pi)E_t\pi_{t+1} + \alpha_\pi\pi_{t-1} + \kappa\hat{y}_t + u_t \tag{1.19}$$

and

$$\hat{y}_t = (1-\alpha_y)E_t\hat{y}_{t+1} + \alpha_y\hat{y}_{t-1} - s[r_t - r] + x_t . \tag{1.20}$$

Later chapters will employ this more general formulation that also gained some empirical support and will refer to more special model formulations (e.g., purely forward-looking or purely backward-looking) by choosing the relevant parameter restrictions.

1.7 The Value Added of the New Neoclassical Synthesis

The *new neoclassical synthesis* denotes a significant step in business cycle analyses. It combines the elements of *Real Business Cycle* analysis and *New Keynesian Macroeconomics*. Its main advantages is that it brings together

[44] See Friedman (2003) on that issue. For a discussion how the consensus model relates to monetarist ideas in which money plays the central role see Meyer (2001).

(again) results of research of different schools of thought formerly confronting each other as irreconcilable. With the NNS at hand they are now able to work within one unified framework and they can exchange their arguments on the basis of quite similar models, while the methodological vicinity makes it far easier to compare positive and normative results in business cycle theory.

The new approach ascribes both schools of thought, 'Keynesian' and 'classical', their importance by assigning each a distinct role within complete dynamic general equilibrium models. But the distinction no longer lies in the fact that the Keynesian theory explains the short run while classical theory explains the long run, as was the case in the 'original' synthesis. Rather, the factors stressed by RBC-theory explain the evolution over time of potential output, while transitory deviations from the potential value result from delays in the adjustment of prices and wages. Since this adjustment process is explicitly modeled, the NNS provides enough space for a thorough dynamic short-run analysis.

In the NNS, real disturbances may play an important role as the ultimate source of short-run variations in economic activity. However, in contrast to the RBC models, this does not mean that the fluctuations in economic activity are necessarily desirable, nor does it imply that there is no rule for monetary policy. Because of the delay in the adjustment process of prices and/or wages, the consequences of real disturbances can be inefficient, which leaves a role for active monetary policy to mitigate the distortions. However, although the NNS framework has become the new paradigm in the sense that almost all research in macroeconomics is carried out in dynamic general equilibrium models with Keynesian elements, this class of models is still evolving.

If the NNS is to gain more influence over actual stabilization policies, then an array of open questions has to be answered with future research, two of which should be mentioned here. First, we need to know more about the specific rigidities that are present empirically, because the specific NNS model results are sensitive to the exact character of the rigidities. Until we succeed in identifying them, the risk is that empirical policy conclusions might be drawn inappropriately. The identification of rigidities also includes the possibility that they may be sector specific, which then precludes a full stabilization of aggregate output by re-active monetary policy, because a single monetary policy stance cannot fit all sectors. This asymmetry in rigidities and the possibility of sector specific shocks bring up the question of whether an internationally coordinated monetary policy might be an issue to be discussed again within the NNS framework. In fact, Canzoneri, Cumby and Diba (2002b) show that the benefits of monetary policy coordination might be higher in open economy versions of NNS models than previously thought by many researchers.

Second, we still need more general empirical tests of the NNS models. So far, the empirical evidence is rather mixed and does not support the new theory in general, as has also been argued with respect to the Phillips curve estimates. More tests are needed to discriminate between the competing theories. One such attempt is Ireland (2002), who investigates whether the correlation between nominal and real variables in the US postwar data is indicative of significant price rigidities or whether it simply reflects the particular way monetary authorities react to developments in the real economy. A model of endogenous money that allows for, but does not require, nominal price rigidities is estimated using a maximum likelihood procedure. The results show that nominal price rigidity, in addition to endogenous money, plays a role in accounting for the key features of the data, which offers significant support for the NNS models.

Appendix A

A Technical Presentation of the New Neoclassical Synthesis

This appendix provides a complete description of the basic model that lies at the heart of the NNS which was employed in the more policy-oriented analysis of the main text. The (closed) economy under consideration consists of households that supply labor, purchase consumption goods, and hold money and bonds. The firms produce differentiated goods by employing labor. For the sake of brevity this appendix abstracts from capital in production. The firms sell their products in monopolistically competitive goods markets. Both, firms and households behave optimally.

Households

Households are characterized by their intertemporal utility that depends on a composite consumption good as in eq. (1.2) in the main text, repeated here for convenience:

$$\text{(A.1)} \qquad C_t = \left[\int_0^1 c_t(j)^{\frac{\theta-1}{\theta}} dj \right]^{\frac{\theta}{\theta-1}},$$

where $\theta > 1$ is the elasticity of substitution between any two given varieties j and j'. Furthermore, real money balances (M/P) and the work effort (N) enter the utility function:[45]

$$\text{(A.2)} \qquad U_t = E_t \sum_{i=0}^{\infty} \beta^i \left[\frac{C_{t+i}^{1-\sigma}}{1-\sigma} + \frac{1}{1-b} \left(\frac{M_s^j}{P_s} \right)^{1-b} - \frac{N_{t+i}^{1+\eta}}{1+\eta} \right].$$

It is convenient the separate the households' decision problem into two parts. First, regardless of the level of total consumption the households have decided on, the optimal combination of individual goods has to be decided on ("expenditure allocation problem"). Second, given this composition allocation of goods, the households have to decide on the level of total consumption, on the amount of work to be supplied to finance the consumption and on the optimal

---

[45] Notice that the leisure is equal to $(1-N_t)$, so that the last term in the utility function can also be interpreted as the (positive) utility stemming from leisure if the "1" in the leisure term is neglected because it is a constant.

money holding ("dynamic programming problem"). Whereas the first choice is static one, the second is an intertemporal allocation problem.

Step 1: optimal (static) expenditure allocation[46]

The representative household's decision problem can be formalized as follows:

$$\text{(A.3)} \qquad \max_{c(i)} \left[\int_0^1 c(j)^{\frac{\theta-1}{\theta}} di \right]^{\frac{\theta}{\theta-1}} \qquad \text{s.t}$$

$$\text{(A.4)} \qquad \Omega = \int_0^1 p(j)c(i)di,$$

where Ω is a given amount of nominal expenditure. The Lagrangian is:

$$\text{(A.5)} \qquad L = \left[\int_0^1 c(j)^{\frac{\theta-1}{\theta}} dj \right]^{\frac{\theta}{\theta-1}} + \lambda\left(\Omega - \int_0^1 p(j)c(j)dj \right).$$

The FOCs are:

$$\text{(A.6)} \qquad \frac{\partial L}{\partial c(j)} = \frac{\theta}{\theta-1}\left[\int_0^1 c(j)^{\frac{\theta-1}{\theta}} di \right]^{\frac{1}{\theta-1}} \frac{\theta-1}{\theta} c(j)^{-\frac{1}{\theta}} - \lambda p(j) = 0$$

and for an other good from the basket $c(j')$, respectively:

$$\text{(A.7)} \qquad \frac{\partial L}{\partial c(j')} = \frac{\theta}{\theta-1}\left[\int_0^1 c(j')^{\frac{\theta-1}{\theta}} di \right]^{\frac{1}{\theta-1}} \frac{\theta-1}{\theta} c(j')^{-\frac{1}{\theta}} - \lambda p(j') = 0$$

and for all goods:

[46] Since the optimization problem in the first step is entirely static and independent of time, it is abstained from explicitly using time subscripts. These are introduced in step 2 further below.

(A.8) $$\frac{\partial L}{\partial \lambda} = \Omega - \int_0^1 p(j)c(j)dj = 0 .$$

Solving the expressions (A.6) and (A.7) with respect to the shadow price and setting them equal leads after some rearranging to:

(A.9) $$c(j) = c(j')\left(\frac{p(j)}{p(j')}\right)^{-\theta} .$$

Substituting expression (A.9) into the constraint (A.4) and using the consumption price index from expression (1.4) in the main text which is derived hereafter leads to:

(A.10) $$c(j) = \left(\frac{p(j)}{P}\right)^{-\theta} \frac{\Omega}{P} .$$

Considering that this price index is to be interpreted as the minimum amount of money for one unit of consumption, so that $\Omega/P = C$, expression (A.10) can also be written as

(A.11) $$c(j) = \left(\frac{p(j)}{P}\right)^{-\theta} C .$$

which is identical to eq. (1.3) in the main text.

Starting point for the derivation of the consumption price index in (1.4) in the main text is the following optimisation problem: minimize the total expenditure for one unit of the composite consumption good given individual prices of the differentiated consumption goods:

(A.12) $$\min_{c(j)} \Omega = \int_0^1 p(j)c(j)dj \qquad \text{s.t.}$$

(A.13) $$1 = \left[\int_0^1 c(j)^{\frac{\theta-1}{\theta}} dj\right]^{\frac{\theta}{\theta-1}} .$$

Then the Lagrangian becomes:

(A.14) $$L=\int_0^1 p(j)c(j)dj+\lambda\left(1-\left[\int_0^1 c(j)^{\frac{\theta-1}{\theta}}dj\right]^{\frac{\theta}{\theta-1}}\right).$$

The FOCs are:

(A.15) $$\frac{\partial L}{\partial c(j)}=p(j)-\lambda\frac{\theta}{\theta-1}\left[\int_0^1 c(j)^{\frac{\theta-1}{\theta}}dj\right]^{\frac{1}{\theta-1}}\frac{\theta-1}{\theta}c(j)^{-\frac{1}{\theta}}=0 \quad \text{and}$$

(A.16) $$\frac{\partial L}{\partial \lambda}=1-\left[\int_0^1 c(j)^{\frac{\theta-1}{\theta}}dj\right]^{\frac{\theta}{\theta-1}}=0.$$

Using the definition of the composite consumption good in (A.1) the expression (A.15) can be simplified to:

(A.17) $$p(j)=\lambda C^{\frac{1}{\theta}}c(j)^{-\frac{1}{\theta}}.$$

Raising this expression to the power of $(1-\theta)$ yields

(A.18) $$p(j)^{1-\theta}=\lambda^{1-\theta}\left(C^{\frac{1}{\theta}}c(j)^{-\frac{1}{\theta}}\right)^{1-\theta}.$$

By integration over all j and using the definition of the composite consumption good this expression becomes:

$$\int_0^1 p(j)^{1-\theta}dj=\lambda^{1-\theta} \qquad \text{or}$$

(A.19) $$\lambda=\left[\int_0^1 p(j)^{1-\theta}dj\right]^{\frac{1}{1-\theta}}.$$

This is identical to expression (1.4) in the text once we interpret the shadow price as the consumption price index P:

(1.4) $$P_t = \left(\int_0^1 p_t(j)^{1-\theta} dj \right)^{\frac{1}{1-\theta}}.$$

Step 2: dynamic optimization problem

For the second part of the dual optimization problem the representative household has to take into account its intetemporal budget constraint:

(A.20) $$C_t + \frac{M_t}{P_t} + \frac{B_t}{P_t} = \left(\frac{W_t}{P_t} \right) \cdot N_t + \frac{M_{t-1}}{P_t} + (1 + i_{t-1}) \frac{B_{t-1}}{P_t} + \Pi_t,$$

where B_t is the households one-period bond holding in nominal terms. Bonds pay a nominal rate of interest of i_t. Real profits from firms are equal to Π_t and W_t is the nominal wage rate. Subject to this budget constraint the representative household maximizes the intertemporal utility function with respect to consumption (C), money holding (M) and the amount of labor (N). This leads to the following conditions for the intertemporal allocation of consumption, money demand and supply of labor which, in addition to the budget constraint, must hold in equilibrium:

(A.21) $$\frac{dU}{\partial C} = 0 \quad \rightarrow \quad C_t^{-\sigma} = \beta(1 + i_t) E_t \left(\frac{P_t}{P_{t+1}} \right) C_{t+1}^{-\sigma}$$

(A.22) $$\frac{dU}{\partial M} = 0 \quad \rightarrow \quad \frac{\left(\frac{M_t}{P_t} \right)^{-b}}{C_t^{-\sigma}} = \frac{i_t}{1 + i_t}$$

(A.23) $$\frac{dU}{\partial N} = 0 \quad \rightarrow \quad \frac{N_t^{\eta}}{C_t^{-\sigma}} = \frac{W_t}{P_t}$$

Equation (A.21) represents the Euler condition for the optimal intertemporal allocation of consumption. Expression (A.22) is a optimally condition that equalizes the marginal rate of substitution between money holding and consumption equal to the opportunity cost of holding money. This expression drives the money demand. Expression (A.23) is the optimality condition for the choice of labor supply by the representative household. It sets the marginal rate of substitution between leisure and consumption equal to the real wage rate.

Firms

It is assumed that each firm has some degree monopolistic power over a differentiated consumption good. Apart from this firms only differ in their ability to adjust prices. According to Calvo's (1983) staggered price setting it is assumed that in each period, the firms that can adjust prices are selected randomly: the fraction of firms that is able to adjust prices in each period is $1-\omega$, while ω denotes the fraction of firms that is not able to change prices in each period. Thus the value of ω defines the degree of price stickiness in the economy. Apart from this, firms are assumed to be identical. They produce their product according to the same constant returns to scale production function in which, for simplicity, capital is ignored:

(A.24) $$c_t(j) = Z_t \cdot N_t(j),$$

where Z is a random productivity shock with E(Z)=1 and N(j) the amount of employed labor by firm j. Firms maximize profits according to the demand is it facing which has already been derived from the households expenditure allocation problem. It is convenient to first describe a representative firm's cost minimisation problem before turning to its optimal pricing decision. Formulated in real terms this problem is:

(A.25) $$\min_{N_t}\left(\frac{W_t}{P_t}\right)N_t + \varphi_t(c_t - Z_t N_t),$$

where φ is the Lagrangian multiplier associated which a change in the amount of production. The first order condition is:

(A.26) $$\varphi_t = \frac{W_t/P_t}{Z_t},$$

from which can immediately been seen that φ_t is equal to the real marginal cost a firm faces. Using this, the firm's decision problem for setting the optimal relative price can be written as:

(A.27) $$\max_{p_t} E_t \sum_{i=0}^{\infty} \omega^i d_{t,t+i}\left[\left(\frac{p_t}{P_{t+i}}\right)\cdot c_{t+i} - \varphi_{t+i}\cdot c_{t+i}\right],$$

where $d_{i,t+i} = \beta^i (C_{t+i}/C_t)^{-\sigma}$ is the real discount factor that can be extracted from the consumption Euler equation derived above. Substituting in the demand for the differentiated consumption good yields:

$$\text{(A.28)} \qquad \max_{p_t} E_t \sum_{i=0}^{\infty} \omega^i d_{i,t+i} \left[\left(\frac{p_t}{P_{t+i}} \right)^{1-\theta} - \varphi_{t+i} \cdot \left(\frac{p_t}{P_{t+i}} \right)^{-\theta} \right] \cdot C_{t+i} \,.$$

The first order condition for the optimal choice of price p_t* is

$$\text{(A.28)} \qquad E_t \sum_{i=0}^{\infty} \omega^i d_{i,t+i} \left[(1-\theta) \cdot \left(\frac{p_t^*}{P_{t+i}} \right)^{1-\theta} + \theta \cdot \varphi_{t+i} \right] \cdot \left(\frac{1}{p_t^*} \right) \left(\frac{p_t^*}{P_{t+i}} \right)^{-\theta} C_{t+i} = 0 \,.$$

Using the definition of the real discount factor and expand (A.28) by $1/P_t$ the previous expression can be rearranged to yield

$$\text{(A.29)} \qquad \left(\frac{p_t^*}{P_t} \right) = \left(\frac{\theta}{\theta - 1} \right) \frac{E \sum_{i=0}^{\infty} (\omega\beta)^i C_{t+i}^{1-\sigma} \varphi_{t+i} \left(\frac{P_{t+i}}{P_t} \right)^{\theta}}{E \sum_{i=0}^{\infty} (\omega\beta)^i C_{t+i}^{1-\sigma} \left(\frac{P_{t+i}}{P_t} \right)^{\theta-1}} \,.$$

In the case in which all firms are able to adjust prices in every period ($\omega = 0$) expression (A.29) reduces to[47]

$$\text{(A.30)} \qquad \left(\frac{p_t^*}{P_t} \right) = \left(\frac{\theta}{\theta - 1} \right) \cdot \varphi_t \,,$$

which equals expression (1.5) in the main text, expect that here it is expressed in real terms ($\varphi_t = \psi_t / P_t$). However, substituting in the definition of the real marginal cost and multiplying both sides of (A.30) immediately leads to expression (1.5).

[47] This is because a value of zero for ω leads to a zero value of the first expression in both expectations, respectively. Zero raised by any power of greater than zero is zero, so that with the exception of period $i = 0$ the elements in both sums vanish, which leaves only the current period ($i = 0$), since zero raised by the power of zero is equal to one. However, in that period P_{t+i} is equal to P_t, so that the last expression is 1 in both the denominator and the enumerator. As a result, everything except the term φ_t cancels out.

Flexible Price (and Flexible Wage) Solution

When all prices are flexible, all firms charge the same price and $p_t^* = P_t$. From (A.30) this means that real marginal costs are equal to the inverse the mark-up ($\mu = \theta/(\theta-1)$). Using the definition of real marginal costs from (A.26), this implies that

(A.31) $$\frac{W_t}{P_t} = \frac{Z_t}{\mu}.$$

From the optimisation of the household we also know that the real wage has to be equal to the marginal rate of substitution between leisure and consumption (see condition (A.23)). Thus, we can also write

(A.32) $$\frac{Z_t}{\mu} = \frac{N_t^{\eta}}{C_t^{-\sigma}}.$$

This can be approximated around the steady state value. Denoting the percentage deviation of each variable X from its steady state value by $\hat{x}$ we can rewrite (A.32):

(A.33) $$\eta \hat{n}_t + \sigma \hat{c}_t = \hat{z}_t.$$

Log-linearizing the production function (A.24) and noticing that actual output y^a must equal total consumption c yields

(A.34) $$\hat{y}_t^a = \hat{z}_t + \hat{n}_t.$$

Combining equations (A.33) and (A.34) leads to the expression of the flexible price equilibrium output:

(A.35) $$\hat{y}_t^f = \left(\frac{1+\eta}{\sigma+\eta}\right) \cdot \hat{z}_t.$$

However, because marginal price exceeds marginal cost, output will by inefficiently low.

Sticky Price (and Flexible Wage) Solution and the New Keynesian Phillips Curve

When prices are sticky, output can differ from the flexible-price equilibrium level in (A.35). Since not all firms are able to adjust their price every period, a firms must take into account not only current marginal costs when it has the opportunity to reset prices but also future marginal costs. Equation (A.29) shows this pricing behavior. The aggregate price level for period *t*, which the price setting in (A.29) is conditioned on, is an average of the prices charged by the fraction 1-ω of firms setting their price in period *t* and the average of the remaining fraction ω of all firms which set their prices in earlier periods. Because the adjusting firms were selected randomly from among all firms, the average price of the non-adjusting firms is just the average price of all firms that prevailed in period *t*-1. Thus, from equation (1.4), the average price in period t satisfies

$$\text{(A.36)} \qquad P_t^{1-\theta} = (1-\omega)(p_t^*)^{1-\theta} + \omega \cdot P_{t-1}^{1-\theta}.$$

Equation (A.36) together with (A.29) determine the behaviour of the aggregate price level. In order to obtain some more insights, both equations can be approximated around a zero average inflation steady-state equilibrium. Let Q_t define the relative price chosen by all firms that adjust prices in period *t*:

$$\text{(A.37)} \qquad Q_t = \frac{p_t^*}{P_t}.$$

The steady state value of Q is Q=1. Combining (A.36) and (A.37) after having divided the latter by P_t, one obtains

$$\text{(A.38)} \qquad 1 = (1-\omega)Q_t^{1-\theta} + \omega \cdot \left(\frac{P_{t-1}}{P_t}\right)^{1-\theta}.$$

Equation (A.38) can be expressed in terms of percentage deviations around the zero-inflation steady state (using the aforementioned notation):

$$\text{(A.39)} \qquad 0 = (1-\omega)\cdot \hat{q}_t - \omega \cdot \pi_t \quad \text{or} \quad \hat{q}_t = \left(\frac{\omega}{1-\omega}\right)\cdot \pi_t,$$

where π_t is the rate of inflation equal $\pi_t = \hat{p}_t - \hat{p}_{t-1}$.

Equation (A.29) can be rewritten as

$$\text{(A.40)} \qquad E\sum_{i=0}^{\infty}(\omega\beta)^i C_{t+i}^{1-\sigma}\left(\frac{P_{t+i}}{P_t}\right)^{\theta-1}\cdot Q_t=\mu\cdot\left[E\sum_{i=0}^{\infty}(\omega\beta)^i C_{t+i}^{1-\sigma}\varphi_{t+i}\left(\frac{P_{t+i}}{P_t}\right)^{\theta}\right].$$

Approximating the left-hand side leads to

(A.41)

$$\left(\frac{C^{1-\sigma}}{1-\omega\beta}\right)+\left(\frac{C^{1-\sigma}}{1-\omega\beta}\right)\cdot\hat{q}_t+C^{1-\sigma}\sum_{1=0}^{\infty}(\omega\beta)^i\left[(1-\sigma)E_t\hat{c}_{t+i}+(\theta-1)(E_t\hat{p}_{t+i}-\hat{p}_t)\right].$$

The right-hand side becomes

(A.42)

$$\mu\left\{\left(\frac{C^{1-\sigma}}{1-\omega\beta}\right)\cdot\varphi+\varphi\cdot C^{1-\sigma}\sum_{1=0}^{\infty}(\omega\beta)^i\left[E_t\hat{\varphi}_{t+i}+(1-\sigma)E_t\hat{c}_{t+i}+\theta(E_t\hat{p}_{t+i}-\hat{p}_t)\right]\right\}.$$

Setting the two previous expressions equal, noting that in the steady state $\mu\cdot\varphi=1$ and cancelling out some terms yields:

$$\text{(A.43)} \qquad \hat{q}_t+\hat{p}_t=(1-\omega\beta)\sum_{i=0}^{\infty}(\omega\beta)^i(E_t\hat{\varphi}_{t+i}+E_t\hat{p}_{t+i})$$

Expression (A.43) can be further simplified. In order to do so, notice that, in general, a first order stochastic differential equation of the following form

$$q_t=ax_t+bE_tq_{t+1}$$

has the solution

$$q_t=a\sum_{k=0}^{\infty}b^kE_tx_{t+k}.$$

The latter functional form equals (A.43) if parameters are matched in the following way:

$$q_t = \hat{q}_t + \hat{p}_t$$

$$x_t = E_t \hat{\varphi}_{t+i} + E_t \hat{p}_{t+i}$$

$$a = (1 - \omega\beta)$$

$$b = \omega\beta .$$

In other words, expression (A.43) can be written in the form

(A.44) $$\hat{q}_t + \hat{p}_t = (1 - \omega\beta)(\hat{\varphi}_t + \hat{p}_t) + \omega\beta(E_t \hat{q}_{t+1} + E_t \hat{p}_{t+1}) .$$

This expression can be further rearranged to

(A.45) $$\hat{q}_t = (1 - \omega\beta)\hat{\varphi}_t + \omega\beta(E_t \hat{q}_{t+1} + E_t \pi_{t+1}) ,$$

where the expected inflation rate is defined as: $E_t \pi_{t+1} = E_t \hat{p}_{t+1} - \hat{p}_t$. Substituting (A.39) into (A.45) yields

(A.46) $$\begin{aligned} \left(\frac{\omega}{1-\omega}\right)\pi_t &= (1 - \omega\beta)\hat{\varphi}_t + \omega\beta(\left(\frac{\omega}{1-\omega}\right)E_t \pi_{t+1} + E_t \pi_{t+1}) \\ &= (1 - \omega\beta)\hat{\varphi}_t + \beta\left(\frac{\omega}{1-\omega}\right)E_t \pi_{t+1} . \end{aligned}$$

Finally, multiplying both sides of the previous equation by $\left(\frac{1-\omega}{\omega}\right)$ leads to

(A.47) $$\pi_t = \kappa \cdot \hat{\varphi}_t + \beta \cdot E_t \pi_{t+1} ,$$

where

$$\kappa = \frac{(1-\omega)(1-\omega\beta)}{\omega} .$$

Expression (A.47) is known as the forward-looking New Keynesian Phillips curve, which is also presented in expression (1.11) in the main text.

Real marginal costs can now be related to a measure of the output gap. Expressed in deviations around the steady state (A.26) can be expressed as

(A.48) $$\hat{\varphi}_t = \hat{w}_t - \hat{p}_t - \hat{z}_t .$$

Using the expression for the production function (A.34), the previous expression can be re-written as

(A.49) $$\hat{\varphi}_t = (\hat{w}_t - \hat{p}_t) - (\hat{y}_t^a - \hat{n}_t).$$

The expression for the deviation of the real wage in (A.49) can be substituted by expression (A.23) after expressing the latter also as deviations around the steady state:

(A.50) $$\hat{w}_t - \hat{p}_t = \eta\hat{n}_t + \sigma\hat{y}_t^a ,$$

so that it becomes

(A.51) $$\hat{\varphi}_t = (\eta\hat{n}_t + \sigma\hat{y}_t^a) - (\hat{y}_t^a - \hat{n}_t) = (1+\eta)\hat{n}_t + (\sigma - 1)\hat{y}_t^a ,$$

which can be further rearranged by, again, making use of (A.34) and substitute for $\hat{n}_t = \hat{y}_t^a - \hat{z}_t$, so that the previous expression becomes

(A.52) $$\hat{\varphi}_t = (1+\eta)(\hat{y}_t^a - \hat{z}_t) + (\sigma - 1)\hat{y}_t^a = (\sigma + \eta)\hat{y}_t^a - (1+\eta)\hat{z}_t .$$

Rewriting (A.52) as

(A.53) $$\hat{\varphi}_t = (\sigma + \eta)\left(\hat{y}_t^a - \left(\frac{(1+\eta)}{(\sigma + \eta)} \right) \hat{z}_t \right)$$

allows to substitute in the solution for the flexible-price equilibrium output (A.35), so that

(A.54) $$\hat{\varphi}_t = (\sigma + \eta)\left(\hat{y}_t^a - \hat{y}_t^f\right),$$

where the last expression of the right-hand side is the gap between actual output and the flexible-price equilibrium output $\hat{y}_t = \left(\hat{y}_t^a - \hat{y}_t^f\right)$, in other words, the output gap. This expression is also given in the main text with $\gamma = \sigma + \eta$. Using (A.55) the Phillips curve in (A.47) becomes

(A.55) $\pi_t = \beta \cdot E_t \pi_{t+1} + \widetilde{\kappa} \cdot \hat{y}_t,$

where

$$\widetilde{\kappa} = \frac{(\sigma + \eta)(1-\omega)(1-\omega\beta)}{\omega}.$$

This equals the expression (1.13) in the main text with the only difference of the disturbance term. This disturbance term is supposed to display a cost push shock. Since the forward-looking Philips curve is derived from optimizing behavior, however, this term has to be rationalized instead of just add it 'ad hoc'. Therefore, expression (A.54) can be slightly modified to

(A.56) $\hat{\varphi}_t = (\sigma + \eta)\left(\hat{y}_t^a - \hat{y}_t^f\right) + u_t.$

The presence of the disturbance term in the relation between real marginal costs and the output gap is justified by the assumption that the relation is not necessarily a deterministic one but can instead subject to stochastic deviation which are then interpreted as cost push shocks. Combining the previous expression with (A.47) then leads to the Phillips curve as presented in the main text of this chapter:

(1.13) $\pi_t = \beta E_t \pi_{t+1} + \widetilde{\kappa} \hat{y}_t + u_t.$

From (1.13) it can be seen that there exists a long-run trade-off in the sense that a positive steady state inflation rate constitutes a permanent deviation of output from potential if $\beta<1$. Let $\widetilde{\pi}$ the steady state level of inflation such that $\widetilde{\pi} = \pi_t = \pi_{t+1}$, it follows that

(A.57) $\hat{y} = \frac{1-\beta}{\kappa} \cdot \widetilde{\pi}.$

The literature solves this "problem" by assuming $\beta=1$. This implies that firms do not discount the future.

The Optimizing IS Curve

Let us first express the consumption Euler equation (A.21) in terms of the real interest rate:

$$(\text{A.58}) \qquad C_t^{-\sigma} = \beta(1+r_t)E_t C_{t+1}^{-\sigma}.$$

Now consider a log-linear approximation to this equation around a steady state with zero inflation:

$$(\text{A.59}) \qquad \hat{c}_t = E_t\hat{c}_{t+1} - \frac{1}{\sigma}\hat{r}_t.$$

If we make use of the market clearing condition $\hat{c}_t = \hat{y}_t^a$ and the definition of the output gap $\hat{y}_t = (\hat{y}_t^a - \hat{y}_t^f)$, we get the forward-looking IS curve:

$$(\text{A.60}) \qquad \hat{y}_t = E_t\hat{y}_{t+1} - \frac{1}{\sigma}(\hat{r}_t) + x_t = E_t\hat{y}_{t+1} - \frac{1}{\sigma}(\hat{i}_t - E_t\pi_{t+1}) + x_t,$$

with $x_t \equiv E_t(\hat{y}_{t+1}^f - \hat{y}_t^f)$ having the interpretation of a productivity shock (see equation (A.35)).[48] Alternatively the IS curve can be written as

$$(\text{A.61}) \qquad \hat{y}_t = E_t\hat{y}_{t+1} - \frac{1}{\sigma}(\hat{i}_t - E\pi_{t+1} - r_t^n),$$

$$\text{where} \quad r_t^n \equiv \sigma(\hat{y}_{t+1}^f - \hat{y}_t^f) = \sigma \cdot \left(\frac{1+\eta}{\sigma+\eta}\right) \cdot E\Delta\hat{z}_{t+1}$$

is the natural real interest rate that depends on the evolution of the productivity parameter.

Adding Sticky Wages to the Model

In the previous sections it was assumed that stickiness in goods prices is the only source of nominal rigidity in the model. This section shows how the model has

[48] Alternatively, the shock term is sometimes includes a government spending shock in order to model effects of fiscal policy. This augmented form can be derived in the same way with additionally including government expenditure in the market clearing condition.

to be modified in order to allow for stickiness in wages. One way how to do this would be following the derivation of the new Phillips curve from the previous section but instead assuming the Calvo price mechanism to be at work in the wage setting process. This derivation would lead to a wage inflation equation comparable with the price inflation equation in (A.47). However, in order to get a result directly comparable to the Phillips curve in (A.56) we will proceed an alternative way.

Suppose each firm now needs to assemble a composite labor input given by differentiated labor types that are monopolistically supplied by households. Under perfect competitive labor markets we saw from expression (A.23) (restated here in log deviations as in (A.50)) that:

$$\text{(A.62)} \qquad \hat{w}_t - \hat{p}_t = \eta \hat{n}_t + \sigma \hat{c}_t = mrs_t,$$

where mrs_t denotes the marginal rate of substitution between consumption and leisure. This is no longer true for the assumption of monopolistic power in the labor market. Condition (A.62) modifies to:

$$\text{(A.63)} \qquad \hat{w}_t - \hat{p}_t = \hat{\mu}_t^l + mrs_t,$$

where $\hat{\mu}_t^l = \log\left(\frac{\theta^l}{\theta^l - 1}\right)$ is the log of the mark-up with θ^l being the elasticity of substitution across differentiated labor types.[49] Using (A.63) together with the definition of real marginal cost from (A.48) we get:

$$\text{(A.64)} \qquad \hat{\varphi}_t = \hat{\mu}_t^l + \eta \hat{n}_t + \sigma \hat{c}_t - z_t.$$

Making use of the market clearing condition $\hat{c}_t = \hat{y}_t^a$ and recognizing from the production function that $\hat{n}_t = \hat{y}_t^a - \hat{z}_t$, we can re-write the previous expression as

$$\text{(A.65)} \qquad \hat{\varphi}_t = \hat{\mu}_t^l + (\eta + \sigma)\hat{y}_t^a - (1+\eta) z_t.$$

This expression directly compares to (A.52). Rearranging it in the same way leads to:

[49] Since the derivation of this monopolistic mark-up in the presence of iso-elastic demand is standard, it is not shown here.

(A.66) $$\hat{\varphi}_t = \hat{\mu}_t^l(\sigma+\eta)\left(\hat{y}_t^a - \left(\frac{(1+\eta)}{(\sigma+\eta)}\right)\hat{z}_t\right)$$

or in terms of the output gap:

(A.67) $$\hat{\varphi}_t = \hat{\mu}_t^l + (\sigma+\eta)\left(\hat{y}_t^a - \hat{y}_t^f\right) = \hat{\mu}_t^l + (\sigma+\eta)\hat{y}_t .$$

From this expression we see that the proportionality between the real marginal costs and the output gap vanishes due to the additional presence of the wage mark-up. Using this modified definition for the real marginal cost in the forward-looking New Keynesian Phillips Curve in (A.47) we get:

(A.68) $$\pi_t = \beta \cdot E_t\pi_{t+1} + \tilde{\kappa}\cdot\hat{y}_t + \kappa\cdot\hat{\mu}_t^l,$$ where again

$$\tilde{\kappa} = \frac{(\sigma+\eta)(1-\omega)(1-\omega\beta)}{\omega} \quad \text{and} \quad \kappa = \frac{(1-\omega)(1-\omega\beta)}{\omega}.$$

Expression (A.68) is the New Keynesian Phillips Curve in the presence of sticky prices and sticky wages. In the particular case of flexible wages but sticky prices which we derived in the previous section, we have $\hat{\mu}_t^l = 0$, and hence equation (A.68) reduces to (A.56). The additional presence of sticky wages has important implications for stabilization policy which were already mentioned in the main text but can be seen more analytically in equation (A.68). To the extent that, in response to shocks, wage stickiness implies movements of the wage mark-up $\hat{\mu}_t^l$, targeting a zero output gap does not imply that the flexible price-zero inflation allocation can be automatically reached, as this is the case in the sticky price-flexible wage case. Instead, the policy makers face a possible trade-off between the output gap and inflation stabilization. Replication the frictionless equilibrium allocation is no longer feasible as long at it requires changes in the real wage. This also means that strict inflation targeting is no longer the optimal policy.[50]

[50] Christiano, Eichenbaum and Evans (2001), and Smets and Wouters (2002) estimated dynamic general equilibrium models for the US and the Euro area, respectively, that specify both wage and price stickiness. Both conclude that wage stickiness, more than price stickiness, is key to the understanding of the dynamics of output and inflation. However, like it is also present in traditional models (like the Friedman misperception model), a model with sticky wages but flexible prices implies that real wages move counter-cyclically. This is not in line with the empirical evidence. For the US, for example, the data suggest a (weak) pro-cyclical movement.

Chapter 2

The Theoretical Foundations of Interest Rate Rules

2.1 Introduction

In the previous chapter, we saw that monetary policy plays an important role in determining the dynamics of a macroeconomic model. More specifically, the 'new consensus model' from section 1.6 which, in turn, stems from a fully specified general equilibrium model includes a monetary policy rule as one of its crucial elements. A monetary policy rule summarizes the policy conducted by the central bank. This chapter builds on the previous one and provides a closer theoretical examination of monetary policy rules and, in particular, of interest rate rules. The next chapter then discusses the empirical evidence of interest rate rules.

In recent years, the modeling of monetary policy rules has gained widespread interest in the field of macroeconomic research. The motivation of this research is twofold. First, researchers want to understand and empirically characterize the behavior of major central banks. This is basically the foundations of most empirical work in this field of research. In this sense, the monetary policy rules are labeled as monetary policy reaction functions. Second, researchers want to characterize and formulate robust monetary policy rules that lead to a stable economic development. This normative aspect motivates most of the theoretical research on monetary policy rules.

The structure of this chapter is as follows. The next section 2.2 briefly discusses the historical roots of monetary policy rules. Section 2.3 proposes a classification scheme for monetary policy rules, in order to provide a systematic framework for monetary policy rules which is employed in more detail in the subsequent chapters. Section 2.4 demonstrates that an optimal interest rate rule can be derived from a small-scale model similar to the one discussed in section 1.6. Section 2.5 presents a formal discussion of the *Taylor principle* that provides the stability condition for any interest rate rule and is, thus, very important for the understanding of interest rate rules. Section 2.6 explicitly discusses the link between money supply (rules) and interest rate rules. Finally, section 2.7 discusses the most relevant caveats for using (mechanical) interest rate rules in practice.

2.2 The Reappearance of Monetary Policy Rules

The idea of formulating a monetary policy rule in the sense of some kind of mechanical adjustment of the instrument of the monetary authority goes back at least to Knut Wicksell (1898):

> *"So long as prices remain unaltered the* [central] *banks' rate of interest is to remain unaltered. If prices rise, the rate of interest is to be raised; and if prices fall, the rate of interest is to be lowered; and the rate of interest is henceforth to be maintained at its new level until a further movement of prices calls for a further change in one direction or the other."*

This quote demonstrates that economists were already early thinking of some kind of mechanical behavior of central banks. Also Milton Friedman's (1968) well-known formulation of the fixed money supply rule has to be considered as an early contribution to the research on monetary policy rules. The motivation of Friedman's research was the comparison of different monetary policy rules motivated by the attempt to identify robust rules that lead to a satisfying macroeconomic outcome even in times of varying and uncertain economic environment.

Since these early contributions, macroeconomists have gained a far deeper theoretical understanding of alternative monetary policy rules. In particular, the introduction of rational expectations into macroeconomics in the mid-1970s has revolutionized macroeconomic research and also its policy recommendations. Based on the solutions to the time-inconsistency problem, one of the results of the literature is that policy rules are superior to discretion (Kydland and Prescott, 1977; Barro and Gordon, 1983). The underlying rationale is that discretion results in either consistent but sub-optimal planning or in economic instability. Given these theoretical insights, one of the key issues for research is to find simple rules that are easily understood such that it is obvious to economic agents when policy makers deviate from that policy rules.

John Taylor's (1993) seminal paper broad the issue of 'rules versus discretion' in practical monetary policy back on the research agenda again. His simple monetary policy rule stipulates that the interest rate instrument of the monetary authority should react to two key macroeconomic variables: the deviation of contemporaneous inflation from a pre-set inflation target (the "inflation gap") and the deviation of contemporaneous real output from its potential level (the "output gap").[51]

[51] Although these rules have become known as "Taylor rules" it should be noted that Henderson and McKibbin (1993) were the first ones to estimate such reaction functions.

In addition to the issue of time-inconsistency other, more indirect motivations for the renewed academic interest in monetary policy rules can be identified. First, in recent years, research in monetary theory has turned away from the empirical identification and theoretical analysis of monetary policy shocks.[52] Instead, research now focuses on the systematic part of monetary policy and its implications for inflation and output dynamics. This systematic part, in turn, is best modeled by empirical reaction functions like the Taylor rule.[53] Second, as discussed in chapter 1, the formulation of the 'new neoclassical synthesis' has renewed the interest in monetary policy as a potentially powerful stabilization policy tool. Opposed to the Real Business Cycles models, in new neoclassical synthesis models monetary policy displays real effects and, thus, has to be studied. Research on monetary policy rules is part of this comprehensive research program.

Expressed more formally, Taylor's (1993) rule for the Federal funds rate is specified as:[54]

$$(2.1) \qquad i_t^{ffr} = r^{*ffr} + \pi_t + \alpha \cdot (\pi_t - \pi^*) + \beta \cdot \tilde{y}_t ,$$

where i^{ffr} is the Federal funds rate (policy instrument of the Federal Reserve System), r^{*ffr} is the equilibrium real Federal funds rate, π^* is the target inflation rate, and $\tilde{y}$ is the deviation of real GDP from its target level. In this framework, the Federal funds rate rises if inflation is currently above its target and/or real GDP is currently above its target level. The size of the interest rate reaction is governed by the size of the two reaction coefficients, α and β. If both macroeconomic variables are on target, the nominal Federal funds rate will be equal to the sum of its real equilibrium level and the target of inflation.[55] For the ease of exposition, the rule in (2.1) is often written as:

---

[52] See, for example, Christiano, Eichenbaum and Evans (1999) for an excellent overview of this line of research.

[53] See Taylor (1999b) for a summary of this research. However, one should keep in mind that both research directions are connected. One possible strategy for identifying monetary policy shocks is to first extract an empirical reaction function as the systematic part of monetary policy and than take the deviations from that rule as the shock components that might be driven by changes in preferences, by strategic considerations or by forecast errors of the central bank.

[54] Since Taylor (1993) has originally formulated his interest rate rule for the Federal Reserve System solely, it is indicated in expression (2.1) with corresponding superscripts. Subsequently however, as it is common in the literature, it will be expressed as a general rule that can also be applied for other central banks.

[55] Note that in this situation: $\pi_t = \pi^*$.

(2.2) $$i_t^{ffr} = \delta + (1+\alpha)\cdot\pi_t + \beta\cdot\tilde{y}_t,$$

where $\delta = r^{*ffr} - \alpha\cdot\pi^*$. Equivalently, the rule can also be expressed in terms of the real interest rate according to the Fisher relation ($r_t = i_t - \pi_t$):

(2.3) $$r_t^{ffr} = \delta + \alpha\cdot\pi_t + \beta\cdot\tilde{y}_t.$$

Taylor (1993) sets both the inflation target and the equilibrium real rate equal to two per cent and assigned equal weights for the reaction coefficients of 0.5, so that the original Taylor rule can after some rearranging be written as:

(2.4) $$i_t^{ffr} = 0.04 + 1.5\cdot(\pi_t - 0.02) + 0.5\cdot\tilde{y}_t.$$

Using these values, Taylor (1993) shows that such a simple rule tracks the Federal fund rate reasonable well. Although having the character of a descriptive reaction function of the Fed's behavior, Taylor argues for the rule's normative significance both on the basis of simulations and on the ground that it describes the U.S. monetary policy in a period in which it is widely judged to have been unusually successful. Starting with the research of Taylor (1993) such interest rate rules have been applied to other major central banks like the Deutsche Bundesbank (up to 1998) and the ECB (since 1999).

2.3 A General Classification of Monetary Policy Rules

The Taylor rule has been subject to considerable attention since its publication, and various extensions have appeared in the academic literature. Before the next section examines the theoretical foundations and implications of such interest rate rules more formally, this section first provides a general classification of monetary policy rules. Monetary policy rules differ with respect to their formulation and their theoretical intention. Figure 2.1 gives an overview of monetary policy rules and proposes a classification scheme of existing monetary policy rules.

In principle, two levels of monetary policy have to be distinguished. These are the target level and the instrument level. This circumstance leads to the first, fundamental distinction of monetary policy rules into *target rules* and *instrument rules*. Although the subsequent theoretical discussion demonstrates that a complementary relation between both classes of monetary policy rules exists, it is nevertheless important to understand their different character and intention.

Fig. 2.1: A Classification Scheme for Monetary Policy Rules

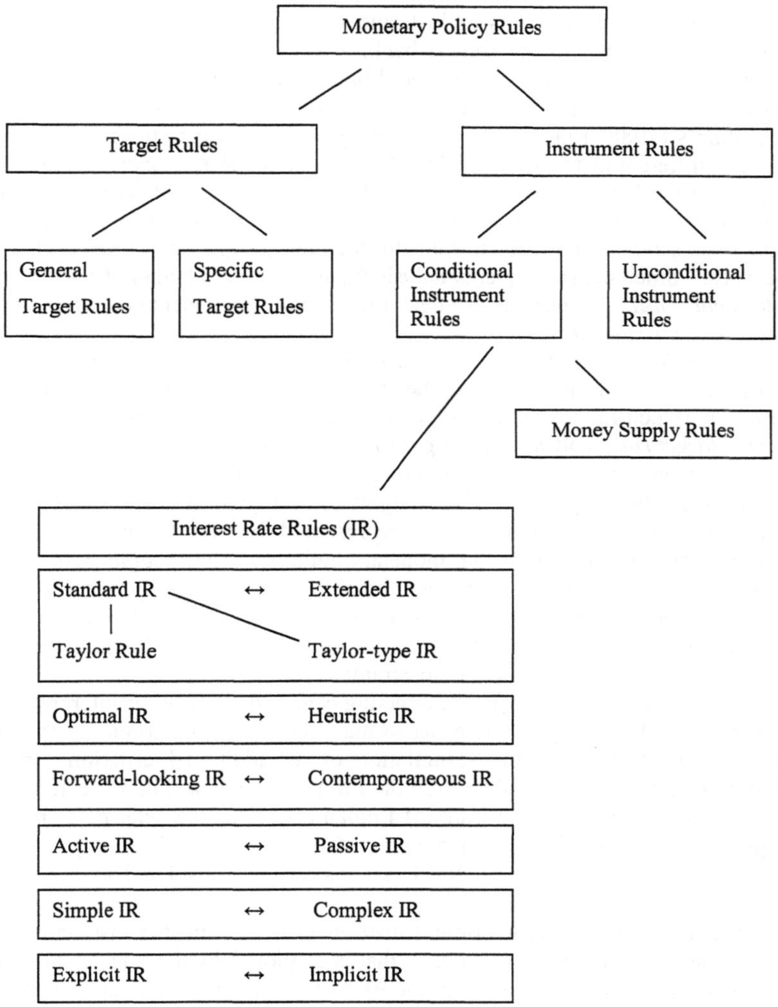

Instrument rules are explicitly formulated monetary policy strategies on the operational level. They can be divided into *conditional instrument rules* and *unconditional instrument rules*. With a *conditional instrument rule* in place, the central bank mechanically sets its instrument as a given function of a subset of information available to the central bank. The instrument, in turn, should be under the exclusive control of the central bank. The Taylor rule for the Federal funds rate in (2.1) is the most prominent *conditional instrument rule*. But also McCallum's (1988) rule for the base money supply belongs to that class, but utilizes a different instrument variable. An *unconditional instrument rule* instead means that the instrument is not directly linked to the present macroeconomic performance. Prominent examples for unconditional instrument rules are "Friedman' s k-% money growth rule" for the money supply and fixed exchange rate rules.[56] Since the subsequent analysis focuses on the subclass of *conditional instrument rules*, the term instrument rule should be understood as being a *conditional instrument rules*.

Target Rules, on the other hand, define a particular goal for monetary policy without being specific about the operational level. According to Svensson (2000), it is helpful to distinguish two subclasses of *target rules*. These are *general target rules* and *specific target rules*. A *general target rule* specifies the goal(s) of monetary rules by giving a quantitative representation and, in case of a set of goals, by attaching specific weights to each goal. It is shown later that, in the theoretical literature, this is represented by the formulation of an intertemporal loss function of the monetary authority. The *specific target rules* go beyond the formulation of a loss function and additionally specify some strategic criteria. In the theoretical literature this corresponds to the formulation of an optimality condition that has to be satisfied after minimizing the loss function subject to some structural constraints.

The strategy of direct inflation targeting can, in that sense, be interpreted as a *target rule*. Depending on the exact formulation, it belongs to one of the two subclasses. For example, the formulation of an additional criterion for the inflation forecast which should match the inflation target within a specific time horizon, as performed by the Bank of England, has the character of a *specific target rule*. The introduction of a pure inflation target without any specific requirement on the operational level can instead be considered as a *general target rule*.

Within the class of (conditional) *instrument rules* a further distinction has to be made according to the instrument that is employed by the rule. Mainly two instrument variables are relevant: the short-term interest rate and (narrow)

[56] However, Figure 2.1 abstains from considering the exchange rate as an instrument variable for monetary policy because, as it is clear in the case of fixed exchange rate, one could argue that no national independent monetary policy is feasible.

monetary aggregates. The first instrument defines the class of *interest rate rules*, while the second class defines *money supply rules*.[57] McCallum's (1988) base money supply rule already mentioned above belongs to the second class. It is based on considerations from the quantity theory of money and employs the base money (currency in circulation plus reserves of the banking system) as the relevant instrument for monetary policy. The rule stipulates that the quantity of base money should be set according to the sum of the inflation target and the 10-year moving average of the growth rate of real GDP minus the 4-year moving average of the velocity of base money.[58] In the recent practice of central banking the main instrument, however, is a short-term interest rate (money market rate) like for example the Federal funds rate in the US. Because of this, most attention within the current research on monetary policy rules is directed towards *interest rate rules*.[59]

The proposed interest rate rules can be further classified according to several dimensions.[60] A first distinction can be made according to the choice of variables to which the central bank reacts. *Standard interest rate rules* are defined as being formulated on the basis of the inflation gap and the output gap. If, additionally, the particular sizes of the reaction coefficients are taken into consideration, these standard rules can be further classified into the Taylor rule itself with its particular coefficients given in (2.4) and so-called *Taylor-type rules* that do have the same structural form but differ with respect to the choice of their particular coefficient values. These rules are displayed by expression (2.1). If additional right-hand side arguments are taken into account, like the real exchange rate or monetary aggregates, the rules fall into the subclass of extended interest rate rules.[61]

---

[57] Notice again that it is abstracted from employing the exchange rate as a monetary policy instrument.

[58] Although being closely related to that concept, it should kept in mind that the money growth concept of the Deutsche Bundesbank from the mid-1970 through 1998 cannot considered as an *instrument rule* in a narrow sense, because the Deutsche Bundesbank targeted a broad monetary aggregate as an intermediate target. Such a target is not under the exclusive control of the central bank and, therefore, cannot be considered as an instrument. The rule-based behavior of the Bundesbank is better described in the above classification as a *specific target rule* in the sense that it comprises some strategic (intermediate) target.

[59] It should be mentioned that in practice the stripline between *money supply rules* and *interest rate rules* cannot be drawn that exactly. Subsequently, it will be shown that a money supply oriented strategy can also be expressed as an *interest rate rule*.

[60] Note that the assignment of a particular rule into one of the following categories is not exclusive, since each category looks at only one particular feature of interest rate rules.

[61] Taking into account the real exchange rate leads to the formulation of a so-called *monetary conditions index* (MCI). However, since the instrument of the MCI is a weighted average of the short-term interest rate and the exchange rate, one also could have defined a particular

Another important distinction is between *optimal interest rate rules* and *heuristic interest rate rules*. The latter are *ad hoc* formulations in the arguments as well as in the size of the coefficients. Again the Taylor rule belongs into this category. Also most estimated empirical reaction functions belong into this category. In most cases their structural formulation is *ad hoc* and the coefficients are determined empirically. The quality of a *heuristic interest rate rule* is measured in two ways depending on the context in which it is formulated. First, if it is formulated as a single equation like in most empirical exercises (monetary policy reaction function), the quality is measured by their ability to *ex post* explain the observed interest rate dynamics. Second, if the rule is part of structural model (like the "consensus model" from chapter 1), the quality is measured by the resulting model dynamics in terms of implied output and inflation volatility based on calibration exercises. *Optimal interest rate rules* instead are extracted from an explicit optimizing model and result as the solution of an optimal control problem. They are normative in nature. The subsequent section 2.4 demonstrates the derivation of such a rule.

A further distinction can be made with respect to the timing of the set of variables the instrument is reacting on. In *contemporaneous interest rate rules* the short-term rate in time t reacts on a set of variables also being determined in that period.[62] In *forward-looking interest rate rules* instead the short rate in time t reacts upon currently (in time t) expected variables' values in time $t+q$, where the length of the forward-looking horizon is represented by q. Such rules are

class of *'mixed' instrument rules* in addition to *interest rate rules* and *money supply rules* in Figure 2.1.

[62] However, as McCallum (1999) has argued, such reaction functions are unrealistic, since policymakers do not have complete information on variables such as output and inflation in the period they must make the decision. One alternative would be a lagged data specification in which the central bank reacts to the last period's observation. Another option would be to form expectations of the current value. For reasons of the clarity of the exposition, the classification in this section implicitly includes both alternatives, the 'lagged data version' and the 'contemporaneous expectations version', into the class of contemporaneous interest rate rules, because the crucial feature of this subclass of rules is that the central bank mainly intends to react on contemporaneous values of the macroeconomic variables. If they are not available, then the central bank departs to one of the mentioned 'second best' strategies. Theoretical analyses support this choice. In Appendix D for section 2.5 it will be shown for the case of Taylor-type rules that all three versions have nearly the same properties with respect to the determinacy of equilibrium. Also empirical analyses show that (due to the high persistence in inflation and output) a distinction of actual period's data and one-period lagged data is of almost no relevance for the results (see the regression results in chapter 3). However, the important issue of data availability is explicitly discussed in section 2.7.

motivated by the observation that central banks react forward-looking in their policy (so-called pre-emptive policy).[63]

As will be shown analytically in section 2.5, the effectiveness of a rule as being stabilizing for the economy crucially depends on the size of the reaction upon an inflationary shock, i.e., on the size of the reaction coefficient of the inflation gap. An *active interest rate rule* that stabilizes the economy after a shock is characterized by a coefficient for the inflation gap bigger than one, whereas a coefficient of smaller than one (in most cases) leads to a *passive interest rate rule* that causes destabilizing dynamics in the economy.[64]

Rules can also be (very) complex if several additional variables rather than only output and inflation are included or several time lags of the macroeconomic variables and/or in the instrument additionally are taken into account. In terms of optimal rules, a rather complex (unrestricted) model with a high number of state variables would then lead to complex *(optimal) interest rate rule*, since all state variables are to be included in the optimal rule. If the model instead is restricted with respect to the number of endogenous variables and if this endogenous variables are the inflation gap and the output gap (like the "consensus model" from section 1.6), a *simple interest rate rule* only in the two standard arguments follows.

Complex models can also lead to the fact that not all right hand side variables are necessarily exogenous. This is, for example, true for the class of forward-looking rules. Depending on the horizon q, the in time t expected future inflation for $t+q$ cannot considered to be independent of the instrument setting in time t itself. Another example is, if the central bank additionally responds to the long-term interest rates. The expectation theory of the term structure of interest rates suggests that the actual value of the long-term interest rate cannot considered to be independent of the actual setting of the short-rate (instrument rate).[65] If variables are endogenous, the rules belong to the class of *implicit interest rate rules*. *Explicit interest rate rules* are characterized by exogenous right hand side variables instead. Again, the Taylor rule is an example of the latter class of interest rate rules.

[63] Here again, it would be possible to define further sub-classes of rules within this category, because it can either be that the central bank reacts to its own inflation forecast or to inflation expectations of the private sector.

[64] As will be shown later, in particular in forward-looking rules, the size of the coefficient of the output gap is of additional importance.

[65] Chapter 4 picks up this issue again.

2.4 An Analytical Foundation of Interest Rate Rules

As already mentioned in the previous section, interest rates rules can have the character of optimal rules. In that sense they can be derived as the explicit solution of an optimal control problem. In order to show this, this section presents a particular model that can be understood as a special (backward-looking) case of the "new consensus model" set out in equations (1.19) and (1.20) of the previous chapter. This particular model is due to Svensson (1997) and has the main advantage that it yields a simple Taylor-type rule as its optimal rule and, thus, the result can be interpreted more easily than more complex rules that result from more elaborated models.[66] A disadvantage of this model is that it is purely backward-looking and somehow contradicts current research under the label 'new neoclassical synthesis' presented in the previous chapter. However, it can nevertheless be seen as a reduced form approximation of more complex forward-looking model formulations that are extracted from the microeconomic optimization problem which was presented in the previous chapter (Taylor, 1999c, p. 662). In addition, as shown by Estrella and Fuhrer (1999, 2002), purely forward-looking models of monetary policy are less successful in matching the data than backward-looking specifications, and they are not necessarily less sensitive to the Lucas critique.[67]

Aggregate demand is described by the conventional dynamic IS-relation of the following form:[68]

$$(2.5) \qquad y_{t+1} = \beta_1 y_t - \beta_2 (i_t - \pi_t) + \eta_{t+1},$$

where y is the output gap defined as the deviation of real GDP from its long-run trend, i is the short-term nominal interest rate that is also the instrument of the central bank and $\pi_t = p_t - p_{t-1}$ is the annual inflation rate with p representing the aggregate price level. All variables except the interest rate are expressed as their natural logarithm. The term η is an i.i.d. shock variable with zero mean representing demand shocks due to, for example, changes in government consumption. The structural parameters are such that $\beta_2>0$ and $0<\beta_1<1$. They govern the sensitivity of future aggregate demand with respect to the current real interest rate and current output gap. According to equation (2.5), the output gap is serially correlated and decreasing in the real interest rate level. In the steady

[66] See Ball (1999) for a similar approach.

[67] Remember the discussion of the forward- versus backward-looking specification of the Phillips curve from chapter 1.

[68] Since the model presented in this section is closely related to the hybrid formulation of consensus model from section 1.6, but does not exactly match it, this section does not precisely adopt the notation from the previous chapter to avoid any false impression.

state the output gap is zero which also implies that the equilibrium real interest rate is normalized to zero.

Aggregate supply is expressed in terms of the Phillips curve relation:

$$\pi_{t+1} = \pi_t + \alpha_1 y_t + \varepsilon_{t+1}, \tag{2.6}$$

where ε represents an i.i.d. random cost-push shock, and the parameter $\alpha_1>0$ determines the slope of the short-run Phillips curve. Equation (2.6) states that inflation changes according to the size of the output gap and supply shocks.

Though being very simple, the model described by equations (2.5) and (2.6) captures several aspects that are important for policymaking in practice. The behavior of output and inflation is subject to random shocks. Output shows persistence because lagged output enters equation (2.5). Inflation is inertial: it is expected to stay at a given level unless output changes or a supply shock hits the economy. The short-term interest rate is the instrument for monetary policy, but it takes the monetary conditions one period to affect output and subsequently one more period for output to affect inflation. Thus, it takes the central bank two periods to influence inflation. This particular structure captures the well demonstrated fact that monetary policy affects output more quickly than inflation.

The central bank aims at minimizing the following intertemporal loss function with the size of inflation and the output gap as the two arguments:

$$\min E_t \sum_{\tau=t}^{\infty} \delta^{\tau-t} L(\pi_\tau, y_\tau), \tag{2.7}$$

where $0<\delta<1$ represents the discount factor. The period loss function is specified as:

$$L(\pi_\tau, y_\tau) = \frac{1}{2}\left[(\pi_\tau - \pi^*)^2 + \lambda y_\tau^2\right], \tag{2.8}$$

where π^* is the target value of inflation defined by the monetary authority and λ is the relative weight that is attached to stabilize output, while the relative weight of the inflation gap is normalized to one. For $\lambda > 0$ such preferences are usually described as *variable inflation targeting*, whereas a zero weight on output expresses a strategy of *strict inflation targeting*. The loss function (2.8) can be interpreted as a *general target rule* as characterized in the classification scheme of the previous section.

Appendix B shows that such a loss function represents the quadratic (second-order Taylor series) approximation to the level of (expected) utility of the representative household in the rational expectation equilibrium associated with a given policy. Thus, there is a direct relation between the goals of monetary policy and the utility function of a representative household that lies at the heart of NNS model presented in the previous chapter. This makes the households' utility a natural normative measure of monetary policy.

Optimizing the intertemporal loss function under the constraints of the structure of the economy displayed by the IS- and the Phillips curve leads to an optimal behavior that is commonly characterized as *inflation-forecast targeting* (see Appendix C):

$$(2.9) \qquad \pi_{t+2|t} - \pi^* = -\frac{\lambda}{\delta \alpha_1 k} y_{t+1|t},$$

$$\text{with} \quad k = \frac{1}{2}\left(1 - \frac{\lambda(1-\delta)}{\delta \alpha_1^2} + \sqrt{\left(1 + \frac{\lambda(1-\delta)}{\delta \alpha_1^2}\right)^2 + \frac{4\lambda}{\alpha_1^2}}\right) \geq 1,$$

where $x_{t+j|t}$ denotes the expectations in time t of a variable x for j periods ahead t.[69] The two-period ahead inflation forecast, $\pi_{t+2|t}$, should equal the inflation target only if the one-period ahead output forecast equals the natural output rate, i.e., the expected next period's output gap, $y_{t+1|t}$, is zero. Otherwise it should exceed (fall short of) the inflation target in proportion to how much the one-period output forecast falls short of (exceeds) the natural level of output. The proportionality is increasing in the relative weight λ.[70] This essentially displays the gradual inflation stabilization strategy under *variable inflation targeting*. A higher weight on output stabilization leads to a slower adjustment of the inflation rate. Equation (2.9) can be interpreted as a *specific target rule* given the characterization in the classification scheme of the previous section.

Solving the demand and supply equations for the respective expectations and substituting them into the optimality condition (2.9) yields a specific reaction function of the form (see also Appendix C):

$$(2.10) \qquad i_t = \pi_t + \tilde{b}_1(\pi_t - \pi^*) + \tilde{b}_2 \cdot y_t,$$

[69] That is, $E_t[x_{t+j}] \equiv x_{t+j|t}$.

[70] It can be proofed that the indirect effect of a change in λ through k in the denominator does not offset the direct effect of λ in the numerator.

where $\widetilde{b}_1 = \dfrac{1-c}{\beta_2 \alpha_1}$,

$$\widetilde{b}_2 = \frac{1-c+\beta_1}{\beta_2} \quad \text{and}$$

$$c = \frac{\lambda}{\lambda + \delta \alpha_1^2 k}.$$

Given that the equilibrium interest rate is normalized to zero, expression (2.10) coincides with Taylor-type rule given in (2.1). Equation (2.10) shows that the reaction coefficients of an optimal rule do have precise structural interpretations. First, they depend on the preferences of the central bank which, in turn, reflect representative household's utility as shown in Appendix B. The higher the weight on output stabilization in the loss function is, the smaller are the reaction coefficients. Second, they depend on the parameters that govern the inflation and the output dynamics. The higher the interest rate sensitivity of output (β_2) is, the smaller are both reaction coefficients. This results because as aggregate demand becomes more responsive to the interest rate, the interest rate will not be required to move as far away from its equilibrium value in order to stabilize the economy. A higher persistence in output (β_1) leads to a more pronounced reaction upon the output gap. The influence of the slope of the Phillips curve (α_1) is best analyzed in the case of strict inflation targeting ($\lambda = 0$) which implies $c = 0$. A stronger response of inflation to the output gap results in a smaller reaction of the short rate with respect to the inflation gap under the optimal policy. This is because the transmission of an interest rate change works through aggregate demand. If the reaction of inflation to the output gap is strong, a smaller interest rate impulse is needed to control inflation.[71]

In general, the precise form and the coefficients of the optimal rule crucially depend on the structural model and the loss function that is chosen. In order to provide a quite simple demonstration effect, the analysis above employed a simple, purely backward-looking model that has the advantage to yield a Taylor-type rule as the associated optimal rule. Studying the forward-looking model version like the one derived in Appendix A comes with the cost

[71] Notice that in the particular case of *strict inflation targeting* the central bank also responses to the output gap although it is not present in the loss function. The central bank has to take care of the output gap even in this case because the output gap is an important determinate of future inflation. Thus, finding a positive and high coefficients for the output gap in empirical analysis does not necessarily imply that the central bank has strong preferences for the output gap itself.

of higher computational burden. The small-scale forward-looking model version from Appendix A would lead to a forward-looking interest rate rule with expected inflation being the argument instead of contemporaneous inflation like in the Taylor rule.[72] However, with an increasing degree of complexity of the model and, thus, of the formal control problem, a more complex optimal rule results because it contains all state variables of the model.[73] Furthermore, depending on the size of the models no closed-form solutions can be obtained. In such cases researchers have to study numerical solutions and draw inference from simulation exercises.[74]

Subsequent research has also been directed to an alternative way of deriving an optimal rule. Given a possibly very complex structural model of the economy, the researchers only focus on deriving the optimal coefficients of a simple rule like the Taylor-type rule. That is, it is assumed that the central bank is able to commit to a simple rule like in (2.1) and then derives the "optimal" coefficients by minimizing the loss function given *ex ante* the form of the interest rate rule.[75] It is important to note that the "optimal" values of the reaction coefficients are only optimal conditional on the central bank following an instrument rule of the given form. This research agenda allows to study the implications of this simple "quasi-optimal" rules in different models compared to the "fully" (often more complex) optimal rule of this particular model. The (relative) quality of a rule in a particular structural model is measured in terms of the implied output and inflation volatility which are the arguments in the central bank's loss function.

It turns out that, within specific models, the performance of simple rules is often nearly as good as the performance of the optimal (model-specific) rule itself. The latter often yields only a marginal reduction in the weighted sum of the variances (Rudebusch and Svensson, 1999). Furthermore, research has shown that the quality of the "fully optimal" rules is highly model-specific, but simple rules instead are robust across models (Levin et al., 1999). Given the model uncertainty we face, this research results also contributed to the relative attractiveness of simple interest rate rules.[76]

---

[72] See, for example, Clarida et al. (1999) for the discussion of optimal rules in this model.

[73] For example, the *Monetary Studies Research Model* of the Fed contains 12 arguments in its optimal rule (Orphanides and Wieland, 1998).

[74] See Walsh (2003, chapter 11) for a presentation. Söderlind (1999) provides the necessary algorithm and the programs for deriving optimal interest rate rules for that kind of models.

[75] The method applied in studying this problem is called "method of undetermined coefficients".

[76] See the volume of Taylor (1999b) for a summary of this research agenda.

2.5 Uniqueness of Equilibrium and the Taylor Principle

Systems of equations like (2.5) plus (2.6) or its forward looking versions from chapter 1, i.e. the 'new consensus model' in eqs. (1.16) plus (1.17), contain three variables: the output gap, the inflation gap and the nominal interest rate. It has been shown that such a model can be closed by the assumption that the central bank controls the nominal interest rate. As argued before, this can be done by an optimal interest rate rule which can be derived from an explicit optimization exercise like in section 2.4, or this rule can be heuristic or exogenous in the sense that the behavior of the central bank is not directly derived from the model, but postulated from outside. However, if a policy rule for the nominal interest rate is added to the model in the latter way, this must be done with some care, because a particular rule may render the system unstable or introduces multiple equilibria. This section picks up this issue of determinacy of the equilibrium and shows how the conditions for stable equilibria can be derived.

The issue of determinacy of a rational expectations equilibrium has been debated in the macroeconomic literature even before the renewed research interest in monetary policy rules emerged. According to the well-known critique of Sargent and Wallace (1975), interest rate rules as such are undesirable, as they lead to indeterminacy of the rational-expectations equilibrium price level. As McCallum (1981) notes, however, their analysis assumes a rule that specifies an exogenous path for the short-term nominal interest rate. In terms of the classification given above, this kind of rules belong to class of *unconditional interest rate rules*. McCallum (1981) argues that determinacy is instead possible in the case of feedback from an endogenous state variable such as the price level; in other words, in case of *conditional interest rate rules*.

It is important to stress the seriousness of these theoretical concerns for the design of stabilization policy.[77] When a candidate class of policy rules may or may not generate indeterminacy, or explosive instability, depending on the particular values of the underlying structural model and of the policy rule, this has to be of a serious concern for policy design, if there is considerable sampling variability about the estimated parameters. Given an estimated structural model of the economy, one might, for instance, recommend a particular rule on the basis that it generates a determinate rational expectations equilibrium, and that the targeted equilibrium would have desirable properties based on other criteria, such as the utility of the representative household from the analysis above. And yet, in reality, important parameters may lie in a region associated with indeterminacy of the equilibrium. Actually implementing the proposed rule could then lead to disastrous consequences. Thus, from the perspective of the design of stabilization policy, one would prefer policy rules that, even if the

[77] See, for instance, Bullard and Mitra (2000) on that issue.

structural parameters actually take on values somewhat different from those that have been estimated, produce a determinate rational expectations equilibrium.

Taylor (1999c) recommends a "leaning against the wind" policy rule which calls for nominal interest rates which are adjusted positively, and more than one-for-one, in response to inflation being above its target level, and positively to levels of production above target. Following Woodford (2001a) this kind of recommendation is called the *Taylor principle*. Taylor's intuition is that under such a rule, a rise in inflation brings about an increase in the real interest rate which, in turn, reduces demand and inflationary pressure, bringing the economy back toward its targeted equilibrium. An interest rate response that falls short of the rise in inflation, on the other hand, leads to a fall in the real interest rate and, thus, adds inflationary pressure to the economy pushing it further away from equilibrium. The following analysis shows that Taylor's intuition can be supported by more formal dynamic analyses.[78]

In order to derive the conditions for determinacy the formal analysis is based on the purely forward-looking version of the IS-LM model that was derived in Appendix A of chapter 1 (see equations (1.17) and A.61)) but, for convenience, employs the notation of the variables of the backward-looking version from the previous section 2.4 (i.e., uncapitalized letters refer to percentage deviations of variables from their steady state levels instead of using "hats" like in chapter 1):

$$(2.11) \qquad y_t = E_t y_{t+1} - \sigma^{-1}\left(i_t - E_t \pi_{t+1} - r_t^n\right)$$

$$(2.12) \qquad \pi_t = \beta E_t \pi_{t+1} + \tilde{\kappa} y_t \, .$$

[78] A related issue to determinacy is the so-called "learnability": even when a determinate equilibrium exists, coordination on that equilibrium cannot be assured if agents do not posses rational expectations at every point in time. It is therefore important to analyze these systems when agents must form expectations concerning economic events using the actual data produced by the economy. The learning approach admits the possibility that expectations might not initially be fully rational, and that, if economic agents make forecast errors and try to correct them over time, the economy may or may not reach the rational expectations equilibrium asymptotically. This issue is not explicitly touched here, because it can be shown that the *Taylor principle* associated with uniqueness and determinacy is also closely linked with stability in the learning process across a variety specifications of the interest rate rules. See Bullard and Mitra (2002) for the formal analysis. They proof that the *Taylor principle* completely characterizes learnability. If agents do not have rational expectations and instead start with some subjective expectations of those variables but learn recursively, then a "leaning against the wind" policy does push the economy towards the rational expectations equilibrium.

The system is closed by an interest rate rule like it was formulated in (2.1) for the Federal funds rate:

(2.13) $$i_t = \varphi_\pi \cdot \pi_t + \varphi_y \cdot y_t ,$$

where the constant term can be omitted, because the nominal interest rate is also formulated in terms of deviation from its steady state value. After substituting (2.13) into (2.11) the equations (2.11) – (2.13) can be rewritten in the following system involving the two endogenous variables π_t and y_t:

(2.14) $$X_t = A + B \cdot E_t X_{t+1} + \Theta \cdot r_t^n ,$$

where $X_t = \begin{bmatrix} y_t \\ \pi_t \end{bmatrix}$, $A = 0$ and

$$B = \frac{1}{\sigma + \varphi_y + \tilde{\kappa}\varphi_\pi} \begin{bmatrix} \sigma & 1 - \beta\varphi_\pi \\ \tilde{\kappa}\sigma & \tilde{\kappa} + \beta(\sigma + \varphi_y) \end{bmatrix}.$$

The exact form of Θ can be omitted since it is not relevant for the following analysis. Since both, π_t and y_t, in the system (2.14) are free, we need both eigenvalues of B to be inside the unit circle in order to insure determinacy. In all other cases the equilibrium will be indeterminate. It follows that the necessary and sufficient condition for the rational expectations equilibrium to be unique is that (see Appendix D for the proof):

(2.15) $$\varphi_\pi + \frac{(1-\beta)}{\tilde{\kappa}} \cdot \varphi_y > 1 ,$$

where it is assumed that $\tilde{\kappa}(\varphi_\pi - 1) + (1-\beta)\varphi_y \neq 0$ in order to rule out non-generic cases. Condition (2.15) has a convenient interpretation. The forward-looking Phillips curve in (2.12) implies that each percentage point of permanently higher inflation results in a permanently higher output gap of $(1-\beta)/\tilde{\kappa}$ percentage points.[79] The left hand side of (2.15) then shows the long-run increase in the nominal interest rate prescribed by the interest rate rule (2.13) for each unit of permanent increase in the inflation rate. Condition (2.15), therefore, closely corresponds to the *Taylor principle* mentioned above: nominal

[79] See equation (A.57) and footnote 27 in chapter 1 on that issue. Because of the long-run trade-off it was argued to assume the discount rate to be equal to unity.

interest rates should rise by more than the increase in the inflation rate. Analytically, it is clear that $\varphi_{\pi} > 1$ is a sufficient condition for (2.15) to be satisfied, and if we further assume that the discount factor is equal to unity, condition (2.15) coincides for the *Taylor principle*. Therefore, in the following the condition $\varphi_{\pi} > 1$ will be referred to as both the *Taylor principle* and the formal stability condition.[80]

This kind of stability proof can also be performed for a variety of alternative interest rate rules, that include the lagged interest rate, lagged values of the inflation and the output gap instead of contemporaneous data like in (2.13), or expectational variables like in so-called forward-looking rules. Appendix D also provides the formal analysis for the latter alternative of the forward-looking specification of the interest rate rule which will be subject to the empirical analysis in the subsequent chapter. In general, it turns out that the condition $\varphi_{\pi} > 1$, respectively, the *Taylor principle* is at least a necessary condition for determinacy in all that cases (see Bullard and Mitra, 2000 and 2002).

2.6 Interest Rate Rules and the Role of Money

So far, the role of money has been left out of the theoretical discussion of monetary policy rules. However, an interest rate rule does not necessarily eliminate a careful analysis of money demand and supply. A money demand function could also easily be integrated into the 'new consensus model' as an additional equation. But as already argued in chapter 1, money in this kind of models is endogenously demand-determined at the level of the nominal interest rate the central bank sets via the interest rate rule, and since the quantity of money is not relevant for the determination of macroeconomic activity, such models are mostly formulated without introducing money at all. However, through the money market equilibrium a close relation of the short-term interest rate and the quantity of money exists. The following section, therefore, demonstrates the theoretical links between interest rate rules and money supply rules. It can be shown that a money supply rule based on arguments of the quantity theory of money can be transformed into an interest rate rule that shares the same arguments as the Taylor rule.[81]

[80] Recall that in the classification scheme this conditions was also the critical value for discriminate between active and passive interest rate rules.

[81] The following derivation is due to Deutsche Bundesbank (1999). As already mentioned before, strictly spoken a money supply rule can only be considered as a monetary policy rule in the sense it is commonly defined in the literature if it is expressed in terms of the base money. The following derivation instead assumes that the central bank targets a broad

Targets for money growth rates are usually derived from the quantity equation expressed here in logarithmic changes:

(2.16) $\Delta m = \pi + \Delta\hat{y} - \Delta v$,

where m is a monetary aggregate, π is the rate of inflation, $\hat{y}$ is the log of output and v is the velocity of circulation of money. The money growth target is then set in accordance with the inflation target, the growth in potential output, and the trend rate in the change of the velocity of circulation:

(2.17) $\Delta m^* = \pi^* + \Delta\hat{y}^* - \Delta v^*$.

If the short-term interest rate is the instrument of the central bank, its changes are oriented to the deviation of actual money growth from its target level:

(2.18) $\Delta i = \xi \cdot (\Delta m - \Delta m^*)$,

with $\xi > 0$. Taking into account equations (2.16) and (2.17), the following expression results:

(2.19) $i = i_{-1} + \xi[(\pi - \pi^*) + (\Delta\hat{y} - \Delta\hat{y}^*) - (\Delta v - \Delta v^*)]$.

This expression can be further modified by employing a standard money demand function (in first differences) of the form:

(2.20) $\Delta m^d = -\gamma_i \cdot \Delta i + \gamma_y \cdot \Delta\hat{y} + \pi + \Delta\varepsilon$,

where $\gamma_i, \gamma_y > 0$ and ε being a stochastic residual. Together with (2.16) money market equilibrium then yields the following expression for the change in the velocity of circulation of money:

(2.21) $\Delta v = \gamma_i \cdot \Delta i + (1 - \gamma_y) \cdot \Delta y - \Delta\varepsilon$.

Accordingly, in the long-run equilibrium for the trend rate of change in the velocity of circulation, a linear relationship with potential output growth follows:[82]

monetary aggregate. This is a valid exercise only if the multiplier between base money and broad money is stable and deterministic.

[82] Keep in mind that in the long-run equilibrium the changes in the instrument rate are zero.

$$(2.22) \qquad \Delta v^* = (1-\gamma_y)\cdot \Delta y^*.$$

Therefore, the interest rate rule in (2.19) can be rewritten as:

$$(2.23) \qquad i = i_{-1} + \alpha_1 \cdot (\pi - \pi^*) + \alpha_2 \cdot (\Delta\hat{y} - \Delta\hat{y}^*) + \alpha_1 \cdot \Delta\varepsilon,$$

$$\text{where} \quad \alpha_1 = \frac{\xi}{1+\xi\cdot\gamma_i} \quad \text{and} \quad \alpha_2 = \alpha_1 \cdot \gamma_y.$$

Just like the Taylor rule, equation (2.23) contains inflation and output gaps as feedback variables for the setting of the short-term interest rate. However, a closer inspection of the rule in (2.23) also reveals some differences. First, in contrast to the Taylor rule, the output target relates to its growth path and not to its level. However, both concepts are closely related, since deviation of output growth from its equilibrium trend implies the opening up of an output gap. Second, the benchmark interest rate is not its equilibrium value like in the Taylor rule, but its level in the preceding period.

Neumann and von Hagen (1990) indeed show that, in the case of the Bundesbank policy from 1979 through 1989, the deviations from the *ex ante* announced money growth target can be explained by deviations of output and inflation from their target levels. Thus, the money supply rule of the Bundesbank is in its arguments empirically very close to the Taylor type rule.[83] Von Hagen (1990), additionally, shows that an interest rate rule can be derived for the forecast of the money multiplier in the context of a strategy of targeting a broad monetary aggregate. Forecasting the value of the multiplier is the crucial problem of the strategy of targeting a broad monetary aggregate. Von Hagen (1990) demonstrates that a close observation of the short-term interest rate can improve the forecast of the multiplier. In addition, the central bank can influence the multiplier through changes in the short-term interest rate. The prerequisite is a close correlation between the short-term interest rate and the multiplier driven, for instance, by portfolio choices of the private banks.[84] Based on these considerations an interest rate rule for influencing the intermediate target of a broad monetary aggregate can be derived.

Also prominent proponents of interest rate rules, like John Taylor himself, argue in favor of analyzing the growth of monetary aggregates in situations in which inflation rates are either extraordinary high or negative.[85] In such

[83] Neumann and von Hagen (1993) additionally find evidence for an exchange rate argument in that rule.

[84] See also von Hagen (1988).

[85] The issue of deflation will be explicitly picked up in the next section.

situations interest rate rules can not be applied, because inflation expectations are quite instable and therefore not easy to be identified. John Taylor (1999d, p. 661) states: "*For this reason it is useful for central banks to keep track of the money supply and perhaps monitor policy rules for the money supply or monetary base even when they are using interest rate rules as a guideline.*" The complementary theoretical analysis to this statement is provided by Christiano and Rostagno (2001). The authors show that the under certain circumstances the implementation of a Taylor-type rule will lead to a higher volatility within the economy. At the same time they demonstrate that this problem can be reduced and even be eliminated if the central bank abandons the interest rate rule and instead monitors the growth rate of money in terms of a money supply rule.

2.7 Limits and Perspectives for the Use of Interest Rate Rules

A natural question that arises after discussing the theoretical foundations of interest rate rules is the one of their applicability in the actual monetary policy. Although mainly being concerned with the theoretical foundations of interest rate rules in this chapter the final section in this chapter briefly discusses the most relevant issues that come along with this question.[86] At least three areas of problems need to be discussed: (i) the issue of parameter uncertainty in the structural model, (ii) the presence of data uncertainty, and (iii) the problem of the zero lower bound on nominal interest rates.

Parameter uncertainty

Parameter uncertainty is a main obstacle for deriving an optimal rule. The previous discussion made clear that the response coefficients of the optimal interest rate rule are convolutions of the structural and the preference parameters. Thus, changes in any structural parameter should result in changes in the interest rate rule's optimal coefficients. Uncertainty about the structural parameters then makes the derivation of the values of optimal parameters very difficult. Traditionally, practitioners believed that according to *Brainard conservatism principle* (Brainard, 1967) such uncertainty about the true value of the structural parameters should translate into a more contained reaction of central banks to inflation and/or output shocks (Goodhart, 1999). However, actual research questions such a conservative behavior.

Söderström (2002) shows that – in contrast to the received wisdom – uncertainty about the parameters in a dynamic macroeconomic model may lead

[86] See Fendel (2004b) for a more comprehensive discussion on the issue of applicability of interest rate rules for central banks

to more aggressive monetary policy. He uses the model outlined in section 2.4 of this chapter. Incorporating uncertainty into this model has important effects on the optimal policy rule derived in section 2.4. If the uncertainty is only additive the optimal rule is not effected. This results from the well-known fact, that optimal policy in a linear-quadratic framework like the model in section 2.4. (i.e., linear restrictions and a quadratic loss function) with only additive uncertainty exhibits *certainty equivalence*. Consequently, the dregee of uncertainty does not effect the optimal policy rule, which only depends on the expected value of the goal variables. Thus, the central banks acts as it would in a non-stochastic environment.

When multiplicative parameter uncertainty is incorporated into the model, *certainty equivalence* ceases to hold, and the variances of the state variables will effect the optimal behavior. Söderström (2002) makes the parameters of the model of section 2.4 stochastic, and therefore time-varying. Based on calibration exercises, he shows that, in particular, when there is uncertainty about the persistence of inflation, it may be optimal to respond to shocks more aggressively.[87] The reason is quite intuitive. If the exact dynamic of the inflation rate in unknown, the degree of uncertainty is increasing with the deviation of the inflation rate from its target level. In order to reduce the degree of uncertainty about future levels of inflation, it is best to bring it back to target as soon as possible, which calls for a more aggressive response to the inflation gap. Uncertainty about the other parameters, however, dampens the policy response, so that the result is mixed.

The issue of the consequences of uncertainty for the optimal rule is, however, unsettled. Some studies support the view of a more aggressive response. Among them are Gianonni (2002), and Tetlow and von zur Mühlen (2001). Other authors support the traditional view of the *Brainard conservatism principle* and recommend a contained response. Among them are Rudebusch (2001), Wieland (1998), and Ehrmann and Smets (2001).

Data and variable uncertainty

Making a particular interest rate rule operational can cause difficulties because of mainly two reasons. The first is the contemporary availability of (high quality) observable data, respectively the degree of uncertainty connected to the available data. The second is the presence of unobservable variables in the interest rate rules, and thus, uncertainty about their true value.

The first issue has already briefly been touched when discussing the use of lagged data or of expectations of contemporaneous data for inflation and output,

[87] In equation (2.7) the persistence parameter has been set to unity by definition. In Söderström's (2002) analysis the parameter is allowed to be different from unity.

respectively. In reality, most data undergo various revisions after their first publication. This fact questions the possibility of prompt reactions of the central bank. On the other hand, it could be argued that central banks have good access to additional data which might allow them the gather a good contemporary grasp of what is going on in the economy. In this respect, the issue of the availability of data is not a prevalent question in the theoretical literature on interest rate rules. It is, however, a crucial issue in empirical work, when researcher try to characterize central banks with empirical reaction functions. The use of *ex post* revised data might not accurately describe the historical decision situation of a central bank (when the revised data was not yet available). Since this chapter is concerned about theoretical aspects of interest rate rules, the issue of real-time data will be picked-up again in the subsequent empirical chapter 3.

Taylor-type rules contain, at least, two unobservable variables: the output gap (respectively the equilibrium output that is needed to calculate it) and the equilibrium real interest rate. If the rule is to be applied, both variables need to be determined. The equilibrium real interest rate can be measured with various methods such as a joint estimation with potential output and trend growth (Laubach and Williams, 2001) or based on inflation-indexed bonds (Bomfim, 2001). For the US, Laubach and Williams (2001) demonstrate that the equilibrium real interest rate is also significantly time-varying.

Potential output, and thus, the output gap is the second unobservable variable within the interest rate rule. Its quantification can also rest on different methods all of which are burdened with significant uncertainty.[88] This uncertainty does not only have consequences for the output gap, but also potentially for the rule itself. Smets (2002) shows that output gap uncertainty can have a significant effect on the optimal response coefficients in quasi-optimal Taylor-type rules. In particular, the efficient response to the current (estimated) output gap is reduced relative to the inflation response (which reduces only marginal).[89] According to his analysis, in the extreme, when measurement errors in the output gap become large, the efficient Taylor rule parameter on the output gap could become zero. Orphanides et al. (1999) obtain similar results within the model of the Federal Reserve Bank for the US economy, although their results do not imply a zero weight on output. They show that even in the presence of measurement error, a small weight on the output gap is still able to produce lower output and inflation variation than those of a zero weight.

[88] See Staiger et al. (1996) for a discussion of estimating natural rates.
[89] Because „quasi-optimal" rules rely on the *ex ante* given functional forms (see section 2.4), in this section it is preferred to call the response coefficients "efficient" rather than "optimal".

Zero lower bound on nominal interest rates

Theoretical considerations and the recent Japanese experience suggest that monetary policy that employs the short-term nominal interest rate is seriously constrained once the interest rate level has reached its zero level, so that no further stimulus can be produced by interest rate cuts. At the so-called zero lower bound of nominal interest rates, no further downward adjustment in the policy rates can occur, since lenders will not accept a negative nominal interest rate when they have the opportunity of holding their wealth in form of cash, on which a zero interest rate is granted.[90]

Eggertsson (2003) argues that, in addition, at the zero lower bound discretionary monetary policy is flawed with a deflation bias that can be viewed as the inverse of the well-known inflation bias analyzed by Kydland and Prescott (1977) and Barro and Gordon (1983). The key idea behind this deflation bias is the following: Aggregate demand depends on the current and future real interest rate. Even at the zero lower bound, the central bank can potentially lower the real interest rate, and thus increase aggregate demand, by increasing inflation expectations possibly through changes in the (announced) target rate of inflation. Therefore, the central bank has an incentive to promise future inflation. However, when the deflationary shock has subsided, the *ex post* optimal rate of inflation is below the promise of the central bank and the central bank has a strong incentive to renege. It follows that, in an environment of discretionary policy decisions, the central bank is unable to commit to future policy when economic agents are rational. This results in an excessive deflation when the zero lower bound is reached.

It is undisputed that the zero lower bound challenges traditional monetary policy, since it has to design alternative instruments and operational targets to escape the deflationary trap. Several options exist, two of which are briefly to be discussed here because they are more or less connected to interest rate rules discussed so far.[91] First, the central bank can target longer-term interest rates in contrast to the short rate. This argument is mainly driven by considerations from

[90] In Japan, interest rates of commercial banks on very short-term deposits temporarily turned negative. This implies that the interest costs must have been lower than the costs of holding cash. Regarding high-powered money, some authors such as Goodfriend (2000), and Buiter and Panigirtzoglou (1999) propose a tax on holding cash. If this can be realized, the zero bound on nominal interest rates would not be a binding constraint and negative interest rates would be possible. Although technically feasible and even recommended by Fukao (2003) for Japan, one could consider this discussion as rather academic and not applicable for monetary policy.

[91] This section will only present these selected options briefly. A comprehensive presentation and discussion can be found in Yates (2004) and Bernanke et al. (2004). Robinson and Stone (2005) demonstrate how the constraint of the zero lower bound can be incorporated into the smale-scale model from chapter 2.4.

the term structure of interest rates. Through its policy instruments, a central bank directly affects the short-term interest rate. However, aggregate demand is mainly influenced by medium and longer-term rates. When short-term interest rates have reached the zero lower bound, medium and longer-term rates can still be significantly positive. The recent experience of Japan suggests that longer-term nominal interest rates may remain at a considerably higher level compared with short term rates and, thereby, hinder economic recovery even when the short-term nominal rate is zero.[92] In this situation, the central bank still has the possibility to support aggregate demand if it succeeds to indirectly lower longer-term interest rates. Theoretically, this implies an augmentation of interest rate rules with arguments from the term structure.

Second, in open economies the exchange rate could in principle be used to stimulate demand and/or generate inflation expectations.[93] McCallum (2001) emphasizes the role of the foreign exchange market. He proposes to shift to a moving exchange rate target, when the zero lower bound is reached. Such a system can be implemented via a policy rule that is formulated similarly to a Taylor rule and that uses the nominal exchange rate as the relevant policy instrument instead of the short-term interest rate. Based on simulations within a calibrated optimizing open-economy model, he demonstrates that the moving exchange rate target, if credible and understood by private agents, can stimulate the economy. In a companion paper, McCallum (2005) considers the use of a policy rule that employs as its instrument variable a weighted average of the interest rate and the rate of depreciation of the nominal exchange rate. With a small weight attached to the depreciation term, it will be nearly irrelevant in normal situations but calls for a strong adjustment when the zero lower bound on the interest rate is reached.

[92] See Fendel and Frenkel (2004) for a discussion. Furthermore, part II of this book relates the issue of term structure effects explicitly to interest rate rules.
[93] See Svensson (2001 and 2003) for explicit recommendation for the Japanese case.

Appendix B

A Second-Order Approximation to Household's Welfare

This appendix demonstrates how a second-order approximation to the household's utility can be used to derive the quadratic objective function in the maximization problem of the central bank.[94] From the previous discussion in chapter 1 we know that due to monopolistic power even under flexible prices equilibrium output in the standard model from Appendix A falls short of the efficient level of output under perfect competition. In the following it is therefore assumed that the fiscal authority guarantees the efficiency of the flexible price steady state by a constant lump-sum subsidy to employment. This assumption implies that the zero inflation steady state in the model from Appendix A also coincides with the efficient one. More technically, we know from (A.39) in Appendix A that real marginal costs are one over the mark-up ($\mu = \theta/(\theta-1)$):

(B.1) $$\varphi = \frac{1}{\mu} = \frac{(\theta-1)}{\theta} = 1 - \frac{1}{\theta}.$$

The subsidy under consideration offsets the last term in (B.1) so that real marginal costs and the mark-up are equal to one in equilibrium. In the following, the analysis is also restricted to a simplified utility function without the real money balance term[95]

(B.2) $$U_t(C,N) = E_t \sum_{i=0}^{\infty} \beta^i \left[\frac{C_{t+i}^{1-\sigma}}{1-\sigma} - \frac{N_{t+i}^{1+\eta}}{1+\eta} \right].$$

This utility function is separable in consumption and labor effort so that cross derivatives $\frac{\partial^2 U}{\partial C \partial N} \equiv U_{CN} = 0$, where the respective subscripts denote partial derivatives. Note also that from this specific form of the utility function it follows that the intertemporal elasticity of substitution in consumption is

[94] I am grateful to Jordi Galí for giving me some useful insights. The derivation is originally due to Woodford (2001b).

[95] This simplification can be justified by the assumption that the utility from holding real money balances is comparably low and, thus, can be neglected.

$\sigma = -\frac{U_{CC,t}}{U_{C,t}} \cdot \overline{C}_t$ and accordingly the intertemporal elasticity of substitution in labor is $\eta = \frac{U_{NN,t}}{U_{N,t}} \cdot \overline{N}_t$.

Notation

In the course of this appendix, the following notation is employed. Let X_t be the actual value of a variable and $\overline{X}_t$ its flexible price allocation. Furthermore, let $\widetilde{X}_t = (X_t - \overline{X}_t)$ and $\hat{X}_t = \log\left(\frac{X_t}{\overline{X}_t}\right)$. The following relations between the variables is used:

$$\widetilde{X}_t = (X_t - \overline{X}_t) = \overline{X}_t\left(\frac{X_t}{\overline{X}_t} - 1\right) = \overline{X}_t\left(\frac{X_t}{\overline{X}_t} - \frac{\overline{X}_t}{\overline{X}_t}\right) = \overline{X}_t\left(\frac{X_t - \overline{X}_t}{\overline{X}_t}\right) = \overline{X}_t\left(\hat{X}_t + \frac{1}{2}\hat{X}_t^2\right)$$

where the last step follows from a second-order approximation of the relative deviation in terms of log deviations that can be written as

$$\frac{X_t - \overline{X}_t}{\overline{X}_t} = \hat{X}_t + \frac{1}{2}\hat{X}_t^2 + o\left(\|a\|^3\right) \approx \hat{X}_t + \frac{1}{2}\hat{X}_t^2,$$

where $o\left(\|a\|^n\right)$ denotes terms of (and higher than) n^{th}, in the bound $\|a\|$ on the amplitude of the relevant shocks. Those terms are then to be ignored depending on the order of the approximation.

The second order Taylor approximation to households utility

For a general function of the form $U_t(C,N)$ the second order approximation of utility around the flexible price allocation can be denoted as:[96]

(B.3) $$U_t - \overline{U}_t = \overline{U}_{C,t} \cdot \widetilde{C}_t - \overline{U}_{N,t} \cdot \widetilde{N}_t + \frac{1}{2}\overline{U}_{CC,t} \cdot \widetilde{C}_t^2 - \frac{1}{2}\overline{U}_{NN,t} \cdot \widetilde{N}_t^2 + o\left(\|a\|^3\right).$$

[96] Notice that work effort enters the utility function with a negative sign.

Using the notation from above this can be expressed as

(B.4)
$$U_t - \overline{U}_t = \overline{U}_{C,t} \cdot \overline{C}_t\left(\hat{C}_t + \frac{1}{2}\hat{C}_t^2\right) - \overline{U}_{N,t} \cdot \overline{N}_t\left(\hat{N}_t + \frac{1}{2}\hat{N}_t^2\right)$$
$$+\frac{1}{2}\overline{U}_{CC,t} \cdot \overline{C}_t^2\left(\hat{C}_t + \frac{1}{2}\hat{C}_t^2\right)^2 - \frac{1}{2}\overline{U}_{NN,t} \cdot \overline{N}_t^2\left(\hat{N}_t + \frac{1}{2}\hat{N}_t^2\right)^2 + o\left(\|a\|^3\right).$$

Rearranging the last expression and ignoring all higher order terms then yields:

(B.5)
$$U_t - \overline{U}_t = \overline{U}_{C,t} \cdot \overline{C}_t\left(\hat{C}_t + \frac{1}{2}\hat{C}_t^2\right) - \overline{U}_{N,t} \cdot \overline{N}_t\left(\hat{N}_t + \frac{1}{2}\hat{N}_t^2\right)$$
$$+\frac{1}{2}\overline{U}_{CC,t} \cdot \overline{C}_t^2 \cdot \hat{C}_t^2 - \frac{1}{2}\overline{U}_{NN,t} \cdot \overline{N}_t^2 \cdot \hat{N}_t^2 + o\left(\|a\|^3\right).$$

Using the particular preference specification from above this can be modified to

(B.6)
$$U_t - \overline{U}_t = \overline{U}_{C,t} \cdot \overline{C}_t\left(\hat{C}_t + \frac{1-\sigma}{2}\hat{C}_t^2\right) - \overline{U}_{N,t} \cdot \overline{N}_t\left(\hat{N}_t + \frac{1+\eta}{2}\hat{N}_t^2\right) + o\left(\|a\|^3\right).$$

The next step consists of rewriting $\hat{N}_t$ in terms of the output gap. Notice from the discussion of the NNS model in chapter 1 and, in particular, from equations (1.8) through (1.10), that the presence of cross-sectional dispersions of prices (the so-called relative price distortion) implies that:

$$\int_0^1 y_t(j)dj = Y_t\int_0^1\left(\frac{p_t(j)}{P_t}\right)^{-\theta} dj = Z_t F(N_t)$$

$$Z_t F(N_t) = Y_t \cdot d_t.$$

where d_t denotes the price distortion. Take a first order Taylor expansion of $Z_t F(N_t) = Y_t \cdot d_t$ around the flexible price allocation:

$$Z_t F(\overline{N}_t) + Z_t F_N(\overline{N}_t)\overline{N}_t\hat{N}_t + F(\overline{N}_t)Z_t\hat{Z}_t = \overline{Y}_t\overline{d}_t + \overline{Y}_t\overline{d}_t\hat{Y}_t + \overline{Y}_t\overline{d}_t\hat{d}_t.$$

Note that $\hat{Z}_t = 0$ and $Z_t F(\overline{N}_t) = \overline{Y}_t \cdot \overline{d}_t$, so we can write

$$\hat{Y}_t + \hat{d}_t = \frac{Z_t F_N(\overline{N}_t)\overline{N}_t \hat{N}_t}{\overline{Y}_t \overline{d}_t}.$$

Furthermore, we have $\overline{d}_t = 1$ (no distortion in the flexible price equilibrium) and, therefore, also $\hat{d}_t = \log d_t$. Given that the production function is linear homogenous, it is also possible to write that $Z_t F_N(\overline{N}_t)\overline{N}_t = \overline{Y}_t$. It then follows:

(B.7) $$\hat{N}_t = \hat{Y}_t + u_t,$$

where, for convenience, $u_t \equiv \log d_t = \log \int_0^1 \left(\frac{p_t(j)}{P_t} \right)^{-\theta} dj$. It can be shown that the dispersion term u_t is proportional to the cross-sectional variance of relative prices and, thus, of second order.

Lemma 1:

$$u_t \approx \frac{\theta}{2} \text{var}_j \{\hat{p}_{j,t}\}$$

Proof:

Let us define $p_{j,t} = \frac{p_t(j)}{P_t}$. Notice that

$$\left(\frac{p_t(j)}{P_t} \right)^{1-\theta} = p_{j,t}^{1-\theta} = 1 + (1-\theta)\hat{p}_{j,t} + \frac{(1-\theta)^2}{2} \hat{p}_{j,t}^2 + o\left(\|a\|^3 \right).$$

Furthermore, from the definition of the composite price index from equation (1.4) of chapter 1, we have that $1 = \int_0^1 \left(\frac{p_t(j)}{P_t} \right)^{1-\theta} dj = \int_0^1 p_{j,t}^{1-\theta} dj$. By taking the cross-sectional average which implies $E_j \{p_{j,t}^{1-\theta}\} = \int_0^1 p_{j,t}^{1-\theta} dj = 1$, it follows that

$$1 = 1 + (1-\theta)E_j \{\hat{p}_{j,t}\} + \frac{(1-\theta)^2}{2} E_j \{\hat{p}_{j,t}^2\} + o\left(\|a\|^3 \right) \text{ or}$$

(B.8) $$E_j\{\hat{p}_{j,t}\}=\frac{(\theta-1)}{2}E_j\{\hat{p}_{j,t}^2\}+o\left(\|a\|^3\right).$$

Consider next the term $p_{j,t}^{-\theta}$. A second-order approximation yields

$$p_{j,t}^{-\theta}=1-\theta\hat{p}_{j,t}+\frac{\theta^2}{2}\hat{p}_{j,t}^2+o\left(\|a\|^3\right).$$

By taking the cross-sectional average and substituting from (B.8) it follows that

$$\begin{aligned}\int_0^1 p_{j,t}^{-\theta}dj &=1-\theta E_j\{\hat{p}_{j,t}\}+\frac{\theta^2}{2}E_j\{\hat{p}_{j,t}^2\}+o\left(\|a\|^3\right)\\ &=1+\frac{\theta}{2}E_j\{\hat{p}_{j,t}^2\}+o\left(\|a\|^3\right)\\ &=1+\frac{\theta}{2}\mathrm{var}_j\{\hat{p}_{j,t}\}+o\left(\|a\|^3\right).\end{aligned}$$

It follows that the dispersion term can be written as

$$\begin{aligned}u_t &=\log\left[1+\frac{\theta}{2}\mathrm{var}_j\{\hat{p}_{j,t}\}\right]\\ &\approx\frac{\theta}{2}\mathrm{var}_j\{\hat{p}_{j,t}\}\end{aligned}$$

and, hence, is of second order.

It is further assumed that the market clearing condition takes the form $Y_t=C_t$ for all t. Under this assumption (B.6) can be rewritten as

(B.9) $$U_t-\overline{U}_t=\overline{U}_{C,t}\cdot\overline{Y}_t\left(\hat{Y}_t+\frac{1-\sigma}{2}\hat{Y}_t^2\right)-\overline{U}_{N,t}\cdot\overline{N}_t\left(\hat{Y}_t+u_t+\frac{1+\eta}{2}\hat{N}_t^2\right)+o\left(\|a\|^3\right).$$

Next, recall that when the optimal subsidy is in place, the flexible price allocation coincides with the efficient one, thus implying $\overline{U}_{N,t}\overline{N}_t=\overline{U}_{C,t}\overline{Y}_t$.[97] Hence, we get:

[97] This follows from a generalized version of equation (A.23) of Appendix A in which the left-hand side is the ratio of marginal disutility of work to the marginal utility of consumption

(B.10) $$U_t - \overline{U}_t = -\overline{U}_{C,t} \cdot \overline{Y}_t \left(u_t + \frac{\sigma + \eta}{2} \hat{Y}_t^2 \right) + o\left(\|a\|^3 \right).$$

We can derive a first-order approximation to $\overline{U}_{C,t}\overline{Y}_t$ about the steady state:[98]

$$\overline{U}_{C,t}\overline{Y}_t = U_C Y + \left(U_{CC} Y + U_C \right) \left(\frac{\overline{Y}_t - Y_t}{Y_t} \right) + o\left(\|a\|^2 \right) = U_C Y + U_C Y (1 - \sigma) \cdot \hat{\overline{Y}}_t + o\left(\|a\|^2 \right),$$

where $\hat{\overline{Y}}_t \equiv \log\left(\frac{\overline{Y}_t}{Y} \right)$,

with Y being the steady state value. It follows then that, up to second order, $\overline{U}_{C,t}\overline{Y}_t = U_C Y$, so that:

(B.11) $$U_t - \overline{U}_t = -U_C C \cdot \left(u_t + \frac{\sigma + \eta}{2} \hat{Y}_t^2 \right) + o\left(\|a\|^3 \right).$$

Accordingly, we can write a second-order approximation to the household's welfare loss resulting from deviations from the flexible price equilibrium, expressed as a fraction of steady state consumption, as:[99]

(B.12) $$W_t = \frac{U_t - \overline{U}_t}{-U_C C} = \frac{1}{2} \left(\theta \operatorname{var}_j \{ \hat{p}_{j,t} \} + (\sigma + \eta) \hat{Y}_t^2 \right),$$

where *Lemma 1* is used. Adding up all expected (discounted) future losses yields the present discounted value of total welfare losses:

(B.13) $$\widetilde{W}_t = \frac{1}{2} E_t \sum_{t=0}^{\infty} \beta^t \left(\theta \operatorname{var}_j \{ \hat{p}_{j,t} \} + (\sigma + \eta) \hat{Y}_t^2 \right).$$

(equal to income in the steady state) together with (A.26) and the normalization of steady state productivity $Z = 1$ (which also implies that $\overline{Y} = \overline{N}$). Furthermore, the assumption of the optimal subsidy leads to real marginal cost φ in (A.26), and therefore the real wage, being equal to unity. Altogether this implies $\overline{U}_{C,t}\overline{Y}_t = \overline{U}_{N,t}\overline{N}_t$.

[98] Note that, for convenience, we leave the minus sign aside in the Taylor expansion.

[99] Notice, that this form defines the loss in positive terms: the higher the *W*, the greater is the loss.

Finally, we can make use of the following Lemma, which shows that the cross-sectional variance of prices is proportional to the squared inflation rate:

Lemma 2:

$$\sum_{t=0}^{\infty} \beta^t \theta \operatorname{var}_j \{\hat{p}_{j,t}\} = \frac{1}{\kappa} \sum_{t=0}^{\infty} \beta^t \pi_t^2 ,$$

where $\kappa = \dfrac{(1-\omega)(1-\omega\beta)}{\omega}$, which coincides to the structural parameter in the new Keynesian Phillips curve in (A.47).

Proof: see Woodford (2001b, NBER WP8071, pp. 22-23).

Thus, we can rewrite (B.13) as

$$\text{(B.14)} \qquad \widetilde{W}_t = \frac{1}{2} E_t \sum_{t=0}^{\infty} \beta^t \left(\frac{\theta}{\kappa} \pi_t^2 + (\sigma + \eta) \hat{Y}_t^2 \right).$$

This welfare measure coincides with the one given in (2.7) and (2.8) which is used in the optimization problem of the central bank, if we, additionally, (i) express inflation relative to its target level instead of the thus far explicitly assumed steady state level of zero, (ii) use the notation of the output gap y_t instead of the deviation of output from its steady state $\hat{Y}_t$, (iii) normalize the weight of the squared inflation to one, which then gives the weight for the output gap in (2.8) as $\lambda = \dfrac{(\sigma + \eta)\kappa}{\theta}$, and (iv) assume that the discount factor of the central bank is equal to the discount factor of the representative household ($\beta = \delta$). The statement (iii) shows that the preference parameters of the central bank are also driven by the structural parameters of the economy.[100]

[100] A second-order approximation along the model that also allows for wage stickiness briefly discussed in chapter 1 and at the end of Appendix A would result in a similar measure of welfare, but with an additionally variable entering the loss function: the variance of wage inflation.

Appendix C

Derivation of an Optimal Interest Rate Rule

A. The Central Bank's Optimization Problem

The central bank's objective is to set i_t so as to minimize (2.7). From (2.5) and (2.6) it is evident that the central bank faces a two-period control lag with π_t and y_t as the two state variables. However, following Svensson (1997), this particular problem can be re-formulated as a quasi one-period optimal control problem that treats $\pi_{t+1|t}$ as the single state variable because $\pi_{t+1|t} = \pi_t + \alpha_1 y_t$ for all t. Also we can treat $y_{t+1|t}$ as the single control variable. Thus the control problem takes the form

(C.1) $$V(\pi_{t+1|t}) = \min_{y_{t+1|t}} \left\{ \frac{1}{2}\left[(\pi_{t+1|t} - \pi^*)^2 + \lambda y^2_{t+1|t}\right] + \delta E_t V(\pi_{t+2|t+1}) \right\}$$

subject to

(C.2) $$E_t \pi_{t+2|t+1} = \pi_{t+2|t} = \pi_{t+1|t} + \alpha_1 y_{t+1|t} .$$

The optimal monetary conditions can then be inferred from

(C.3) $$i_t - \pi_t = -\frac{1}{\beta_2} y_{t+1|t} + \frac{\beta_1}{\beta_2} y_t ,$$

which follows from the aggregate demand specification (2.5).

Because the period loss function is quadratic and the constraint is linear, the indirect loss function $V(\pi_{t+1})$ will be quadratic:

(C.4) $$V(\pi_{t+1|t}) = k_0 + \frac{1}{2} k (\pi_{t+1|t} - \pi^*)^2 ,$$

where the two coefficients k and k_0 remain to be determined. The linear quadratic nature of the optimal control problem gives rise to the property of certainty equivalence. Therefore, the solution does not depend on variance of the shock variables.

The first order condition is

(C.5)
$$\frac{\partial V(\pi_{t+1|t})}{\partial y_{t+1|t}} = \lambda y_{t+1|t} + \frac{\partial\left(\delta E_t V(\pi_{t+2|t})\right)}{\partial y_{t+1|t}} = \lambda y_{t+1|t} + \delta E_t V_{\pi_{t+2|t+1}}(\pi_{t+2|t+1}) \cdot \alpha_1$$
$$= \lambda y_{t+1|t} + \delta\alpha_1 k(\pi_{t+2|t} - \pi^*) = 0.$$

This expression can than be rearranged to the optimality condition

(2.9) $$\pi_{t+2|t} - \pi^* = -\frac{\lambda}{\delta\alpha_1 k} y_{t+1|t}.$$

In order to determine the parameter k we write the decision rule for output as

(C.6) $$y_{t+1|t} = -\frac{\delta\alpha_1 k}{\lambda}(\pi_{t+2|t} - \pi^*).$$

Substituting (C.2) into this expression yields after some rearranging

(C.7) $$y_{t+1|t} = -\frac{\delta\alpha_1 k}{\lambda + \delta\alpha_1^2 k}(\pi_{t+1|t} - \pi^*).$$

This can be substituted back into the inflation forecast (C.2) to get

(C.8) $$\pi_{t+2|t} = \frac{\lambda}{\lambda + \delta\alpha_1^2 k}(\pi_{t+1|t} - \pi^*) + \pi^*.$$

We next employ the envelope theorem to see that from (C.1) and (C.4) jointly follows

(C.9) $$V_{\pi_{t+1|t}} = k(\pi_{t+1|t} - \pi^*) = (\pi_{t+1|t} - \pi^*) + \delta k(\pi_{t+2|t} - \pi^*).$$

Here we used the fact that $\frac{\partial E_t V(\pi_{t+2})}{\partial \pi_{t+1|t}} = \frac{\partial E_t V(\pi_{t+2})}{\partial \pi_{t+2|t}} \cdot \frac{\partial \pi_{t+2|t}}{\partial \pi_{t+1|t}}$, where the last term is equal to one by (C.2). Substitution of (C.8) into this expression yields

(C.10) $$V_{\pi_{t+1|t}} = \left[1 + \frac{\delta k \lambda}{\lambda + \delta \alpha_1^2 k}\right](\pi_{t+1|t} - \pi^*).$$

Thus, it follows that

(C.11) $$k = 1 + \frac{\delta k \lambda}{\lambda + \delta \alpha_1^2 k}.$$

In order to find the solution for k, we rearrange this expression to

(C.12) $$k(\lambda + \delta \alpha_1^2 k) = (\lambda + \delta \alpha_1^2 k) + \delta \lambda k,$$

which yields the quadratic function

(C.13) $$k^2 - \left(1 - \frac{(1-\delta)\lambda}{\delta \alpha_1^2}\right) \cdot k - \frac{\lambda}{\delta \alpha_1^2} = 0.$$

Using the standard technique and only considering the positive solution for the reason of plausibility this equation yields the solution

(C.14) $$k = \frac{1}{2}\left(1 - \frac{\lambda(1-\delta)}{\delta \alpha_1^2} + \sqrt{\left(1 + \frac{\lambda(1-\delta)}{\delta \alpha_1^2}\right)^2 + \frac{4\lambda}{\alpha_1^2}}\right) \geq 1.$$

This coincides with the parameterisation given for expression (2.9) given in the main text.

B. Derivation of the Interest Rate Rule

Expression (2.9) can be further modified in order to yield an optimal reaction function with only contemporaneous arguments. Therefore using (2.5) the one-year output forecast is expressed as

(C.15) $$y_{t+1|t} = \beta_1 y_t - \beta_2 (i_t - \pi_t).$$

Substituting this into (2.9) and solving for the short-term interest rates yields after some rearranging:

$$\text{(C.16)} \qquad i_t = \pi_t + \frac{\delta\alpha_1 k}{\beta_2\lambda}\cdot\left(\pi_{t+2|t} - \pi^*\right) + \frac{\beta_1}{\beta_2}\cdot y_t\,.$$

From (2.6) with (C.15) the two-year inflation forecast can be expressed as

$$\text{(C.17)} \qquad \pi_{t+2|t} = \pi_t + \alpha_1(1+\beta_1)y_t + \alpha_1\beta_2(i_t - \pi_t).$$

Substituting the inflation forecast into (C.16) yields after sorting terms:

$$i_t\left(1+\frac{\delta\alpha_1^2 k}{\lambda}\right) = \left(\frac{\delta\alpha_1^2 k(1+\beta_1)}{\beta_2\lambda} + \frac{\beta_1}{\beta_2}\right)\cdot y_t - \frac{\delta\alpha_1 k}{\beta_2\lambda}\cdot\pi^* + \left(1+\frac{\delta\alpha_1^2 k}{\lambda}\right)\cdot\pi_t + \frac{\delta\alpha_1 k}{\beta_2\lambda}\cdot\pi_t\,.$$

Let us next define

$$\left(1+\frac{\delta\alpha_1^2 k}{\lambda}\right) = \left(\frac{\lambda+\delta\alpha_1^2 k}{\lambda}\right) \equiv \frac{1}{c}$$

and rewrite the former expression as

$$\text{(C.18)} \qquad i_t\cdot\frac{1}{c} = \left(\frac{\delta\alpha_1^2 k(1+\beta_1)}{\beta_2\lambda} + \frac{\beta_1}{\beta_2}\right)\cdot y_t + \frac{\delta\alpha_1 k}{\beta_2\lambda}\cdot(\pi_t - \pi^*) + \frac{1}{c}\cdot\pi_t\,.$$

The term in front of the inflation gap can also be written as

$$\frac{\delta\alpha_1 k}{\beta_2\lambda} = \frac{1-c}{c\alpha_1\beta_2}\,.$$

Proof:

$$\frac{1}{c} = 1+\frac{\delta\alpha_1^2 k}{\lambda} \quad => \quad \frac{1-c}{c} = \frac{\delta\alpha_1^2 k}{\lambda} \quad => \quad \frac{1-c}{c\alpha_1\beta_2} = \frac{\delta\alpha_1 k}{\beta_2\lambda}\,.$$

The term in front of the output gap can also be written in the following form:

$$\frac{\delta\alpha_1^2 k(1+\beta_1)}{\beta_2\lambda}+\frac{\beta_1}{\beta_2}=\frac{(1-c)\cdot(1+\beta_1)}{c\beta_2}+\frac{\beta_1}{\beta_2}.$$

Proof:

$$\frac{1-c}{c}=\frac{\delta\alpha_1^2 k}{\lambda} \quad => \quad \frac{(1-c)\cdot(1+\beta_1)}{c}=\frac{\delta\alpha_1^2 k(1+\beta_1)}{\lambda} \quad =>$$

$$\frac{(1-c)\cdot(1+\beta_1)}{c\beta_2}=\frac{\delta\alpha_1^2 k(1+\beta_1)}{\lambda\beta_2}$$

Given the two redefinitions, we can express (C.18) as

$$i_t\cdot\frac{1}{c}=\left(\frac{(1-c)\cdot(1+\beta_1)}{c\beta_2}+\frac{\beta_1}{\beta_2}\right)\cdot y_t+\frac{1-c}{c\alpha_1\beta_2}\cdot(\pi_t-\pi^*)+\frac{1}{c}\cdot\pi_t.$$

Multiplication of both sides of the previous equation by c and some further rearranging yields

$$i_t=\left(\frac{1-c+\beta_1}{\beta_2}\right)\cdot y_t+\frac{1-c}{\alpha_1\beta_2}\cdot(\pi_t-\pi^*)+\pi_t.$$

This coincides with the Taylor-type rule in (2.10) in the main text:

(2.10) $$i_t=\pi_t+\tilde{b}_1(\pi_t-\pi^*)+\tilde{b}_2\cdot y_t,$$

where $\tilde{b}_1=\frac{1-c}{\beta_2\alpha_1}$ and

$$\tilde{b}_2=\frac{1-c+\beta_1}{\beta_2}.$$

Appendix D

The Analytical Foundation of the 'Taylor Principle'

This appendix derives the *Taylor principle*, respectively the condition (2.15). In addition to the main text also the forward-looking expectations version which will be employed in the empirical analysis in the subsequent chapters is explicitly considered.

Contemporaneous Data Version

In this section the small-scale macroeconomic model from section 2.5 repeated here for convenience is studied:

(2.11) $$y_t = E_t y_{t+1} - \sigma^{-1}\left(i_t - E_t \pi_{t+1} - r_t^n\right)$$

(2.12) $$\pi_t = \beta E_t \pi_{t+1} + \tilde{\kappa} y_t,$$

which is closed by the Taylor-type rule based on contemporaneous data

(2.13) $$i_t = \varphi_\pi \cdot \pi_t + \varphi_y \cdot y_t.$$

Such a system can be written in a more comprehensive form already given in the main text:

(2.14) $$X_t = A + B \cdot E_t X_{t+1} + \Theta \cdot r_t^n,$$

$$\text{with} \quad B = \frac{1}{\sigma + \varphi_y + \tilde{\kappa}\varphi_\pi} \begin{bmatrix} \sigma & 1 - \beta\varphi_\pi \\ \tilde{\kappa}\sigma & \tilde{\kappa} + \beta(\sigma + \varphi_y) \end{bmatrix},$$

where the characteristics of matrix B is crucial for ensuring the uniqueness of the equilibrium.
In order to derive the stability conditions more generally, consider first the general form of matrix B:

(D.1) $$B = \begin{bmatrix} a_{11} & a_{12} \\ a_{21} & a_{22} \end{bmatrix}.$$

The characteristic polynomial of B is given by:

$$\text{(D.2)} \qquad \det(B-\lambda I)=\begin{vmatrix} a_{11}-\lambda & a_{12} \\ a_{21} & a_{22}-\lambda \end{vmatrix},$$

where I is the identity matrix. Calculating for the determinant yields:

$$\det(B-\lambda I)=(a_{11}-\lambda)\cdot(a_{22}-\lambda)-a_{21}\cdot a_{12}$$

$$=a_{11}\cdot a_{22}-a_{11}\cdot\lambda-a_{22}\cdot\lambda+\lambda^2-a_{21}\cdot a_{12}$$

$$=\lambda^2+a_1\cdot\lambda+a_0,$$

with $a_1\equiv -a_{11}-a_{22}$ and $a_0\equiv(a_{11}\cdot a_{22}-a_{21}\cdot a_{12})$. The eigenvalues are then given by the characteristic equation:

$$\text{(D.3)} \qquad \lambda^2+a_1\cdot\lambda+a_0=0.$$

As already stated in the main text both eigenvalues have to be inside the unit circle. This is the case if and only if both of the following two conditions are satisfied (see LaSalle 1986, p.28):

$$\text{(D.4)} \qquad |a_0|<1 \qquad \text{and}$$

$$\text{(D.5)} \qquad |a_1|<1+a_0.$$

Under the contemporaneous data version of (2.13) the elements of the matrix B are:

$$a_{11}=\frac{\sigma}{\sigma+\varphi_y+\tilde{\kappa}\varphi_\pi}, \qquad a_{12}=\frac{(1-\beta\varphi_\pi)}{\sigma+\varphi_y+\tilde{\kappa}\varphi_\pi},$$

$$a_{21}=\frac{\tilde{\kappa}\sigma}{\sigma+\varphi_y+\tilde{\kappa}\varphi_\pi}, \qquad a_{22}=\frac{\tilde{\kappa}+\beta(\sigma+\varphi_y)}{\sigma+\varphi_y+\tilde{\kappa}\varphi_\pi}.$$

It follows for the coefficients in the characteristic equation:

$$a_0 = \frac{\beta\sigma}{\sigma + \varphi_y + \widetilde{\kappa}\varphi_\pi} \text{ and } \quad a_1 = \frac{-\sigma - (\widetilde{\kappa} + \beta(\sigma + \varphi_y))}{\sigma + \varphi_y + \widetilde{\kappa}\varphi_\pi}.$$

From condition (D.4) it immediately follows that:

(D.6) $$-(1-\beta) < \varphi_y + \widetilde{\kappa}\varphi_\pi,$$

which is trivially satisfied since $0 < \beta < 1$. From condition (D.5) it follows:

(2.15) $$\varphi_\pi + \frac{(1-\beta)}{\widetilde{\kappa}} \cdot \varphi_y > 1,$$

which has been already stated in the main text.[101]

Interestingly, it turns out that a contemporaneous expectation version of the Taylor-type of the form:

(D.7) $$i_t = \varphi_\pi \cdot E_{t-1}\pi_t + \varphi_y \cdot E_{t-1}y_t,$$

that takes into account the informational problem of the central bank puts the same restrictions upon the coefficients in order to ensure determinacy of the rational expectation equilibrium (see Bullard and Mitra, 2002, for the proof). The informational problem of the central bank could alternatively been fixed by using historical data. Studying a lagged data version of the Taylor-type rule of the form:

(D.8) $$i_t = \varphi_\pi \cdot \pi_{t-1} + \varphi_y \cdot y_{t-1}$$

also lead to the Taylor principle with the additional condition that the response to the output gap needs to be sufficiently small (see Bullard and Mitra, 2002, for the formal proof).[102]

Forward-looking Expectations Version

The empirical analysis of the subsequent chapters will employ a forward-looking version of interest rate rules. Therefore, its stability conditions are also

---

[101] Furthermore, $\widetilde{\kappa}(\varphi_\pi - 1) + (1-\beta)\varphi_y \neq 0$ rules out eigenvalues that are on the unit circle.

[102] It is abstained from discussing the latter two cases in detail because they are not applied in the analysis of the subsequent chapters.

derived in this appendix. For convenience, a horizon of one period for the forecast is assumed. Thus, the rule can be formalized as:

(D.9) $$i_t = \varphi_\pi \cdot E_t \pi_{t+1} + \varphi_y \cdot E_t y_{t+1}.$$

Combining this version of the interest rate rule with equations (2.11) and (2.12) leads to the reduced system given by:

$$X_t = A + B \cdot E_t X_{t+1} + \Theta \cdot r_t^n,$$

where $X_t = \begin{bmatrix} y_t \\ \pi_t \end{bmatrix}$, $A = 0$, $\Theta = \begin{bmatrix} \sigma^{-1} \\ \tilde{\kappa}\sigma^{-1} \end{bmatrix}$ and

$$B = \begin{bmatrix} 1-\sigma^{-1}\varphi_y & \sigma^{-1}(1-\varphi_\pi) \\ \tilde{\kappa}(1-\sigma^{-1}\varphi_y) & \beta + \tilde{\kappa}\sigma^{-1}(1-\varphi_\pi) \end{bmatrix}.$$

Since π_t and y_t are free variables, both eigenvalues need to be inside the unit circle for uniqueness. In this case we get:

$$a_0 = \left(1-\sigma^{-1}\varphi_y\right)\cdot\left(\beta + \tilde{\kappa}\sigma^{-1}(1-\varphi_\pi)\right) - \left(\tilde{\kappa}(1-\sigma^{-1}\varphi_y)\cdot\left(\sigma^{-1}(1-\varphi_\pi)\right)\right)$$

which can be reduced to:

(D.10) $$a_0 = \beta(1-\sigma^{-1}\varphi_y)$$

together with condition (D.4) this yields:

(D.11) $$\varphi_y < \sigma(1+\beta^{-1}).$$

This condition implies that the value of φ_y is of primary importance for determinacy. An aggressive response to the output gap can lead to indeterminacy, independently of the value of coefficient φ_π.
Furthermore, we get:

(D.12) $$a_1 = \tilde{\kappa}\sigma^{-1}(\varphi_\pi - 1) + \sigma^{-1}\varphi_y - 1 - \beta.$$

Together with (D.5) this implies the following two conditions:

(D.13) $\tilde{\kappa}(\varphi_\pi - 1) + (1+\beta)\varphi_y < 2\sigma(1+\beta)$ and

(D.14) $\varphi_\pi + \frac{(1-\beta)}{\tilde{\kappa}} \cdot \varphi_y > 1,$

where the latter conditions is equal to condition (2.15) of the contemporaneous data specification, which we labelled the *Taylor principle.* Taking the three conditions together, in turns out that the forward-looking specification is more restrictive than the contemporaneous data version. Again the *Taylor principle* has to hold, but in addition the output response has to be sufficiently low by equation (D.12). Also too large values of φ_π can lead to indeterminacy by condition (D.13).

Chapter 3

Estimating Empirical Reaction Functions for the Deutsche Bundesbank and the European Central Bank

3.1 Introduction

This chapter complements the theoretical analysis of the previous chapter and provides estimates of reaction functions for the Deutsche Bundesbank from 1979 through 1998 and the European Central Bank (ECB) from 1999 through 2003. Since most of the empirical literature is concerned about testing monetary policy rules for the US Federal Reserve System (Fed), this chapter does not discuss empirical evidence of the Fed's behavior. An excellent overview of the literature on monetary policy reaction functions with respect to the Fed is provided by Hamalainen (2004).

The empirical characterization of the ECB via estimating reaction functions is of particular interest, since the ECB is a newly established central bank with almost no track record. Thus, this chapter is an attempt to characterize the first years of the single monetary policy in the European Monetary Union (EMU) empirically.[103] Additionally, providing empirical reaction functions of the Deutsche Bundesbank for the pre-EMU era is worthwhile task, because the ECB is often compared to the Deutsche Bundesbank and, therefore, the estimation results for the Deutsche Bundesbank can serve as benchmarks for the ECB estimates.

This chapter, however, does not aim at providing a comprehensive empirical analysis for both central banks. Instead it has two main intentions. First, it briefly introduces the estimation method of generalized methods of moments with which monetary policy rules have mostly been estimated in the literature. Second, the empirical results of this chapter serve as benchmarks for the analysis in part two of this book. Therein, chapters 4 through 6 will extend the interest rate rules discussed so far by arguments of the term structure of interest rates. The theoretical findings of chapter 4 are then tested in chapter 5, while chapter 6 provides an alternative estimation approach for monetary policy rules based on no-arbitrage consideration. The empirical results of chapters 5 and 6 are then compared to the ones in the present chapter.

The present chapter has the following structure. Section 3.2 derives the estimation equation and describes the estimation procedure. Section 3.3 provides

[103] This chapter partly draws on the estimations from Fendel and Frenkel (2005a). However, Fendel and Frenkel (2005a) explicitly link the estimation results to the debate on the monetary policy strategy of the ECB. This discussion will be touched only briefly in this chapter.

estimates for the Deutsche Bundesbank. Section 3.4 examines whether a specific monetary policy rule can be identified for the ECB. It also compares the findings on such a rule with the strategy that the ECB defined for its monetary policy.

3.2 The Estimation Procedure

Among the empirical reaction functions, the forward-looking monetary policy rules are the most popular ones. This chapter follows this direction and mainly presents estimates of forward-looking reaction functions. Following Clarida et al. (1998 and 2000), the general policy rule then takes the form:

$$i^* = \bar{i} + \alpha_1 E_t(\pi_{t+k} - \pi^*) + \alpha_2 E_t(y_{t+q} - y_{t+q}^*), \tag{3.1}$$

where i^* is the desired level of the nominal short-term interest rate, and $\bar{i}$ is its equilibrium level. The second term on the right-hand side is the expected deviation of the k-period ahead inflation rate (π) from the target rate (π^*) which is assumed to be constant over time, while the third term is the expected deviation of output (y) from its natural level (y*) q periods ahead (i.e., the output gap). The coefficients α_1 and α_2 represent the intensity with which the desired interest rate of the central bank reacts to the inflation and the output gap. The contemporaneous data Taylor-type rule which was the main concern of the previous chapter follows as the special case of equation (3.1) with $k = q = 0$.

In the empirical literature on monetary policy rules it is often argued that central banks do not adjust the interest rate towards its desired level given by equation (3.1) immediately but in smaller steps, in order to avoid too large changes in the interest rate that might disrupt financial markets.[104] However, the existing theory, by and large, does not readily account for why central banks should adjust their instrument in a sluggish fashion. Possible alternative explanations are model uncertainties (Clarida, Galí and Gertler, 1999), data uncertainties (Orphanides, 1998) or an optimal smoothing behavior of the central bank in the sense that lagged dependency of the short-term interest rate provides a leverage with respect to longer-term rates which permits the central bank to better manipulate aggregate demand (Rotemberg and Woodford, 1997).[105] The assumption of interest rate smoothing behavior leads to

[104] The statistical significance of the lagged interest rate could have a very different interpretation than the interest smoothing behavior determinants mentioned before. Based on evidence from the term structure of interest rates, Rudebusch (2002) believes that the reason might be the serial correlation of shocks rather than interest rate smoothing behavior of central banks.

[105] See also Woodford (1999). Chapter 4 picks up this issue again.

(3.2) $$i_t = (1-\rho)i_t{}^* + \rho i_{t-1} + \upsilon_t,$$

where the parameter $0 \le \rho < 1$ describes the degree of interest rate smoothing behavior and υ_t is an i.i.d. exogenous random shock to the interest rate.[106] Combining (3.1) and (3.2) leads to

(3.3) $$i_t = (1-\rho)\left(\bar{i} + \alpha_1 E_t(\pi_{t+k} - \pi^*) + \alpha_2 E_t(y_{t+q} - y_{t+q}{}^*)\right) + \rho i_{t-1} + \upsilon_t.$$

In order to arrive at a testable relationship, the unobservable terms in equation (3.3) have to be eliminated. Therefore, rewrite equation (3.3) as:

(3.4) $$i_t = (1-\rho)\alpha_0 + \alpha_1(1-\rho)\pi_{t+k} + \alpha_2(1-\rho)\left(y_{t+q} - y_{t+q}{}^*\right) + \rho i_{t-1} + \varepsilon_t,$$

where

$$\alpha_0 = \bar{i} - \alpha_1\pi^* \text{ and } \varepsilon_t = \upsilon_t - \alpha_1(1-\rho)\left(\pi_{t+k} - E_t\pi_{t+k}\right) - \alpha_2(1-\rho)\left(y_{t+q} - E_t y_{t+q}\right).$$

The error term, thus, includes interest rate shocks and the forecast error of the central bank. Furthermore it is assumed that

(3.5) $$E_t\left[\varepsilon_t \middle| I_t\right] = 0,$$

where I_t is the central bank's information set available at time t. Equation (3.5) simply states that the central bank uses its best possible guess about future inflation and output in its interest rate decisions. The forecast error is assumed to be uncorrelated with the information set. Equation (3.5) defines a set of orthogonality conditions which can be used for the estimation based on the generalized methods of moments (GMM).

Given that the equilibrium real interest rate is defined by $\bar{r} = \bar{i} - \pi^*$ and that $\alpha_0 = \bar{i} - \alpha_1\pi^*$, the implicit inflation target can be extracted from the regressions according to

[106] Bullard and Mitra (2000) have shown that monetary policy inertia (interest rate smoothing) generally has a beneficial effect for the determinacy of a rational expectations equilibrium. For the sake of brevity the analysis of lagged interest rate versions was not explicitly included into section 2.5 of the previous chapter.

(3.6) $$\pi^* = \frac{\bar{r} - \alpha_0}{\alpha_1 - 1},$$

once a value of the equilibrium real interest rate is exogeneously alleged.

Equation (3.4) cannot be estimated with the ordinary least squares (OLS), because the right-hand side variables are not independent from the error term. In this case, the explanatory variables are not weakly exogenous. The literature proposes to use the generalized methods of moments (GMM) alternatively. This estimation technique nests many common estimators and can be chosen to avoid a possible correlation between the right-hand side variables and the error term (the so-called simultaneity bias). This is done by making use of appropriate instruments. Generally speaking, the set of instruments should contain variables that are known to the central bank at the time of the decision about the value of the instrument rate and that are orthogonal to the error term. In this context, lagged values of the explanatory variables are natural candidates for the set of instruments.

In order to ensure the identification of the parameters to be estimated, the number of instruments n has to be at least as high as the number of parameters p. If the number of instruments is greater than the number of parameters ($n > p$) the system is called over-identified. The optimization problem at the heart of the GMM estimation than produces a system of n equations with only p unknowns, which calls for an appropriate weighting matrix. Hanson (1982) has shown that a necessary (but not sufficient) condition to obtain asymptotically efficient parameter estimates is to set the weighting matrix equal to the inverse of the covariance matrix of the sample moments. In the following estimation this weighting matrix is chosen using the method of Newey and West (1987), who have proposed a general covariance matrix estimator that is consistent in the presence of both heteroskedasticity and autocorrelation of unknown form (so-called *HAC Covariances*).

An advantage is that the GMM estimator requires no information about the exact distribution of the error term. This implies that the normality assumption which is a crucial precondition for many other estimation techniques is not required. All what is required is that an orthogonality condition such as (3.5) holds. Furthermore, the *J-statistics* can be used to test the validity of over-identifying restrictions.[107] Under the null hypothesis that the over-identifying restrictions are satisfied, the *J-statistics* multiplied with the number of observations is asymptotically χ^2 distributed with degrees of freedom equal to

[107] The value of J is the minimized value from the criterion function.

the number over-identifying restrictions, i.e. $(n - p)$.[108] The estimations of the following two sections are based on the outlined GMM technique.[109]

3.3 Empirical Reaction Functions for the Deutsche Bundesbank

The data set for the Deutsche Bundesbank regressions is monthly and covers the period from 1:1979 to 12:1998. This period represents what we might call the 'Bundesbank regime' in which the Bundesbank was responsible for interest rate setting in Germany. The sample starts in 1979, because this represents the starting of the European Exchange Rate Mechanism and ends in 1998, when the ECB took over responsibility for monetary policy in the euro area. The start of the sample is chosen in order to leave out the period of the Bretton Woods system (which constrained monetary policy due to world-wide fixed exchange rates) as well as the period immediately after the breakdown of the Bretton Woods system which was a period of instability in international financial markets. For the period after 1998 the same analysis is performed for the interest rate setting of the European Central Bank in a subsequent section.

The data set is constructed as follows. The short-term interest rate is the German overnight money market rate. The inflation rate is based of the consumer price index. The output gap is based on the monthly index of industrial production. Although being aware that industrial output is more volatile than, say GDP, this section follows the usual practice and opts for this variable in order to obtain monthly figures. The output gap is constructed on the basis of a linear trend. In order to avoid starting point and end point problems, the trend between the longer period from 1970 through 2003 is computed.[110] Figures 3.1 shows the developments of the output gap.

---

[108] See Johnston and Di Nardo (1997, p. 337ff).

[109] The Eviews 5.0 software was used to perform the estimations.

[110] Also a HP filter was used and the reported results are robust against this change. Furthermore, it turned out that a quadratic trend did not change our measure of the output gap, since the quadratic term turned out to be insignificant. Thus, the linear trend was chosen.

Figure 3.1: The Output Gap for Germany 1979 - 1998

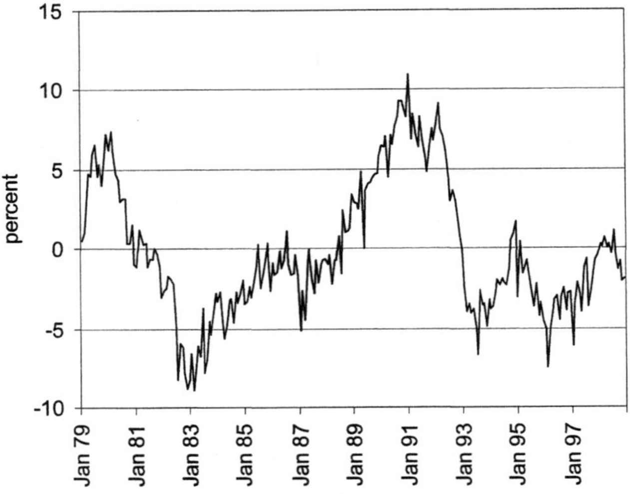

Table 3.1 reports estimation results of the contemporaneous data version of the Taylor-type rule as it was discussed in the previous chapter. It is also abstained from including an interest rate smoothing term in the first two specifications. In particular, this means an estimation of equation (3.4) with $k = q = \rho = 0$ (Regression I). Additionally, Table 3.1 provides an estimation with lagged data, i.e. $k = q = -1$ and $\rho = 0$ (Regression II). Regressions III and IV then extend specifications I and II by allowing for interest rate smoothing (ρ is not restricted to zero). As already indicated the estimations are based on the GMM procedure. However, in the contemporaneous data version no instruments are required and GMM then exactly nests the OLS estimator.

Table 3.1: Estimates on Contemporaneous and Lagged Version of the Taylor-type Rule (Deutsche Bundesbank, 1979-1998)

Coefficient	Regression I (Contemp. data with no smoothing)	Regression II (Lagged data with no smoothing)	Regression III (Contemp. data with smoothing)	Regression IV (Lagged data with smoothing)
ρ (smoothing)	set to zero	set to zero	0.95 (0.017)	0.95 (0.018)
α_0 (constant)	2.74 (0.182)	2.68 (0.181)	1.38 (1.138)	1.56 (1.19)
α_1 (inflation)	1.12 (0.047)	1.12 (0.047)	1.13 (0.263)	1.08 (0.287)
α_2 (output gap)	0.05 (0.015)	0.07 (0.016)	0.29 (0.128)	0.29 (0.136)
Adj. R^2	0.72	0.72	0.98	0.98
DW	0.14	0.13	1.64	1.60

Standard errors are in parentheses

The results of the Regressions I through IV can be interpreted in the light of the theoretical discussion of the previous chapter 2. The coefficient that displays the response to inflation is greater than one in all cases. Thus, the Deutsche Bundesbank did follow the *Taylor principle*. The response to the output gap is quite small but significant in all specifications. Comparing Regressions I and II with their counterparts III and IV shows that interest rate smoothing is a strong empirical feature of the interest rate policy of the Deutsche Bundesbank. The explanatory power of the regressions improve significantly once it is allowed for a smoothing term. Also the Dubin Watson (DW) value is significantly improving with the additional smoothing term.[111] Comparing the contemporaneous versions with their respective lagged data version counterparts

[111] It should be noted that from economic intuition a DW value of still smaller than two makes sense and indicates towards a successive adjustment towards the long-term value of the interest rate after a disturbance. Only a value of greater than two would be counterintuitive.

(i.e., comparing I with III, and II with IV), validates to claim of the classification scheme from chapter 2 that they are almost identical.

Table 3.2: Estimates of Forward-Looking Taylor-type Rules with Different Horizons (Deutsche Bundesbank, 1979-1998)

Coefficient	Regression V (k = 12 and q = 0)	Regression VI (k = 12 and q = 3)	Regression VII (k = 12 and q = 6)	Regression VIII (k = 9 and q = 3)
ρ (smoothing)	0.91 (0.012)	0.91 (0.012)	0.91 (0.012)	0.91 (0.013)
α_0 (constant)	1.14 (0.546)	0.91 (0.597)	0.86 (0.64)	1.88 (0.497)
α_1 (inflation)	1.57 (0.147)	1.60 (0.146)	1.62 (0.149)	1.30 (0.124)
α_2 (output gap)	0.07 (0.047)	0.09 (0.049)	0.09 (0.052)	0.10 (0.047)
Adj. R^2	0.98	0.98	0.98	0.98
Implied π^*	2.5	2.8	2.84	1.4
DW	1.59	1.56	1.53	1.72
J-statistics	13.629	12.878	12.104	14.76

Standard errors are in parentheses
Instruments: constant; 1st-6th, 9th and 12th lag of output gap; 1st-6th, 9th and 12th lag of inflation; 1st, 6th, 9th and 12th lag money market rate; 1st-6th, 9th and 12th lag of IMF commodity price index.

Table 3.2 shows the results of regressions of the forward-looking specification of equation (3.4). The regressions vary with respect to their forward-looking horizon: Regression V sets $k = 12$ and $q = 0$, Regression VI sets $k = 12$ and $q = 3$, Regression VII sets $k = 12$ and $q = 6$, and finally Regression VIII sets $k = 9$ and $q = 3$. All specifications allow for interest rate smoothing. In the GMM estimation the correction for heteroscedasticity and autocorrelation of unknown form with a lag truncation parameter of 12 is used. In addition, Bartlett weights are chosen to ensure positive definiteness of the estimated variance-covariance matrix.

The results in Table 3.2 again support the claim that the Deutsche Bundesbank followed the *Taylor principle*. This claim is robust across different horizons of the inflation and the output forecast. Also the parameter for the output gap is in line with the theoretical consideration of chapter 2. Its value is significant but sufficiently low in order to ensure determinancy.[112] Also the test statistics are satisfactory. The *J-statistics* indicate that a valid set of instruments has been chosen.[113] Table 3.2 also contains an estimate of the implicit inflation target of the Bundesbank over the sample period. It is calculated according to equation (3.6) under the assumption that the equilibrium real interest rate is about 3 percent.[114] Except for Regression VIII the values of the implicit inflation targets are of reasonable values that coincide with the announcements of the Deutsche Bundesbank.

An alterative estimation approach, however, is to explicitly take care of the inflation target which the Deutsche Bundesbank announced yearly. The estimation according to equation (3.4) so far was formulated on the basis of the absolute inflation rate as the relevant right-hand side variable, leaving the implicit inflation target endogenously. The latter was extracted based on an assumption on the equilibrium real interest rate. This estimation specification, however, does not allow for time varying inflation targets and, thus, Table 3.2 only reports an average value over the sample period. Because the inflation target might not have been constant, an alternative regression specification based in an explicit inflation target complements the analysis of the behavior of the Bundesbank with. Therefore, equation (3.4) is slightly rewritten as:

$$(3.7)\quad i_t = (1-\rho)\alpha_0 + \alpha_1(1-\rho)\left(\pi_{t+k} - \pi_t^{norm}\right) + \alpha_2(1-\rho)\left(y_{t+q} - y_{t+q}{}^*\right) + \rho i_{t-1} + \varepsilon_t,$$

$$\text{where } \alpha_0 = \bar{i} \text{ and } \varepsilon_t = \upsilon_t - \alpha_1(1-\rho)\left(\pi_{t+k} - E_t\pi_{t+k}\right) - \alpha_2(1-\rho)\left(y_{t+q} - E_t y_{t+q}\right).$$

Notice that in contrast to specification (3.4) the inflation target has been relabeled to π_t^{norm} and now explicitly contains a time index. Due to the

[112] See condition (D.11) in Appendix D.

[113] The critical χ^2 value for a p-value of 0.05 and 25 degrees of freedom (29 instruments minus 4 coefficients) is 14.61. The reported J-statistic has to be smaller in order to accept the validity of the instruments.

[114] This value approximately coincides with the average *ex post* real interest rate over the sample period which is 3.1 percent.

formulation based on the inflation gap rather than inflation only, the coefficient α_0 can now be interpreted as the equilibrium nominal interest rate.

The data on the inflation gap is constructed using the difference of the consumer price index which has been used before and the so-called price norm that has been announced by the Deutsche Bundesbank on a yearly basis. This could be interpreted as a kind of inflation target, although the Deutsche Bundesbank did not explicitly target inflation but the money growth rate. Nevertheless, the inflation values were used as inputs into the derivation of the money growth target and price stability was the final target. Whenever the Bundesbank announced ranges instead of values of the price norm it was opted for the middle of the range.[115] Table 3.3 reports the price norm.

Table 3.3: Price Norm of the Deutsche Bundesbank 1979 – 1998

Year	Price Norm	Year	Price Norm
1979	4.0	1989	2.0
1980	4.0	1990	2.0
1981	3.5 – 4.0	1991	2.0
1982	3.5	1992	2.0
1983	3.5	1993	2.0
1984	3.0	1994	2.0
1985	2.0	1995	2.0
1986	2.0	1996	2.0
1987	2.0	1997	1.5 – 2.0
1988	2.0	1998	1.5 – 2.0

Source: Deutsche Bundesbank, monthly reports

Table 3.4 reports the results of complementary regressions based on specification (3.7). The chosen values for k and q are identical to those in Table 3.2. Also the estimation method (i.e., the lag truncation of 12, chosen Bartlett weights and the set of instruments) is identical. The results are in line with the ones from Table 3.2. The *Taylor principle* significantly holds through the

[115] Until 1984, the price norm, or price assumption, reflected the Deutsche Bundesbank's view of the "unavoidable" level of inflation, while from 1985 onwards, it was defined as the maximum rate of inflation to be tolerated over the medium term. Conceptually, the price norm should refer to the GNP/GDP deflator rather the CPI, since it was related to the price term in the quantity equation. However, it is a good approximation for the implicit target of the consumer price inflation. Over the sample period the price norm ranged from 4 percent (at the beginning) to 2 percent (since the mid 1980s). Thus, the extracted (average) implicit inflation targets from Table 3.2 are quite reasonable.

specifications IX to XI. The coefficients for the output gap in this specifications are also sufficiently low and significant. The *J-statistics* indicate again that the set of instruments is valid. Regression XII, however, indicates that shorten the horizon of the inflation gap forecast leads to a violation of the *Taylor principle* and the results become insignificant. This is in line with the related Regression VIII from Table 3.2, where the shortening of the inflation forecast led to an implausible value of the implicit inflation target.

Table 3.4: Estimates of Forward-Looking Taylor-type Rule with Price Norm Incorporated (Deutsche Bundesbank 1979-1998)

Coefficient	Regression IX (k = 12 and q = 0 with price norm)	Regression X (k = 12 and q = 3 with price norm)	Regression XI (k = 12 and q = 6 with price norm)	Regression XII (k = 9 and q = 3 with price norm)
ρ (smoothing)	0.95 (0.012)	0.89 (0.016)	0.88 (0.019)	0.97 (0.016)
α_0 (constant)	3.11 (0.693)	4.05 (0.344)	4.1 (0.359)	2.19 (2.425)
α_1 (inflation)	1.64 (0.188)	1.68 (0.131)	1.71 (0.128)	0.85 (0.581)
α_2 (output gap)	0.14 (0.106)	0.09 (0.041)	0.09 (0.047)	0.32 (0.263)
Adj. R^2	0.98	0.98	0.98	0.98
Implied π^*	price norm	price norm	price norm	price norm
DW	1.46	1.15	1.07	1.52
J-statistics	13.261	12.138	11.191	13.745

Standard errors are in parentheses
Instruments: constant; 1st-6th , 9th and 12th lag of output gap; 1st-6th, 9th and 12th lag of inflation; 1st, 6th, 9th and 12th lag money market rate; 1st-6th , 9th and 12th lag of IMF commodity price index.

Taking this evidence together, it seems that the Deutsche Bundesbank followed the *Taylor principle* and acted forward-looking with a horizon of about 1 year in targeting inflation. This result is in line with the literature on estimated reaction functions for the Bundesbank based on a variety of sample periods and data sets.[116] However, the estimates in this chapter and in much of the literature are performed by using *ex post* revised data. Orphanides (2001) shows that estimation results might change substantially when one considers the data on which a central bank historically had to decide, i.e. data that had not (yet) went through *ex post* data revisions. Gerberding et al. (2004) construct a (quarterly) real-time data set for the Bundesbank, that matches the Deutsche Bundesbank's real-time information set. They find that the *Taylor principle* also holds on basis of real-time data. The most significant forward-looking horizon is about 5 quarters. In contrast to the analysis in this chapter the estimator for the output gap turns insignificant. However, when adding the change of output rather than the value, they find a significant response. This result is in line with the transformation of the Deutsche Bundesbank monetary target strategy into a Taylor-type rule in section 2.6.[117]

3.4 Empirical Reaction Functions for the European Central Bank

The European Central Bank (ECB) was established in June 1998 and began its operations in January 1999, when European Monetary Union (EMU) was established and the euro was launched. Since then, the ECB has been responsible for monetary policy in the euro area and it seems a natural exercise to estimate monetary policy rules for the ECB. The ECB itself does not seem to totally reject the usefulness of monetary policy rules. In its Monthly Bulletin of October 2001 (ECB, 2001, p. 38), the ECB states: "*The emphasis* [...] *on rule-guided monetary policy* [...] *is generally welcome* [, because] *it provides a salutary antidote to the perennial risks of a discretionary, ad hoc approach to monetary policy.*" This statement by itself provides enough motivation for the search of the monetary policy rule of the ECB.

Due to the relatively short sample period, direct econometric estimates of the empirical reaction function of the ECB have been very limited so far. An exception is Hayo and Hofmann (2003) who compare the ECB reaction function to the Bundesbank reaction function over the period 1979:04 to 1998:12. However, they present only a single estimation specification for both central

[116] See, for example, Neumann and von Hagen (2002), Faust et. al. (2001) and Surico (2003a/b).

[117] See equation (2.23). However, the coefficient of lagged interest rate is not forced to one, which a test of the monetary policy rule in (2.23) would call for.

banks. They do not examine alternative specifications nor do they test for different data representations within their given regression specification (e.g., different de-trending methods). Fourçans and Vranceanu (2004) also estimate reaction functions for the ECB but use different specifications and data compared to the study in this chapter.

Most other existing studies do not investigate 'real ECB' policy reaction function but rather focus on a 'fictitious euro area central bank' by using aggregated and synthetic euro zone data extended backwards to include time periods prior to the start of the common monetary policy. Among those studies are Gerdesmeier and Roffia (2003), Gerlach-Kirsten (2003) and Gerlach and Schnabel (1999). While the method applied in these studies eliminates the otherwise occurring small-sample problem, it appears to be a relatively unreliable approach to generate conclusions for the ECB policy after 1999.

The reaction function (3.4) is also estimated with the GMM estimator. Data are monthly and range from 1:1999 to 10:2003.[118] The inflation rate is the harmonized index of consumer prices (HICP), output is the industrial production in the euro area and the short-term interest rate is the European over-night index average (EONIA). Three different trend-generating processes for industrial output are used because the short sample period may lead to an inconsistent construction of the output gap. The use of a set of different de-trending methods potentially leads to more robust results. On the basis of the logarithm of industrial production the output gap is constructed on the basis of a quadratic trend (eurogap1), a linear trend (eurogap2) and a Hodrick-Prescott filter with the penalty parameter set to 14400 (eurogap3).[119]

In addition to the three output gaps based on industrial production, monthly euro area-wide unemployment rates are also taken as an indicator of real activity in the ECB reaction function. In this case, the output gap (eurogap4) is calculated on the basis of a Hodrick-Prescott filter (again with penalty parameter of 14400).[120] One has to be aware of the fact that the unemployment rate has a high structural share. However, given the short time period under consideration it can be assumed that the structural share remained fairly constant during this

[118] This sample period is chosen because it coincides with the ECB presidency of Willem F. Duisenberg. However, Fendel and Frenkel (2005b) show that the results stay the same if an extended period from 1:1999 through 08:2004 is employed. The latter period is, therefore, employed in the empirical analysis in chapter 5.

[119] The value of 14400 for monthly data is standard in the literature.

[120] The so-called "end point problem" renders the Hodrick-Prescott procedure a somewhat inadequate choice especially when central banks face decision problems in real time. However, the Hodrick-Prescott filter was considered as a supplement for the other de-trending methods in order to check for the robustness of results.

period so that all variations can be interpreted as cyclical. Figure 3.2 displays the development of the constructed output gaps.[121]

Figure 3.2: Different Output Gaps for the Euro Area

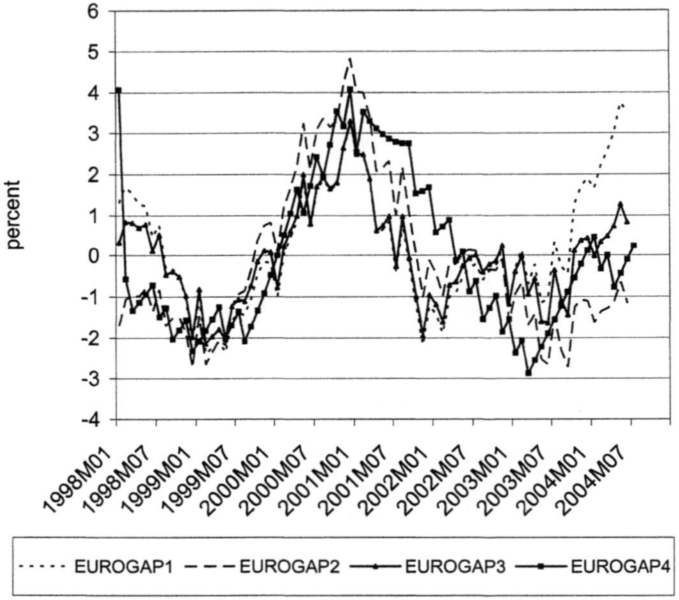

The approach of using a variety of output gap measures takes also into account the critique of Orphanides (1999), who has extensively considered the problem of the output gap to show that different behavior by the Fed in the 1979s and 1980s can be explained by different measures of the output gap rather than by different parameters in the reaction function.

The GMM estimation is implemented using the correction for heteroscedasticity and autocorrelation of unknown form with a lag truncation

[121] Figure 3.2 shows the output gap for a longer period than the sample period. This is because of avoiding the already mentioned end-point problem. In chapter 5, however, augmented reaction functions for the ECB over the extended sample period shown here will estimated. A comparison of the estimations indicates that the results are robust against the change in the sample period.

parameter of 12. Bartlett weights are chosen to ensure positive definiteness of our estimated variance-covariance matrix.[122] Following Clarida, Galí and Gertler (2000) the forward-looking horizons are set as k =12 and q = 0.[123] In the first set of regressions, the same set of instruments as for the regressions of the Deutsche Bundesbank are used with the only exception of the IMF commodity price index, because the *J-statistics* indicated that this is not a valid instrument. Due to the use of the twelve month-ahead inflation rate in the regression analysis, the effective sample period is reduced to 1999:01 to 2002:10. The use of the lagged instrument variables does not shorten our sample since we are able to use the 1998 values as instruments for 1999 (the beginning of the period of interest) regardless of the ECB regime.[124]

The regression results are shown in Table 3.5 on the next page. They differ with respect to the output gap concept. The statistical properties appear quite remarkable, although one must be aware that the short sample period can cause difficulties in the estimation. The coefficient of inflation is always significant and higher than one, reflecting that the *Taylor principle* holds.[125] The output gap also significantly enters the reaction function of the ECB. This is independent of the concept of type of concept that is employed for the output gap. The interest-smoothing parameter is also significant and of a magnitude suggested by the recent literature. An exception is specification (XIV) with the linear trend. The smoothing parameter is unusually low, but the Durbin Watson statistic suggests that there is some serious autocorrelation left in the residuals.

[122] This is identical to the estimation of the Deutsche Bundesbank reaction functions.

[123] The horizons have also been varied as in the case of the Deutsche Bundesbank. It turned out that the values of k =12 and q = 0 provided the best fit. It is abstained from reporting the other specifications including the contemporaneous data specifications.

[124] The initial values are set as follows: ρ=0.8, α_0=1, α_1=2 and α_2=1.5. The initial coefficient values for inflation and the output gap are in a range that a Taylor rule would normally suggest and are also in line with the previous results based on other data sets and countries. However, since the estimation results might be somewhat sensitive to the initial values of the coefficients in the iteration process, it was also experimented with variations of the initial values which indicated that the results are indeed robust to changes up to +/- 50 % of the above values. However, for the smoothing parameter, only values ranging from 0.6 to 0.95 were used, since the condition for stability is that $0<\rho<1$.

[125] One should not compare the size of the inflation coefficient of the ECB to the one obtained for the Bundesbank in order to make a statement about the relative stabilization preferences of the two central banks. This is because from chapter 2 we know that the coefficients in the optimal interest rate rules are convolutions of the preference parameters and the structural parameters, so that no direct inference from the size of the estimated parameters to the preferences is possible.

Table 3.5: Estimation Results of Forward-Looking Specification for the ECB (1999 – 2004; $k = 12$ and $q = 0$)

Coefficient	Regression XIII	Regression XIV	Regression XV	Regression XVI
ρ (smoothing)	0.92 (0.01)	0.69 (0.05)	0.84 (0.01)	0.95 (0.02)
α_0 (constant)	- 0.91 (0.97)	0.44 (0.94)	- 0.68 (0.65)	- 4.83 (4.92)
α_1 (inflation)	2.54 (0.49)	1.43 (0.44)	2.00 (0.30)	4.32 (2.45)
α_2 (eurogap1)	1.69 (0.26)			
α_2 (eurogap2)		0.29 (0.02)		
α_2 (eurogap3)			0.53 (0.03)	
α_2 (eurogap4)				0.65 (0.14)
Implied π*	1.56	2.46	2.18	1.96
Adj. R^2	0.94	0.90	0.96	0.95
DW	1.49	0.8	1.84	1.52
J-Statistic 16df	5.04	4.19	4.5	5.09

Standard errors are in parentheses
Instruments: constant; 1st-6th, 9th and 12th lag of output gap; 1st-6th, 9th and 12th lag of inflation; 1st, 6th, 9th and 12th lag of EONIA.

Table 3.5 also presents the result of specification (XVI) based on the 'unemployment gap' (eurogap4). The coefficients have again the expected values, although the response to the inflation gap seems very high and less significant in that specification. The *J-statistics* indicates the validity of the set of instruments.[126] The results of the implicit inflation targets are also reported in Table 3.5. They are based on the assumption that the equilibrium real interest rate for the euro area is 1.5 percent.[127] The implicit inflation target ranges between 1.56 and 2.46. These values are also quite impressive since they lie exactly in the range of the definition of price stability of 'near two percent'.[128]

Another question that seems to be worthwhile to examine in this framework is the role of money growth in the reaction function of the ECB. According to the strategy of the ECB, the growth rate of M3 relative to the reference value of 4½ % per annum should be of some significance. The GMM estimation provides a straightforward test of the importance of money growth rate in form of a test of the validity of instruments. This test is based on the *J-statistics*. In order to perform the test, the baseline regressions shown in Table 3.5 are re-estimated with additional instruments. We take the first six lags, the ninth and the twelfth lag of the excess money growth.[129] The latter is defined as the difference between the seasonally adjusted three-month moving average growth rate of M3 in the euro area and its reference value of 4.5 percent. Table 3.6 (on the next page) presents the results. Because of its inferior result, the regression based on the linear trend of industrial production (eurogap2) is excluded.

The results are quite comparable to their respective baseline regressions reported in Table 3.5. Although the parameter values for inflation and the output gap are somewhat lower, all main features (e.g. the *Taylor principle*) again hold significantly. In addition, the range of the implied inflation target is again fairly close to the expected value indicating the relative robustness of our estimation. Given that a valid set of instruments was chosen in the regressions of Table 3.5, the results of the *J-statistics* for the test of overidentifying restrictions in Table 3.6 does not reject the null hypothesis of validity of the additional instruments.[130] This indicates that excess money growth did not affect the ECB's

[126] The critical χ^2 value with 17 degrees of freedom (21 instruments minus 4 coefficients) for the 5 percent significance level is about 9.

[127] Again this value is chosen in accordance with the average ex post level of the real interest rate over the sample period.

[128] Notice, that the ECB changed the formulation of its inflation target from "below 2 percent" to "below, but near 2 percent" in 2003 (see ECB, 2003). Because the ECB did not vary its inflation target, no complement analysis with an exogenous inflation gap based on equation (3.7) is performed. However, in the empirical analysis of chapter 5, an inflation target of 1.5 percent for the ECB will be adopted.

[129] Other lag structures were also stepwise tested which had no major influence on the results.

[130] The critical χ^2 value for a p-value of 0.05 and 25 degrees of freedom (29 instruments minus 4 coefficients) is 14.61. The reported J-statistics has to be smaller in order accepted the validity of the instruments.

behavior directly but instead served as a good instrument for the right-hand side variables.[131]

Table 3.6: Supplementary Regression Results for the ECB with Excess Money Growth as an Additional Instrument

coefficient	Regression XVII	Regression XVIII	Regression XIX
ρ (smoothing)	0.85	0.75	0.91
	(0.01)	(0.01)	(0.01)
α_0 (constant)	0.20	1.19	0.63
	(0.30)	(0.16)	(0.56)
α_1 (inflation)	1.84	1.24	1.60
	(0.15)	(0.07)	(0.29)
α_2 (eurogap1)	0.49		
	(0.03)		
α_2 (eurogap3)		0.45	
		(0.02)	
α_2 (eurogap4)			0.56
			(0.04)
Implied π*	1,54	1.29	1.45
Adj. R^2	0.95	0.93	0.94
DW	1.43	1.10	1.40
J-Statistic 24 df	4.43	4.47	5.33

Standard errors are in parentheses
Instruments: constant; 1st-6th, 9th and 12th lag of output gap; 1st-6th, 9th and 12th lag of inflation; 1st, 6th, 9th and 12th lag of EONIA; and 1st-6th, 9th and 12th lag of excess money growth rate.

[131] From a purely econometric point of view, excess money growth could be highly correlated with inflation, the output gap, or the lagged interest rate. Further tests did not enable me to draw final conclusions as to which variable exactly is instrumented for by which particular lag. Excess money with various leads and lags were also included as additional explanatory variable but a significant influence could not be detected. This supports the result of the J-test.

The absence of a direct link between monetary aggregates and interest rate reactions might have two reasons. First, ECB could well have reacted to monetary figures which were purged from the influence of portfolio shifts and precautionary money holdings that the ECB (2004) identified as special effects. Second, the ECB has emphasized on various occasions and has also clarified in the revision of its strategy that the monetary analysis is of medium to longer term nature. In these cases, it is not surprising that no mechanical link between interest rate setting and monetary developments can be detected econometrically. With this in mind, our result does not contradict the two pillar strategy.

Certainly, for the ECB estimation the issue of real-time data has to be raised, too. Gerdesmeier and Roffia (2004) investigate this for the ECB. They find that when using real time data the *Taylor principle* is only satisfied in the case of forward-looking rules. Estimations based on the contemporaneous specification do not support that the ECB followed the *Taylor principle*. However, they also draw the conclusion that the forward-looking specifications of the form that where presented in this section generally provide a better fit for the actual behavior of the ECB compared to contemporaneous ones.

A explicit comparison of the point estimates for the reaction coefficients of the Bundesbank and the ECB and, in turn, drawing conclusions about their relative preferences towards inflation and output stabilization is not possible. As shown in chapter 2, the reaction coefficients in optimal rules are not only determined by preferences but also by structural parameters of the economy which reflect the transmission process. Only if euro area and German economic structure were identical a valid inference would be possible. However, the latter is obviously not the case.

Part II: Interest Rate Rules and the Term Structure of Interest Rates

Chapter 4

Optimal Monetary Policy Rules in the Presence of Term Structure Effects

4.1 Introduction

As discussed in the previous chapters, the debate on optimal monetary policy has been vitally influenced by Taylor (1993), who argues that a simple monetary policy rule based on setting the short-term nominal interest rate in accordance with both the contemporary inflation and the output gap leads to a good stabilization performance in the economy. It has also been shown that a Taylor-type rule can be extracted from a small-scale optimizing model. The model in this chapter extends and generalizes the one from chapter 2 by taking into account that interest rates may differ for different maturities. This allows us to consider the fact that, on the one hand, longer-term interest rates are the more important rates when it comes to affecting aggregate demand and future inflation, while, on the other hand, the short-term interest rate represents the instrument of the central bank. The whole set of interest rates differing in their maturity together represent the term structure of interest rates, i.e., the yield curve.

The presence of yield curve effects on the transmission of monetary policy cannot be captured by simply assuming time-lags in the transmission process. This would only represent the effect that a given change in the instrument will take some time until the monetary action will translate into longer-term interest rates and, thus, into aggregate demand and inflation. It cannot describe the possibility that the change in the longer-term interest rates might not mimic the change in the instrument one for one, which means that the yield curve might change its shape in response to monetary policy actions of the central bank. Therefore, the present chapter explicitly considers the term structure of interest rates.

The rest of this chapter is structured as follows. Section 4.2 discusses the role of the term structure in monetary policy more generally. Section 4.3 extends the model from section 2.4 and derives an optimal interest rate rule in the presence of term structure effects. Applying the purely backward-looking case is necessary to derive a closed form solution for the optimal rule which is to be compared to the optimal rule from chapter 2.4. Section 4.4 additionally presents a general (hybrid) model from section 1.6 which allows for backward-looking and forward-looking behavior. From this model only a "quasi-optimal" rule can be derived if the long term bond is restricted to have a maturity of only two periods. However, the resulting optimal rule allows to crosscheck whether the findings from the backward-looking model are likely to hold in forward-looking case.

4.2 The Term Structure of Interest Rates and Monetary Policy

The term structure of interest rates, i.e., the relation of short-term and long-term interest rates, is an important feature for the operation of monetary policy.[132] To date, many central banks commonly use a short-term interest rate (typically an overnight rate) as their direct operating instrument in order to reach their final goal of price stability (and may be an additional output goal). Monetary policy in this sense is intended to work through aggregate demand. Of course, none of the important sectors of real spending – investment, consumption, or housing – depends directly on the overnight rate. Instead, aggregate spending depends on longer-term interest rates, possibly with different horizons across countries. Therefore, gauging how changes in the short rate triggered by the central bank affect the longer-term interest rates and, thus, the entire term structure of interest rates is important for understanding the monetary transmission mechanism.

For the conduct of monetary policy three crucial questions are closely related to the existence of the term structure.

(1) How should monetary authorities interpret and use the information of a particular term structure?

(2) How does monetary policy, especially changes of the short-term interest rate, affect the term structure of interest rates and, in turn, other aggregate variables of pivotal importance that represent the final objectives of monetary policy, like inflation and possibly output?

(3) Given the fact that today monetary policy is often described and analyzed by monetary policy rules, how do term structure effects fit into this theoretical considerations?

---

[132] For an extensive theoretical treatment of the term structure of interest rates see Shiller (1990).

There exists a huge literature that gives answers to the first two questions which is briefly surveyed in section 4.2. The third question, however, has only gained little attention so far and is the main scope of the present chapter.

4.2.1 *Interpreting the term structure of interest rates*

According to the first question, central banks are interested in obtaining information about current expectations from forward-looking financial markets in order to help predict the future path for inflation and output. For this reason, central banks often rely on the so-called expectations theory of the term structure of interest rates, which in its pure version states that longer-term interest rates are set according to market expectations of future shorter-term rates. Abstracting from any liquidity preference that normally puts a possibly time-varying term premium on longer-term rates, interest rates will be determined by the market in a way such that a representative investor is indifferent between holding either a long-term bond or a sequence of short-term bonds covering the same length of time.[133]

The yield curve and the underlying market expectations contain important information for monetary policy makers. But the information content at the short end differs in its general characteristics from the one at the long end. At the short end, according to the expectations theory, interest rates primarily reflect market expectations about very near-term monetary policy settings of the overnight rate (Rudebusch, 1995). At this horizon, central banks are especially interested in the implied forward rates in order to understand market expectations of the immediate path of the instrument rate. Given such expectations, central banks can evaluate whether their near-term policy intentions are being appropriately communicated to market participants.

As demonstrated for the Bundesbank and the ECB in chapter 3, central banks move short-term rates in steps so that they (among possible other intensions) can observe the consequences of their action and assess sequentially

[133] The segmented market hypothesis stands in sharp contrast to the pure expectations theory (Culbertson, 1957). According to the extreme version of this theory, the overall credit market is split into a series of segments based on the maturity of loans, without any substitution by either creditors or lenders. This can be reasoned by particular preferences of market participants for only one maturity together with extremely high risk aversion and severe uncertainty in credit markets. Therefore, the yield in any one market for a given maturity cannot influence the yield in any other market for another maturity. A compromise between the expectations hypothesis of perfect substitutability and the segmented market hypothesis of zero substitutability is the preferred habit hypothesis proposed by Modigliani and Sutch (1966 and 1967).

the need for each incremental rate change.[134] Using the implied forward rates, a central bank can see whether its initial rate increase (decrease) carries with it expectations of a whole sequence of increases (decreases). Thus, not only the first rate change but a whole sequence of projected changes in short terms is put into the 'pipeline' in the moment a series of changes is initiated. To the extent that a central bank's subsequent interest rate moves were predicted, they would not constitute new policy impulses by themselves (Goodfriend, 1998). Any subsequent change should then *ex ante* be priced into the longer-term rates. If the central bank observes that this is not the case, this might call then for even stronger interest rate steps and/or a more pronounced communication of policy intentions. Insofar as the future monetary policy is understood by the private sector, markets can to a large extent "do the central bank's work for it", in that the actual changes in overnight rates required to achieve the desired incentives can be much more modest when expected future rates move as well (Woodford, 2004, p. 17).

It could also be that, for some reason, an interest rate step that is intended as being a singular one is misunderstood as being the starting point of several subsequent steps in the same direction. Consider, for example, the case of an interest rate increase. The false prediction of future interest rate increases would result in an outcome that is too tight compared to the central bank's intention. The presence of the term structure gives central banks the possibility to recognize this and to counteract such developments, for example, by a well-directed communication effort. In general, the yield curve is an indicator of how well – if at all – the central bank's intentions are understand by financial markets.

At the medium- and longer-end (say, a three-to-ten-year horizon), the term structure provides an indication of the market's inflation expectations. According to the Fisher-relation, it is common wisdom that the nominal yield of a bond approximately equals the long-term real yield plus the expected average inflation rate over the same maturity. Assuming that the real interest rate is constant in the medium to the long run, changes in inflation expectations translate into changes in nominal rates. Central banks extract inflation expectations both as inputs for forecasting future inflation and economic activity, and as a measure of the credibility of the current stance of monetary policy in achieving the long-run goal of price stability. Schich (1996), indeed, finds evidence that the German medium segment of the term structure contains significant information about future inflation development. Research by Estrella and Mishkin (1995) yields similar results for a set of European countries. Goodfriend (1993) argues that inflation expectations obtained from the term

[134] For a extended discussion of interest rate smoothing see Goodhart (1997).

structure had a major influence on the monetary policy conducted by the Federal Reserve, too.

In addition, extensive empirical research motivated by the expectations theory of the term structure of interest rates suggests that the yield curve also has predictive power with respect to future real activity. Bernard and Gerlach (1996) study the ability of the term structure to predict recessions in eight countries. They find that the term spreads are useful for predicting recessions as much as two years ahead.[135]

4.2.2 *How does monetary policy affect the term structure of interest rates?*

Besides interpreting the information content of the term structure of interest rates, central banks are also interested in how changes of the short-term rate affect the yield curve, or even in altering it actively through monetary policy actions. Central banks are very interested in this 'leverage-effect' because the longer-term rates are more important for influencing aggregate demand. The interrelation of short-term and long-term rates is mainly an empirical issue. Cook and Hahn (1989) investigate the effects of monetary policy on the term structure. They find a substantial correlation between actual changes in longer-term rates and the funds rate changes induced by the Federal Reserve. As the maturity of the longer-term securities increases, the correlation diminishes but never disappears. For example, even the yield on a 10-year bond would typically rise 10 to 15 basis points for any one-percentage point increase of the funds rate. But changes in the longer-run rates following a policy action are not always identical since they reflect both the immediate change in the short-term rate and changes in expectations about future policy actions. For example, Campbell (1995) reports that the 10-year rate jumped by almost twice as much as the increase in the funds rate at the time of the Fed tightening in spring 1994 instead of the typical muted response described by Cook and Hahn (1989).[136]

Anecdotical evidence also shows the possibility of asymmetric movements in short-term and long-term rates, mostly driven by dramatically changing inflation expectations. For the European economies, Estrella and Mishkin (1995) also indicate that the relationship between monetary policy action and the term structure spread is unlikely to remain invariant over time. Such variability in

[135] See also Estrella and Mishkin (1995) for similar results.

[136] In January 1994, the Fed drove up the federal funds rate by a quarter of a percentage point, but the 6-month, 5-year, and 10-year yields each rose by a half point, while the 30-year yield also rose by about a quarter point. The response to a second policy move was similar, while later steps again displayed the general finding of a less violently reaction of longer maturities (Campbell, 1995, p. 144). This anecdotic evidence might also be seen as support for the aforementioned 'policy in the pipeline' argument.

financial markets responses is an important source of uncertainty associated with the real effects of monetary policy.

The perspectives of how to look at the term structure are compatible in principle, although reconciling them sometimes creates difficulties of interpretation in practice, and there is always some ambiguity left. For example, does a steepening yield curve indicate a loss of confidence in the central bank's commitment to fight inflation, or does it indicate that markets expect tighter policy in form of higher short-term interest rates in the future? In sum, the yield curve contains useful information for monetary policy, but it needs to be interpreted in light of judicious 'identifying' conditions, together with other data on the economy (Goodfriend, 1998). For this reason, notwithstanding the positive empirical results on the predictive power of the term structure, a compelling case for giving the latter a formal role in monetary policy, such as an intermediate target, cannot be made.

4.2.3 *Implications of the term structure of interest rates for monetary policy rules*

Since monetary policy is often described by monetary policy rules in theoretical and in empirical research as it has been demonstrated in the first part of this study, it seems necessary to ask the question whether the presence of term structure effects does have any implications for those rules. At first glance, there seems to be a major inconsistency between the presence of monetary policy rules and the complexity of term structure effects discussed before. Monetary policy rules, on the one hand, imply some kind of mechanical usage of the monetary policy instrument in response to the cyclical state of the economy. Term structure effects, on the other hand, contain some degree of ambiguity that might not easy be reconciled with mechanic monetary policy rules. This kind of contradiction leaves us with some discomfort and concerns about the use of monetary policy rules. In order to underpin our argument, the next section formulates a very simple model that shows that the presence of term structure effects is not always consistent with the derivation of explicit monetary policy rules.

4.3 An Optimal Interest Rate Rule with Term Structure Effects

This section extends the model discussed in section 2.4. The difference to the model discussed there is that now it is additionally allowed for the long-term interest rate to play a crucial role in the economy. Aggregate demand is described by the conventional dynamic IS-relation of the following form:

(4.1) $$y_{t+1} = \beta_1 y_t - \beta_2 (i_t - \pi_t) + \eta_{t+1}$$

where y is the output gap defined as the deviation of real GDP from its long-run trend. In contrast to section 2.4 the interest rate i is now to be understood as a weighted nominal interest rate defined below in equation (4.2), and $\pi_t = p_t - p_{t-1}$ is the annual inflation rate corresponding to the maturity of i with p representing the aggregate price level. All variables except interest rates are again expressed as their natural logarithm. The term η is an i.i.d. shock variable with zero mean representing demand shocks due to, for example, changes in government consumption. The structural parameters are such that $\beta_2>0$ and $0<\beta_1<1$ hold. They govern the sensitivity of future aggregate demand with respect to the current real interest rate and current output gap. According to equation (4.1), the output gap is serially correlated and decreasing in the real interest rate level. In the steady state the output gap is zero which also implies that the equilibrium real interest rate is normalized to zero.

The weighted interest rate in (4.1) is formulated to capture the monetary conditions within the economy in general. The latter are a function of interest rates of different maturities within the economy. For simplicity the set of interest rates is defined to consist of a short-term interest rate and a long-term interest rate:

(4.2) $$i_t = \rho \cdot i_{n,t}^l + (1-\rho) \cdot i_t^s,$$

where $i_{n,t}^l$ is the yield of a (long-term) n-period bond and i_t^s is the (short-term) one period holdings' interest rate which is the instrument of the central bank. Thus, the monetary conditions i_t implicitly represent a weighted average interest rate over all maturities. This captures the effect that aggregate demand in equation (4.1) is simultaneously influenced by the short-term interest rate and by the long-term interest rate. The parameter $0 \le \rho \le 1$ determines the relative weight. It is well-known that the importance of different maturities differ across countries, for example, due to differing financing practices.[137] Alternatively, one

[137] For example, in the United Kingdom, unlike in the United States, expenditure is more sensitive to short-term than to long-term interest rates, owing to the prevalence of floating-rate debt instruments (Batini and Haldane, 1999, p. 164). In the model the US economy would then be characterized by a higher value of ρ compared to the UK. Differences in this structural feature of economies could also be modelled by choosing differing values of n, since the chosen value need not be identical with the longest maturity available in the

can think that different categories of expenditure within the whole expenditure basket are affected by different interest rates. While consumption expenditure is more related to the short-term and medium-term interest rates, investment is more related to longer-term financing conditions.

The expectations theory of the term structure of interest rates relates interest rates of different maturities according to the subsequent expression:

$$1+i_{n,t}^{l}=\sqrt[n]{\prod_{j=0}^{n-1}\left(1+E_t[i_{t+j}^{s}]\right)}.$$

The term $E_t[i_{t+j}^{s}]$ represents the expected short-term interest rate at time t for the holding period $t+j$, i.e., the implied forward rate for that period. The equation represents the intertemporal arbitrage condition that equalizes the yield on a n-period-holding of the long-term bond and the expected yield on a sequence of one-period-holdings of short-term investments over n periods. For pure convenience, this expression abstracts from the presence of a liquidity premium term. Under the assumption that such a premium would be a stable function of the maturities of the contracts, its inclusion would not alter our main results. Taking logs of both sides and using the common approximation, we can express the long-term interest rate as:

$$\text{(4.3)}\qquad i_{n,t}^{l}=\frac{1}{n}\sum_{j=0}^{n-1}E_t[i_{t+j}^{s}]=\frac{1}{n}i_t^{s}+\frac{1}{n}\sum_{j=1}^{n-1}E_t[i_{t+j}^{s}].$$

The second equality follows from the fact that, for the first period, the implied forward rate coincides with the prevailing short-term spot rate.

Aggregate supply is identical to the one from section 2.4 and is expressed in terms of the Phillips curve relation:

$$\text{(4.4)}\qquad \pi_{t+1}=\pi_t+\alpha_1 y_t+\varepsilon_{t+1},$$

where ε represents an i.i.d. random cost-push shock, and the parameter $\alpha_1>0$ determines the slope of the short-run Phillips curve. Equation (4.4) states that inflation changes according to the size of the output gap and supply shocks.

As already mentioned in section 2.4, the model described by equations (4.1) through (4.4) captures several aspects that are important for policymaking in practice. The behavior of output and inflation is subject to random shocks.

economy. Instead, the choice should be driven by considerations about the transmission process.

Output shows persistence because lagged output enters equation (4.1). Inflation is inertial: it is expected to stay at a given level unless output changes or a supply shock hits the economy. In contrast to section 2.4, monetary policy is now handicapped by two circumstances. First, as already modeled in section 2.4 it and is also subject to time lags: it takes the monetary conditions one period to affect output and subsequently one more period for output to affect inflation. Second, monetary policy has non-perfect control over the monetary conditions. If the short-term interest rate is the instrument for monetary policy, it is not the only argument that determines the weighted interest rate.

The central bank aims at minimizing the following intertemporal loss function with the size of inflation and the output gap as the two arguments:

$$(4.5) \qquad \min E_t \sum_{\tau=t}^{\infty} \delta^{\tau-t} L(\pi_\tau, y_\tau),$$

where $0 < \delta < 1$ represents the discount factor. The period loss function is specified as

$$(4.6) \qquad L(\pi_\tau, y_\tau) = \frac{1}{2}\left[(\pi_\tau - \pi^*)^2 + \lambda y_\tau^2\right],$$

where π^* is the target value of inflation defined by the monetary authority and λ is the relative weight that is attached to stabilize output. For $\lambda>0$ such preferences are usually described as *variable inflation targeting*, whereas a zero weight on output expresses a strategy of *strict inflation targeting*. Optimizing the intertemporal loss function under the constraints of the structure of the economy displayed by the IS- and the Phillips curve leads again to an optimal behavior that was already characterized as *inflation-forecast targeting* (see again Appendix C):

$$(4.7) \qquad \pi_{t+2|t} - \pi^* = -\frac{\lambda}{\delta \alpha_1 k} y_{t+1|t},$$

$$\text{with} \quad k = \frac{1}{2}\left(1 - \frac{\lambda(1-\delta)}{\delta \alpha_1^2} + \sqrt{\left(1 + \frac{\lambda(1-\delta)}{\delta \alpha_1^2}\right)^2 + \frac{4\lambda}{\alpha_1^2}}\right) \geq 1,$$

where again the shorter notation of the expectations is employed such that $x_{t+j|t}$ denotes the j-period ahead expectations for any variable x.

The inflation forecast can be controlled by the central bank via the value of the weighted interest rate, i_t. Here, in contrast to section 2.4, we must consider that the central bank can only set the short-term interest rate and must take into account the interest rate relationships that prevail in the economy. Thus, the next step is to find the (short-term) interest rate rule that satisfies condition (4.7). From (4.1) and (4.2) we know that the forecast for the one-period ahead output gap is

$$y_{t+1|t} = \beta_1 y_t - \beta_2 \left(\rho \cdot i^l_{n,t} + (1-\rho) \cdot i^s_t - \pi_t\right). \tag{4.8}$$

Using expression (4.8) in (4.7) leads to the following relationship for the short-term interest rate:[138]

$$i^s_t = \frac{\delta \alpha_1 k}{\lambda \beta_2 (1-\rho)} \cdot \left[\pi_{t+2|t} - \pi^*\right] + \frac{1}{1-\rho} \cdot \pi_t - \frac{\rho}{1-\rho} \cdot i^l_{n,t} + \frac{\beta_1}{\beta_2 (1-\rho)} \cdot y_t . \tag{4.9}$$

According to (4.4) the two-period ahead inflation forecast is

$$\pi_{t+2|t} = \pi_t + \alpha_1 y_t + \alpha_1 y_{t+1|t} ,$$

which after taking into account (4.8) becomes:

$$\pi_{t+2|t} = (1+\alpha_1 \beta_2) \cdot \pi_t + \alpha_1 (1+\beta_1) \cdot y_t - \alpha_1 \beta_2 \rho \cdot i^l_{n,t} - \alpha_1 \beta_2 (1-\rho) \cdot i^s_t . \tag{4.10}$$

This expression can be substituted into (4.9) and after some re-arranging we arrive at:

$$i^s_t = \frac{1}{(1-\rho)} \cdot \pi_t + \frac{\widetilde{b}_1}{(1-\rho)} \cdot (\pi_t - \pi^*) + \frac{\widetilde{b}_2}{(1-\rho)} \cdot y_t - \frac{\rho}{(1-\rho)} \cdot i^l_{n,t} , \tag{4.11}$$

$$\text{where } \widetilde{b}_1 = \frac{1-c}{\beta_2 \alpha_1}, \quad \widetilde{b}_2 = \frac{1-c+\beta_1}{\beta_2} \quad \text{and} \quad c = \frac{\lambda}{\lambda + \delta \alpha_1^2 k} .$$

This expression for the optimal short-term interest rate coincides with expression (2.10) from section 2.4, if $\rho = 0$ and $i^s_t = i^l_{n,t}$. The latter is the condition for a horizontal yield curve.

[138] For the more detailed derivation of the subsequent equations see Appendix E.

In order to eliminate the expression for the long-term interest rate in (4.11), we can use its approximation in equation (4.3) and after some intuitive steps, the optimal short-term interest rate can be expressed as

$$(4.12) \qquad i_t^s = \gamma \cdot \pi_t + \gamma \cdot \widetilde{b}_1 \cdot (\pi_t - \pi^*) + \gamma \cdot \widetilde{b}_2 \cdot y_t - \gamma \cdot \rho \cdot \frac{1}{n} \sum_{j=1}^{n-1} E_t[i_{t+j}^s],$$

$$\text{where} \quad \gamma = \frac{1}{(1-\rho) + \frac{\rho}{n}} \geq 1, \text{ because } n \geq 1.$$

The optimal response function (4.12) is a generalized version of the one derived in Svensson (1997) and also presented in section 2.4. For $\rho = 0$ and/or $E_t i_{t+j}^s = i_t^s, \forall j$ (i.e., a horizontal yield curve), the previous result from (2.10) is re-established. Two points of difference are noteworthy. First, the reaction coefficients for current inflation and the output gap are larger than those derived in (2.10) implying a more aggressive reaction of the central bank. Ceteris paribus, the coefficient γ grows with (i) a higher weight of the long-term interest rate in the monetary conditions, and (ii) a longer maturity of the long-term interest rate. Second, due to the presence of term structure effects an additional term representing the role of the implied forward rates emerges in the optimal policy rule. This term *ceteris paribus* reduces the interest rate response due to its negative sign. The size of this dampening effect depends on the parameters γ and ρ.

The implications of the modified reaction coefficients and the additional term are straightforward. On the one hand, the fact that the central bank can only control the short-term interest rate while the latter only jointly affects the aggregate demand together with the long-term interest rate calls for a more aggressive movement in the short rate. On the other hand, the long-term interest rate may mimic the change in the short-term rate if the change in the instrument also affects the implied forward rates. If this is the case, the last term dampens the size of the required change in the instrument rate.[139] This reaction function indicates that the central bank has to guess, respectively to project, how a shift in the instrument affects the implied forward rates. Thus, this rule belongs to the class of so-called *implicit instrument rules* as coined by Rudebusch and Svensson (1999), since the right-hand side is endogenous and depends on the rule itself. This self-referential, rational expectations nature of the rule complicates its analytical derivation in terms of an explicit instrument rule.

[139] Such a case would be graphically represented by a parallel shift in the yield curve without any change in its slope.

It is important to distinguish the commitment environment from the discretionary environment: a commitment environment would imply that both i_t and $E[i_{t+j}]$ are policy instruments of the central bank. In a discretionary environment, however, i_t is the only instrument and the expectations term must be taken as given because the policymaker at time t cannot bind policy making at any time $t+j$. But time t expectations of time $t+j$ interest rates, of course, depend on the actual policy of the central bank. In the following a discretionary environment is considered, which is believed to be closer to reality.[140]

How can the central bank gauge with this endogeneity problem of the implicit optimal rule? One possible reaction is to move the policy instrument in several steps and simultaneously observe the reaction of the term structure, since the evidence mentioned earlier suggests that the reaction of the yield curve to monetary policy changes is not time-invariant. Such policy would be a reason for the empirically observed interest rate smoothing. It also coincides with the 'policy in the pipeline' argument because an interest rate step that is expected to serve as the starting point of a sequence of further steps will have a greater impact on all segments of the yield curve and, thus, on aggregate demand than comparable already anticipated steps (within the sequence) that may already be priced into the yield curve.[141]

According to our previous discussion, a positively sloped yield curve (i.e., implied forward rates that exceed the actual value of the short-term interest rate)[142] does not necessarily (purely) indicate expectations of a future tightening of monetary policy. Especially in the medium and long-term segment of the yield curve, it can also be a sign for a rise in expected future inflation (and an expected boom situation) by market participants. But the present model cannot account for this, because the price adjustment function (4.4) is purely backward looking. Looking at (4.12) the derived policy rule would even be counterintuitive: a rise in future interest rates driven by higher future inflation would ceteris paribus call for an interest rate decline.

To be consistent with the model formulation one rather applies here the interpretation that is connected to the shorter end of the yield curve, for which – according to the line of argumentation above – previous research showed that the interest rates are mainly driven by expectation about the next interest rate

140 Clarida et al. (1999, p. 1671), for example, also belief that the "scenario without commitment accords best with reality. In practice, no major central bank makes any kind of binding commitment over the course of its future monetary policy."

141 Note that this reasoning differs from the explanation of Woodford (1999) and Rotemberg and Woodford (1997) for optimal interest rate smoothing that is based on the leverage that a smooth adjustment rule may provide the central bank over the longer term interest rates. In their analysis the main idea is that lagged dependence of the short rate permits the central bank to manipulate long term rates.

142 Recall that this section abstracts from a liquidity premium.

steps. This somehow arbitrary reasoning might be unsatisfactory to the reader, but it is nothing but the theoretical counterpart of the fact the yield curve cannot be interpreted mechanically when integrated into an interest rate rule, which, in turn, cannot be used mechanically by central banks. As argued above, with the knowledge of this fact central banks sympathize with a policy of prudent interest rate moves which, in turn, are observed ex post as interest rate smoothing.

The derivation of the Taylor-type rule in the form of equation (4.12) has the advantage that we are able to isolate the two contrary effects in the presence of the yield curve on the optimal interest rate setting, i.e., the level effect on the coefficients and dampening effect of the additional forward-looking term. This is very helpful for discussing the implications of the presence of yield curve effects for monetary policy. But expression (4.12) is ambiguous with respect to the net effect on the interest rate. To gain further inside, redefine the implied forward rates as

$$(4.13) \qquad E_t[i^s_{t+j}] = i^s_t + E_t[\phi_{t+j}],$$

where the term ϕ_{t+j} represents the difference between time $t+j$ forward rate and the actual time t short-term interest rate, so that expression (4.13) splits the implied forward rate into the actual short-term rate and the expected deviation from this value in future periods. Substituting this expression in (4.12) yields, after some rearranging,

$$(4.14) \qquad i^s_t = \pi_t + \widetilde{b}_1 \cdot (\pi_t - \pi^*) + \widetilde{b}_2 \cdot y_t - \frac{\rho}{n} \cdot \sum_{j=1}^{n-1} E_t[\phi_{t+j}].$$

This expression equals the Taylor-type rule derived in (2.10) except for the last term, which represents the yield curve effect. This effect increases with a rise of the parameter ρ. If the sum of expected deviation of future short-term rates from the present one is positive, i.e., on average the short-term rate is expected to rise above its actual value, then the optimal interest rate response is dampened, and vice versa. Nevertheless, the monetary policy rule remains an implicit one, since the right hand side is endogenous.[143] For a flat yield curve, represented by $E_t[\phi_{t+j}] = 0, \forall j$, and/or a zero weight on the long-term interest rate in the

[143] When the expectations term is broad to the left hand side of the rule one could alternatively think of expression (4.14) as a policy rule that sets the path of (expected) short-term interest rates in accordance with the cyclical state of the economy. Since the last term also stands for the longer-term interest rates, the resulting left-hand side can be interpreted as the desired monetary conditions given the state of the economy.

specification of the monetary conditions, the result from (2.10) can again be re-established.

4.4 A "Quasi Optimal" Rule in a Generalized (Hybrid) Model

This section briefly provides the analysis of term structure effects in a generalized version of the model from the previous section which has been already studied in the literature.[144] This model has a hybrid form in the sense that it allows for forward-looking as well as for backward-looking agents in the economy. A closed form solution can only be derived when two crucial assumption are made: (i) compared to the analysis from before, the long-term interest rate only refers to a two-period interest rate; (ii) the functional form of the optimal rule is *ex ante* assumed to be of the Taylor-type, that is, only a "quasi optimal" rule can be derived. In that sense, the analysis in this section, although starting from a generalized version of the model, is far more restrictive than the previous one. However, presenting both model variants provides an deeper understanding of the consequences of the term structure for the optimal rule.

The structure of the economy is captured by the following equations:

$$(4.15)\quad y_{t+1} = \beta_1\left[(1-\mu_y)y_t + \mu_y y_{t+1|t}\right] - \beta_2 r_t^l + \eta_{t+1},$$

where again a the shorter notation of the expectations is used, such that $x_{t+j|t}$ denotes the j-period ahead expectations for any variable x. Equation (4.15) is a partly forward-looking version of the IS curve from (4.1). The parameter $\mu_y \in [0,1]$ governs the degree of forward-looking. Notice that a particular timing of the expectations is chosen that deviates from the timing of the hybrid form of the optimizing IS-LM model given in section 1.6. This "semi-forward-looking" form is necessary in order to support a closed form solution. The IS curve in (4.15) includes only the long-term real interest rate. This only for convenience differs from the assumption in (4.1) where a weighted interest rate was modeled. In (4.15) it is assumed that $\rho = 1$.[145] However, as already indicated it is crucial to assume that the long-term interest rate has a maturity of only two periods:

$$(4.16)\quad r_t^l = (1-\mu_r)(i_t - \pi_t) + \mu_r(i_{t+1|t} - \pi_{t+1|t}),$$

[144] The model version in this section is due to Lansing and Trehan (2003).
[145] The equilibrium real rate is again normalized to zero.

where i_t is the nominal short-rate. If the parameter μ_r is 0.5, then (4.16) is again the approximation of the expectations theory as in (4.3).
The Phillips curve is given by:

$$(4.17)\quad \pi_{t+1} = (1-\mu_\pi)\pi_t + \mu_\pi \pi_{t+1|t} + \alpha_1 y_t + \varepsilon_{t+1},$$

where the parameter $\mu_\pi \in [0,1]$ governs the degree of forward-looking. Note again the particular timing assumption that differs from section 1.6. This assumption can be motivated by the "sticky information" Phillips curve from Mankiw and Reis (2002). If the parameter μ_y is equal to zero, than (4.17) reduces to (4.4). When $\mu_\pi = \mu_y = \mu_r = 0$, the system of equations (4.15) through (4.17) reduces to the purely backward-looking model from section 2.4 (see equations (2.5) and (2.6)).

Using again the same optimization approach as in sections 2.4 and 4.3 based on the preferences of the central bank stated in (4.5) and (4.6) and pre-condition that the optimal rule takes the particular Taylor-type form the central bank's optimal interest rate rule under discretion is given by:[146]

$$(4.18)\quad i_t = \pi^* + b_\pi \cdot (\pi_t - \pi^*) + b_y \cdot y_t$$

with

$$b_\pi = 1 + \frac{\left[1 - \dfrac{\beta_1(\mu_y - \mu_r)}{1-\mu_r}\right] \cdot \delta k \left(\dfrac{\alpha_1}{1-\mu_\pi}\right)}{\beta_2 \left[\lambda + (1-\mu_r)\,\delta k \left(\dfrac{\alpha_1}{1-\mu_\pi}\right)^2\right]}$$

$$b_y = \frac{(1-\beta_1\mu_y)\delta k \left(\dfrac{\alpha_1}{1-\mu_\pi}\right)^2 + \dfrac{\beta_1(1-\mu_y)}{1-\mu_r}\left[\lambda + \delta k \left(\dfrac{\alpha_1}{1-\mu_\pi}\right)^2\right]}{\beta_2 \left[\lambda + (1-\mu_r)\delta k \left(\dfrac{\alpha_1}{1-\mu_\pi}\right)^2\right]}$$

146 See Lansing and Trehan (2003) for the details of the derivation. Because the derivation generally follows the lines of Appendices C and E with the additional feature that it is assumed that private agents form their expectations based on the knowledge of the functional form of (4.18), it is abstracted from presenting its details.

and

$$k = \frac{1}{2}\left(1 - \frac{\lambda(1-\delta)}{\delta\left(\frac{\alpha_1}{1-\mu_\pi}\right)^2} + \sqrt{\left(1 + \frac{\lambda(1-\delta)}{\delta\left(\frac{\alpha_1}{1-\mu_\pi}\right)^2}\right)^2 + \frac{4\lambda}{\left(\frac{\alpha_1}{1-\mu_\pi}\right)^2}} \right) \geq 1.$$

It can be shown that in the case when $\mu_\pi = \mu_y = \mu_r = 0$, the interest rate rule in (4.18) reduced to the one from the purely backward-looking model in section 2.4.

From (4.18), it is possible to interpret the influence of the parameters on the (optimal) coefficients in the interest rate rule (see Lansing and Trahan (2003) for details). An increase in the parameter μ_y (i.e., the forward-looking component in the IS curve) leads to a decrease in both reaction coefficients. The intuition is quite clear. A higher forward-looking component in output also means a reduction in the persistence of output. This, in turn, means that the output gap makes are more pronounced jump in response to a change in the interest rate, which means that output can be brought back to zero with a smaller interest rate response to the output gap itself. Moreover, given that the central bank exerts control over inflation via interest rate-induced changes in the output gap, this improved control over the output gap allows to bring back inflation to its target level with a smaller response to rising inflation as well.

An increase in the parameter μ_r (i.e., the relevance of longer term interest rates, and thus, the term structure) leads to stronger responses to the output gap and the inflation gap. This result has already been discovered in the *n*-maturity case of the previous section (see equation (4.12) in comparison to (2.10)). Since the central bank has only indirect control over the long-term interest rate which drives aggregate demand, the central bank is forced to react more pronounced to produce the same impact.[147] In this sense, the results established on the basis of the purely backward-looking model in the previous section are confirmed within a hybrid model.

The result of an increase in μ_π is not obvious. Only for the particular case $\lambda = 0$ (and, thus, $k = 1$), the reaction to the inflation gap decreases, while the reaction of the output gap remains unchanged. The intuition is as follows. An increase in the forward-looking term of the Phillips curve makes inflation more

[147] See also Eijfinger et al. (2000) for this result.

responsive to expected inflation, which, in turn can be influenced by the central bank via the output gap, which is influenced by changing the interest rate. So, the future inflation is more responsive to the interest rate, which allows the central bank to bring back inflation with a smaller reaction to inflation itself. Moreover, the direct response to the output gap does not change when $\lambda = 0$, because the central bank just does not care about the output gap in their preferences.[148]

[148] For the general case of $\lambda > 0$ Lansing and Trehan (2003) based on quantitative simulation show that the optimal response for the central bank is to react less to inflation (as already in the special case) and more to the output gap.

Appendix E

Derivation of an Optimal Rule with Term Structure Effects

The starting point is the optimality condition which has been derived in Appendix C:

$$\text{(4.7)} \qquad \pi_{t+2|t} - \pi^* = -\frac{\lambda}{\delta\alpha_1 k} y_{t+1|t},$$

in which we can substitute the forecast for the one-period ahead output gap that is derived from (4.1) and (4.2):

$$\text{(4.8)} \qquad y_{t+1|t} = \beta_1 y_t - \beta_2\left(\rho \cdot i^l_{n,t} + (1-\rho)\cdot i^s_t - \pi_t\right).$$

This yields

$$\text{(E.1)} \qquad \pi_{t+2|t} - \pi^* = -\frac{\lambda}{\delta\alpha_1 k}\left[\beta_1 y_t - \beta_2\left(\rho \cdot i^l_t + (1-\rho)\cdot i^s_t - \pi_t\right)\right],$$

which can be solved for the short-term interest rate to get

$$\text{(4.9)} \qquad i^s_t = \frac{\delta\alpha_1 k}{\lambda\beta_2(1-\rho)}\cdot\left[\pi_{t+2|t} - \pi^*\right] + \frac{1}{1-\rho}\cdot\pi_t - \frac{\rho}{1-\rho}\cdot i^l_{n,t} + \frac{\beta_1}{\beta_2(1-\rho)}\cdot y_t .$$

The next step is to get ride of the term of expected inflation that can also be expressed as

$$\text{(4.10)} \qquad \pi_{t+2|t} = (1+\alpha_1\beta_2)\cdot\pi_t + \alpha_1(1+\beta_1)\cdot y_t - \alpha_1\beta_2\rho\cdot i^l_{n,t} - \alpha_1\beta_2(1-\rho)\cdot i^s_t ,$$

where use of (4.4) and (4.8) is made. Substituting this into (4.9) and sorting the terms yields

$$\text{(E.2)} \qquad \begin{aligned} \left(1+\frac{\delta\alpha_1^2 k}{\lambda}\right)\cdot i^s_t &= \frac{\delta\alpha_1 k}{\lambda\beta_2(1-\rho)}\cdot(\pi_t - \pi^*) + \left(\frac{1}{(1-\rho)} + \frac{\delta\alpha_1^2 k}{\lambda(1-\rho)}\right)\cdot\pi_t \\ &+ \left(\frac{\delta\alpha_1^2 k(1+\beta_1)}{\lambda\beta_2(1-\rho)} + \frac{\beta_1}{\beta_2(1-\rho)}\right)\cdot y_t - \left(\frac{\rho}{1-\rho} + \frac{\delta\alpha_1^2 k\rho}{\lambda(1-\rho)}\right)\cdot i^l_t . \end{aligned}$$

By defining $\left(1+\frac{\delta\alpha_1^2 k}{\lambda}\right)=\frac{\lambda+\delta\alpha_1^2 k}{\lambda}\equiv\frac{1}{c}$ it is possible to rearrange this expression as

$$\frac{1}{c}\cdot i_t^s=\frac{1-c}{c\cdot\alpha_1\beta_2(1-\rho)}\cdot(\pi_t-\pi^*)+\frac{1}{c\cdot(1-\rho)}\cdot\pi_t$$

(E.3)
$$+\left(\frac{(1-c)(1+\beta_1)}{c\cdot\beta_2(1-\rho)}+\frac{\beta_1}{\beta_2(1-\rho)}\right)\cdot y_t$$

$$-\left(\frac{\rho}{1-\rho}+\frac{(1-c)\rho}{c\cdot(1-\rho)}\right)\cdot i_t^l.$$

This can be rewritten as

(E.4)
$$i_t^s=\frac{1-c}{\alpha_1\beta_2(1-\rho)}\cdot(\pi_t-\pi^*)+\frac{1}{1-\rho}\cdot\pi_t+\frac{1-c-\beta_1}{\beta_2(1-\rho)}\cdot y_t-\frac{\rho}{1-\rho}\cdot i_t^l,$$

which is

(4.11)
$$i_t^s=\frac{1}{(1-\rho)}\cdot\pi_t+\frac{\widetilde{b}_1}{(1-\rho)}\cdot(\pi_t-\pi^*)+\frac{\widetilde{b}_2}{(1-\rho)}\cdot y_t-\frac{\rho}{(1-\rho)}\cdot i_{n,t}^l,$$

where $\widetilde{b}_1=\frac{1-c}{\beta_2\alpha_1}$ and $\widetilde{b}_2=\frac{1-c+\beta_1}{\beta_2}$.

Using the expectations theory in (4.3) this is

(E.5)

$$i_t^s=\frac{1}{(1-\rho)}\cdot\pi_t+\frac{\widetilde{b}_1}{(1-\rho)}\cdot(\pi_t-\pi^*)+\frac{\widetilde{b}_2}{(1-\rho)}\cdot y_t-\frac{\rho}{1-\rho}\left[\frac{1}{n}\cdot i_t^s+\frac{1}{n}\cdot\sum_{j=1}^{n-1}E_t\left[i_{t+j}^s\right]\right].$$

Solving for i_t^s then yields

(E.6)

$$i_t^s = \frac{1}{(1-\rho)+\frac{\rho}{n}} \cdot \pi_t + \frac{\widetilde{b}_1}{(1-\rho)+\frac{\rho}{n}} \cdot (\pi_t - \pi^*) +$$
$$\frac{\widetilde{b}_2}{(1-\rho)+\frac{\rho}{n}} \cdot y_t - \frac{1}{(1-\rho)\cdot\frac{\rho}{n}+1} \cdot \sum_{j=1}^{n-1} E_t\left[i_{t+j}^s\right]$$

which can also be expressed as

(4.12)
$$i_t^s = \gamma \cdot \pi_t + \gamma \cdot \widetilde{b}_1 \cdot (\pi_t - \pi^*) + \gamma \cdot \widetilde{b}_2 \cdot y_t - \gamma \cdot \rho \cdot \frac{1}{n} \sum_{j=1}^{n-1} E_t[i_{t+j}^s],$$
$$\text{with} \quad \gamma = \frac{1}{(1-\rho)+\frac{\rho}{n}} \geq 1.$$

The last step is to split the expression for the implicit forward rate into the actual value of the short-term interest rate plus a difference term

(4.13)
$$E_t[i_{t+j}^s] = i_t^s + E_t[\phi_{t+j}].$$

Substituting this into (4.12) and again solving for the short-term interest rate yields

(E.7)
$$i_t^s\left(1+\gamma\frac{\rho}{n}(n-1)\right) = \gamma \cdot \pi_t + \gamma \cdot \widetilde{b}_1 \cdot (\pi_t - \pi^*) + \gamma \cdot \widetilde{b}_2 \cdot y_t - \gamma \cdot \rho \cdot \frac{1}{n} \sum_{j=1}^{n-1} E_t[\phi_{t+j}].$$

Note that with the definition of γ given above I can rewrite this expression as

(E.8)

$$i_t^s\left(1+\frac{1}{1+\frac{n(1-\rho)}{\rho}} \cdot (n-1)\right) = \gamma \cdot \pi_t + \gamma \cdot \widetilde{b}_1 \cdot (\pi_t - \pi^*) + \gamma \cdot \widetilde{b}_2 \cdot y_t - \gamma \cdot \rho \cdot \frac{1}{n} \sum_{j=1}^{n-1} E_t[\phi_{t+j}]$$

which is equal to

(E.9)

$$i_t^s\left(1+\frac{1}{\frac{\rho}{n}+(1-\rho)}\right)=\gamma\cdot\pi_t+\gamma\cdot\widetilde{b}_1\cdot(\pi_t-\pi^*)+\gamma\cdot\widetilde{b}_2\cdot y_t-\gamma\cdot\rho\cdot\frac{1}{n}\sum_{j=1}^{n-1}E_t[\phi_{t+j}],$$

so that the coefficient of the short-term interest rate equals γ. After dividing both sides by γ we arrive at the final expression in the main text:

(4.14) $$i_t^s=\pi_t+\widetilde{b}_1\cdot(\pi_t-\pi^*)+\widetilde{b}_2\cdot y_t-\frac{\rho}{n}\cdot\sum_{j=1}^{n-1}E_t[\phi_{t+j}].$$

Chapter 5

The Empirics of Monetary Reaction Functions and Term Structure

5.1 Introduction

The traditional Taylor-type rules that were discussed in part I of this study state that the monetary authority should set the short-term interest rate in proportion to the output gap and the gap between the actual level of inflation and its target. Since the seminal paper of John B. Taylor empirical reaction functions have been formulated for all major central banks. Several papers suggest to extend the benchmark Taylor rule in different directions. Most importantly, some authors claim that central banks reveal a forward-looking behavior and, additionally, show a strong tendency to smooth the interest rate (Clarida et al., 1998). Chapter 3 showed that the Deutsche Bundesbank and the European Central Bank can also be characterized by these forward-looking Taylor-type rules.

Less attention has been paid to the presence of yield curve effects so far. However, the yield curve could play an important role for determining monetary policy. The theoretical discussion in the previous chapter demonstrated that point. This chapter complements the theoretical discussion of the previous chapter and investigates the role the term structure of interest rates played for the monetary policy of the Deutsche Bundesbank and the European Central Bank empirically. It is based on the theoretical finding of the previous chapter and augments the empirical analysis from chapter 3. It has the following structure. Section 5.2 briefly picks up the theoretical considerations from the previous chapter from the perspective of empirical testing. Section 5.3 presents the results of the regression analysis that explicitly allows for the presence of the term structure of interest rates.

5.2 Theoretical Considerations

The term structure of interest rates is an important feature for the conduct of monetary policy. Although monetary policy is intended to work through aggregate demand, none of the important sectors of real spending depends directly on the overnight rate. Instead, aggregate spending depends on longer-term interest rates. Therefore, gauging how changes in the short rate triggered by the central bank affect the longer-term interest rates and, thus, the entire term structure of interest rates is important for understanding the monetary transmission mechanism.

The yield curve contains important information for monetary policy makers, but the information content at the short end differs from the one at the long end. At the short end, interest rates primarily reflect market expectations about very near-term monetary policy settings of the overnight rate. At this horizon, central banks are especially interested in the implied forward rates in order to understand market expectations regarding future changes in the interest rate instrument. Given such expectations, central banks can evaluate whether their near-term policy intentions are being appropriately communicated to market participants.

It was already argued in the previous chapter that an important reason for central banks to move short-term rates in steps is that they can observe the consequences of their action and assess sequentially the need for each incremental rate change. Using the implied forward rates, a central bank can see whether its initial rate increase (decrease) carries with it expectations of a whole sequence of increases (decreases) of anticipated future increases. To the extent that a central bank's subsequent interest rate moves were predicted, they would not constitute new policy impulses (Goodfriend, 1998). Any subsequent change should then ex ante be priced into the longer term rates. Insofar as the future monetary policy is understood by the private sector, markets can to a large extent "do the central bank's work for it", in that the actual changes in overnight rates required to achieve the desired incentives can be much more modest when expected future rates move as well (Woodford, 2004, p. 17).

At the medium- and longer-end, say, in a three-to-ten-year horizon, the term structure provides an indication of the market's inflation expectations. Central banks extract inflation expectations both as input for forecasting future inflation and economic activity, and as a measure of the credibility of the current stance of monetary policy in achieving the long-run goal of price stability. Schich (1996), for instance, finds evidence that the German medium segment of the term structure contains significant information about future inflation development.

Since monetary policy of the ECB and the Deutsche Bundesbank have empirically been described by monetary policy rules in chapter 3, it seems worthwhile to examine whether the presence of term structure effects do have any implications for those rules. At first glance, there seems to be a major inconsistency between the presence of monetary policy rules and the complexity of term structure effects described above. Monetary policy rules, on the one hand, imply some kind of mechanical usage of the monetary policy instrument in response to the cyclical state of the economy. Term structure effects, on the other hand, contain some degree of ambiguity that might not easily be reconciled with mechanic monetary policy rules. However, the next section demonstrates that term structure-augmented monetary policy rules can be estimated in a way that is consistent with the way central bankers think about the term structure.

5.3 Estimation Results

Following the analysis of chapter 3, and in particular equation (3.7), the general representation of the forward-looking reaction function can be written as:

$$(5.1)\quad i_t = (1-\rho)\alpha_0 + \alpha_1(1-\rho)\left(\pi_{t+k} - \pi_{(t)}*\right) + \alpha_2(1-\rho)\left(y_{t+q} - y_{t+q}*\right) + \rho i_{t-1} + \varepsilon_t,$$

$$\text{with}\quad \alpha_0 = \bar{i} \quad\text{and}\quad \varepsilon_t = \upsilon_t - \alpha_1(1-\rho)\left(\pi_{t+k} - E_t\pi_{t+k}\right) - \alpha_2(1-\rho)\left(y_{t+q} - E_t y_{t+q}\right),$$

where i is the short-term interest rate, y is the output level (with the star indicating potential output), π is inflation (with a star indicating the target level),[149] ρ represents the smoothing parameter, E is the expectation operator given the information set I_t, α_1 again represents the reaction parameter with respect to the inflation gap, α_2 represents the reaction parameter with respect to the output gap, q and l are the horizons of the forward-looking behavior, and ε is the error term. this reaction function was employed in the empirical analysis of the Deutsche Bundesbank (see equation (3.7)).

The empirical analysis in this chapter employs the identical data as in chapter 3. The data are monthly and cover the period from 1:1979 to 12:1998 for the Deutsche Bundesbank reaction function and 1:1999 to 8:2004 for the ECB reaction function.[150] The data on the German inflation gap is constructed using the difference of the consumer price index and the so-called price norm that was announced by the Bundesbank on an annual basis. The European inflation gap is the difference between the harmonized index of consumer prices (HICP) and 1.5 which proxies the inflation target the ECB had in mind during the period under consideration. The output gaps are based on the monthly index of German and European industrial production respectively and are constructed on the basis of a linear trend.[151] In the estimation, the short-term interest rate is

[149] The parentheses of the time subscript of the inflation gap should indicate that a time-variable inflation target is only used in the case of the Deutsche Bundesbank. For the ECB, a constant inflation target is assumed.

[150] Note that the sample period for the ECB is extended compared to section 3.4.

[151] In order to avoid starting point and end point problems, the trend is computed over an extended period covering 1970 through 2003 for the German output gap. For the European

the German overnight money market rate for the Deutsche Bundesbank reaction function and the EONIA (European Overnight Index Average) for the ECB reaction function. In order to estimate the forward-looking monetary policy rule, again a GMM estimation is applied.[152] The forward-looking horizon is set $k = 12$ and $q = 0$, and the same set of instruments as in chapter 3 is used: a constant as well as lagged values of the output gap, the inflation gap, the IMF commodity price index and the short-term interest rate.[153]

Table 5.1: Benchmark Regressions for the Deutsche Bundesbank and the ECB

Coefficient	Regression XX Bundesbank	Regression XXI ECB
α_0 (constant term)	3.11	2.66
	(0.693)	(0.233)
α_1 (inflation gap)	1.64	1.15
	(0.188)	(0.322)
α_2 (output gap)	0.14	0.28
	(0.065)	(0.028)
ρ (smoothing parameter)	0.95	0.73
	(0.012)	(0.047)
Durbin Watson	1.46	1.06
J-statistics	13.3	8.5
Adj.R^2	0.98	0.94

Standard errors in parentheses
Instruments: constant; 1st-6th, 9th and 12th lag of output gap; 1st-6th, 9th and 12th lag of inflation; 1st, 6th, 9th and 12th lag money market rate; for Deutsche Bundesbank only: 1st-6th, 9th and 12th lag of IMF commodity price index.

trend the period under consideration is not extented. A HP filter was also used in in both cases and the reported results were robust against this change.

152 As in chapter 3, the estimation procedure corrects for heteroscedasticity and autocorrelation of unknown form. In addition, Bartlett weights are chosen to ensure positive definiteness of our estimated variance-covariance matrix.

153 See bottom of Table 5.1 for details.

Table 5.1 shows the estimation result of our benchmark regression. The estimation for the case of the Deutsche Bundesbank already appeared in chapter 3 as Regression IX in Table 3.3. The ECB estimation slightly differs from those in Table 3.4 in chapter 3 because of the extended sample period and the use of an exogenous inflation target of 1.5 percent.

The benchmark regressions show that the Bundesbank and the ECB responded to the inflation and the output gap. The coefficients of the inflation gaps imply that the *Taylor principle* holds in both cases. However, as argued in the theoretical considerations above stemming from the analysis in chapter 4, the benchmark specification lacks important arguments from the term structure. Therefore, it is tested whether information from the term structure can explain part of the residuals from the benchmark regressions. Since it was argued above that the information content of the term structure differs between the short end and the medium-to-long end, the study employs in the next step simultaneously two kinds of term structure information.[154] First, the 5-year interest rate, i_t^{5y}, is taken. This is a proxy for expected inflation over horizons of the medium term or, more specifically, for horizons of more than 12 month, which is not covered by the forward-looking inflation term. Figure 5.1 shows the development of the 5-year interest rate in comparison to the overnight rate. The later is the German overnight money market rate until 12:1998 and the EONIA thereafter.

Second, the spread between the monthly money market rate and the one year interest rate is calculated to serve as information on the short end of the yield curve. The estimation employs the difference between its time *t* and time *t*-1 value as a proxy for the "change in the short-end spread" (denoted as $\Delta\, i_t^{1y\text{-}spread}$). Assuming that the risk premium is constant over time an increasing spread means that implied forward rates (i.e., the expected future short-term interest rates) are increasing more than the actual short rate. Figure 5.2 shows the development of the spread over the sample period.

[154] The estimation relies on the German yield curve data also for the ECB reaction function because it can be argued that the German yield curve is a reasonable approximation for the Euro area yield curve. The estimates of the German yield curve are based on the parameters of the Svensson (1994) smoothing technique as made available by the Deutsche Bundesbank.

Figure 5.1: Medium-Term and Short-Term Interest Rates

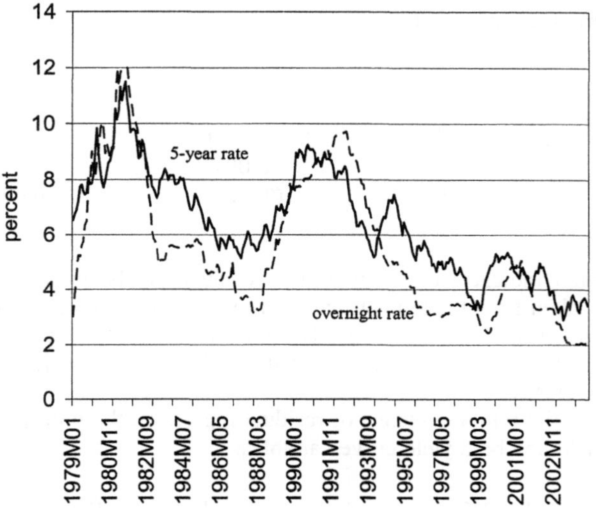

Figure 5.2: Development of the 1-Year-Spread

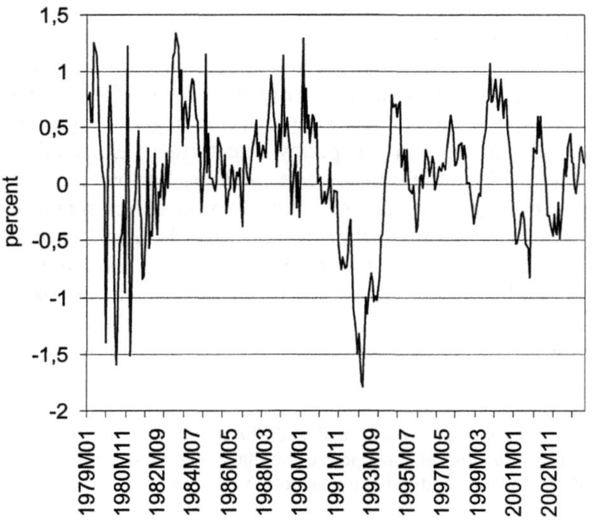

An OLS regression of the residual from the previous regression for the Deutsche Bundesbank reaction function on the two yield curve variables yield (standard errors are in parentheses):

$$\text{Residual } (\varepsilon) = \underset{(0.049)}{\underset{-0.21}{\alpha_{I} * \Delta i_t^{1y-spread}}} + \underset{(0.0027)}{\underset{0.0071}{\alpha_{II} * i_t^{5y}}} \qquad \text{adj. } R^2\text{: } 0.09 .$$

The estimation indicates that part of the residual can be explained with the information taken from the term structure of interest rates so that our benchmark regression is not specified correctly. But the influence of the two yield curve variables differs in signs. This indicates the ambiguity in the interpretation of term structure movements.[155]

Based on the initial evidence of residual regression the policy rules are re-estimated including both yield curve variables:

$$i_t = (1-\rho)\alpha_0 + \alpha_1(1-\rho)\left(\pi_{t+k} - \pi_{(t)}*\right) + \alpha_2(1-\rho)\left(y_{t+q} - y_{t+q}*\right)$$
$$(5.2) \qquad + \alpha_3(1-\rho)\cdot\Delta i_t^{1y-spread} + \alpha_4(1-\rho)\cdot i_t^{5y} + \rho i_{t-1} + \varepsilon_t .$$

The results of equation (5.2) for both the Deutsche Bundesbank and the ECB are shown as specifications XXII and XXIII in Table 5.2. The parameters on the expected inflation gap and the output gap remain broadly unchanged although the ECB now slightly fails the *Taylor principle*. The parameters on the "change in the short end spread" have the expected negative signs in both cases. If, for instance, an increase in the policy rate triggers expectations of future increases, the initial increase can, *ceteris paribus*, be lower but still has the desired effects on aggregate demand. Both central banks managed to create expectations of a sequence of further interest rate changes ("leverage effect"). However, the coefficients for the medium-term interest rate are positive indicating that both central banks additionally reacted to rising inflation expectation at horizons greater than that captured by the included forward-looking inflation gap term.

---

[155] Regressions of (5.1) were also performed with the term structure variables as additional instruments and the *J-statistics* also supported the claim that these are no valid instruments but instead should included as additional explanatory variables.

Table 5.2: Augmented Regressions Based for the Bundesbank and the ECB

Coefficients	Regression XXII Bundesbank	Regression XXIII ECB
α_0 (constant term)	1.33	-0.70
	(0.977)	(0.612)
α_1 (inflation gap)	1.26	0.95
	(0.124)	(0.239)
α_2 (output gap)	0.05	0.31
	(0.033)	(0.032)
α_3 (change in the short-end spread)	-1.81	-2.58
	(0.528)	(0.439)
α_4 (medium-term rate)	0.48	0.75
	(0.127)	(0.114)
smoothing parameter	0.87	0.87
	(0.02)	(0.012)
Durbin Watson	1.22	2.31
J-statistics	11.4	10.1
Adj.R^2	0.98	0.98

Standard errors in parentheses
Instruments: constant; 1st-6th , 9th and 12th lag of output gap; 1st-6th, 9th and 12th lag of inflation; 1st, 6th, 9th and 12th lag money market rate; for Deutsche Bundesbank only: 1st-6th, 9th and 12th lag of IMF commodity price index.

In sum, the augmented regression analysis support the theoretical consideration from above and the previous chapter. The term structure plays an important role for monetary policy and has thus to be included into empirical reaction function. In doing so, term structure effects are found to be empirically significant for the Deutsche Bundesbank as well as for the ECB. The next chapter, however, presents an alternative method for incorporating term structure effects into empirical monetary reaction function that is based on considerations from the finance literature.

Chapter 6

A Joint Determination of Interest Rate Rules and the Dynamics of the Term Structure of Interest Rates

6.1 Introduction

In this chapter, the empirical determination of interest rate rule that has been extensively discussed in the previous chapters is combined with a modeling approach that stems from the finance literature.[156] This approach that models the dynamics of the term structure of interest rates describes a popular strand of the finance literature, that has also been growing rapidly in recent years. These are no-arbitrage models of the term structure of interest rates. The so-called affine term structure models (ATSM) are the most popular ones within this literature. They explain the dynamics of the term structure of interest rates by (mostly) unobserved stochastic (risk) factors, while yields of different maturities are connected by the absence of arbitrage opportunities.

Although a vast variety of affine term structure models exists due to the number of latent factors and the explicit formulation of their stochastic processes, they all share a common feature: in the single-factor case the only risk factor equals the short rate, whereas in multi-factor cases the short rate is a (additive) combination of multiple risk factors. Monetary policy rules share the same (functional) structure, once the risk factors are interpreted as macroeconomic variables. Therefore, the short-term interest rate is a critical point of intersection between the two lines of research.

Together, the two perspectives suggest that understanding the manner in which central banks move the short rate (respectively, the policy rate) in response to fundamental macroeconomic variables should explain movements in the short end of the yield curve. With the consistency between long and short rates enforced by the no-arbitrage assumption, (expected) macroeconomic variations should amount for movements farther out of the yield curve as well. Combining the two lines of research could sharpen our understanding of the dynamics of the term structure of interest rates, respectively, the yield curve.

Understanding what moves the bond yields is important for at least four reasons. A first one is forecasting. When adjusted for risk, yields of long-maturity bonds represent expected values of average future short-term yields. Therefore, the yield curve contains information about the expected future path of

[156] This chapter is an extended version of the article "An affine three-factor model of the Germn term structure of interest rates with macroeconomic content" published in *Applied Financial Economics Letters*, Vol. 1 (2005), 151-156.

the economy. The second reason is connected to monetary policy and to the discussion of chapters 4 and 5. Central banks are only able to move the short end of the yield curve via their interest rate decisions. However, what matters more for aggregate demand, and thus, for targeting inflation are the longer-term yields. A model of the dynamics of the yield curve helps to understand how movements at the short end translate into changes of longer-term yields. This knowledge helps central banks to conduct monetary policy. Debt policy is a third reason. When issuing new debt, governments need to decide about the maturity of the new bonds. Thus, they need an idea how the term structure of interest rates develops over time. A fourth reason is derivative pricing and hedging. Prices of complex securities, such as swaps, caps and floors, options on interest rates, and futures can be computed from a given model of the yield curve. Furthermore, banks need to manage the risk of paying short-term interest rates on deposits while receiving long-term interest rates on loans. Hedging strategies involve contracts that are contingent on future short rates, such as swap contracts. To compute appropriate strategies, banks need to know how the price of derivative securities depends on the state of the economy.

This chapter combines two popular strands of the literature, i.e., it sets out a model that is able to capture the dynamics of the German term structure of interest rates very well and additionally generates reaction coefficients in the short rate equation that are very close to the magnitudes that are observed in empirical models discussed so far, but which abstracted from arbitrage-free dynamics of the term structure of interest rates.[157] However, in the formulation of the model a trade-off exists: the aim is to sufficiently characterize the dynamics of the term structure of interest rates but keep the model as tractable as possible, i.e., keeping the number of parameters to be estimated as low as possible. For this reason, the analysis is restricted to the class of constant volatility models with time-invariant term premia.

Several other papers have recently also combined the two lines of research.[158] Ang and Piazessi (2003) estimate the dynamics of the US yield curve also based on macroeconomic factors as well as unobservable factors. They show that macroeconomic factors primarily explain movements at the short end and the middle of the yield curve while unobservable factors account mostly for movements at the long end. However, they do not jointly estimate the coefficients of the macroeconomic factors and the latent factors. They first estimate the coefficients of the monetary policy rule and estimate the remaining parameters in a second step holding the pre-estimated parameters constant.

[157] In contrast to previous chapters, the estimations in this chapter are only based only the sample of the Bundesbank regime. This is due to the exploit estimation technique which requires a critical length of the sample period.
[158] See Diebold et al. (2005) for an excellent introduction into this new area of research.

Rudebusch and Wu (2003) estimate a two-factor Gaussian term structure model for the U.S. Based on a subsequent OLS analysis they show that the extracted factors are correlated with factors that typically enter a monetary policy rule.

This chapter departs from those 'two step analyses' by estimating an empirical model that jointly incorporates observable as well as unobservable factors. It also takes into account the term structure dynamics up to a maturity of 10 years, while those studies take 6 years as the longest maturity. The present analysis draws on the study of Cassola and Luis (2003) who show that the dynamics of the German term structure from 1972 through 1998 can be well explained by a two-factor Gaussian model with time-invariant risk premia and adds explicit economic content to their model. Hördahl et al. (2003) also construct a joint model of German macroeconomic factors and the yield curve. However, they estimate the macroeconomic and the yield curve dynamics within the framework of the new neo-classical synthesis outlined in chapter 1. The approach in the present lacks such a structural model but has the advantage to link macroeconomic and latent term structure factors more explicitly.

This chapter is structured as follows. The subsequent section briefly characterizes the class of affine term structure models as well as the concept of the absence of arbitrage and its consequences for the pricing of bonds. Section 6.3 introduces the general multi-factor affine term structure model in discrete time (the Duffie Kan model) which nests most of the known affine term structure models. In section 6.4, this general model is tailored to a particular Gaussian version that serves as my empirical model. Section 6.5 relates the reaction coefficients monetary policy rules to the parameter of the affine term structure model. The estimation procedure based on a Kalman filter and the results are presented in section 6.6.

6. 2 An Arbitrage-Free Perspective of the Term Structure of Interest Rates

6.2.1 A Non-technical Characterization of Affine Term Structure Models

The term structure of interest rates can be characterized by affine term structure models.[159] These models are based on an explicit no-arbitrage condition in financial markets. The assumption of the absence of arbitrage opportunities seems quite natural for bond yields. Most bond markets are extremely liquid, and arbitrage opportunities are traded away immediately. Tractability is the main advantage of affine models: they assume bond yields to be affine (i.e., constant-plus-linear) functions of some state vector (the risk factors), so that models can easily be solved either in closed form or numerically using standard

[159] See Maes (2004) and Piazessi (2003) for excellent overviews.

procedures.[160] The models of Vasicek (1977) and Cox, Ingersoll and Ross (or CIR, 1985) are the pioneers of the class of affine term structure models. Both focus on closed form solutions and show how the term structure of interest rates at a moment in time reflects regularities of interest rate movements over time. In the simplest versions of such models, the so-called one-factor models, the short-term interest rate is the single factor that drives the movements of the term structure.

The underlying diffusion process of the short rate is modeled as a Markov process, which means that its history contains no information about its future value that cannot be extracted from its current value. The Markov property is consistent with the so-called weak form of market efficiency, which generally says that extraordinary returns cannot be achieved by the use of the precise historical evolution in the price of a particular asset. The Markov process makes it possible that prices of zero coupon bonds of any maturity can also be written as a function of the short rate and their time to maturity. In this sense, the zero coupon bonds are derivative securities, i.e. securities deriving their value from the underlying short rate dynamics. Bond pricing can, thus, be performed along the well-known logic of derivative pricing including the Black and Scholes (1973) model of stock option pricing.

If the short rate follows a particular diffusion process and bond prices are a function of the short rate, then, by *Ito's Lemma*, the latter will also follow a diffusion process whose drift and variance can be characterized by the drift and variance of the short rate diffusion process.[161] Given a set of risky bonds, it is possible to design a risk-free self-financing portfolio that has to yield the instantaneously risk-free (short) rate within the interval *dt* in order to be consistent with the absence of arbitrage. This riskless portfolio is fully characterized in terms of the portfolio weights that have to be attached to the single assets. It turns out that the excess return per unit of risk for each asset has to be identical. This defines the market price of risk. In a setting with more than one risk factor, one market price of risk is associated with each factor. Formally, the existence of a unique (vector of the) market price(s) of risk requires the absence of arbitrage.

The market price of risk relates the expected return of a particular bond to its volatility, both of which can be expressed in terms of the drift and the volatility of the underlying short rate process (by *Ito's Lemma*). Expressing the

---

160 A function $f(\cdot)$ is defined to be affine if it is constant-plus-linear in its arguments (strictly speaking, linear would suffice). A univariate example would be: $f(x) = a + bx$, for all real parameters a and b.

161 Ito's Lemma requires additionally that the bond pricing functions have to be twice differentiable. See Bolder (2001) for an in-depth illustration of the particular steps involved in the solution of ATSM.

market price of risk in terms of the latter derives the fundamental partial differential equation that each interest rate derivative has to satisfy in the absence of arbitrage: the so-called *term structure partial differential equation.* However, a unique solution for this term structure partial differential equation does not always exist. But it can be shown that an affine structure of bond prices guarantees a solution. This feature makes the class of affine term structure models particularly attractive.[162]

The logic that single-factor affine term structure models are based on the dynamics of the short rate indicates that the formulation of the nature of the diffusion process for the short rate is crucial for any term structure model. The Vasicek (1977) model assumes that the short rate's volatility is constant, whereas in the CIR (1985) model the short rate's volatility is to be proportional to the square root of the short rate itself. This has the advantage of ruling out negative values of the interest rate because short rate volatility declines to zero when the short rate is zero. Thus, its future value is only determined by its drift which is positive. Both models have in common that the short rate exhibits mean reversion. A stochastic process that shows such dynamics is known as an *Ornstein-Uhlenbeck* process. Chan et al. (1992) provide empirical evidence that interest rates do indeed have the feature of mean reversion.

However, one-factor models have some unrealistic properties. First, they are not able to generate all the shapes of the yield curve that are observed in practice. For example, the one-factor Vasicek and CIR models can only produce increasing yield curves, decreasing yield curves and yield curves with a small hump (i.e, $\cap$-shaped). Typically, yield curves have one of these shapes. However, they can occasionally differ from these, e.g. the yield curve is sometimes decreasing for short maturities and then increasing for longer maturities. Such an inverse hump (i.e., $\cup$-shaped) or any other yield curve cannot be generated by one-factor models. Second, one-factor models do not allow for the twist of the term structure of interest rates, i.e. yield curve changes where short-maturity yields move in the opposite direction of long-maturity yields. This is because all yields are driven by a single factor, meaning that they have to be highly correlated. Intuitively, multi-factor models are much more flexible and are able to generate additional yield curve shapes and yield curve dynamics.[163]

[162] In particular, the affine structure decomposes the term structure equation into two separate differential equations that together form a so-called *Ricatti problem* that is quite easy to handle.

[163] Empirical evidence strongly points towards multi-factor extensions of the model. See Dewachter and Maes (2000) and Dai and Singleton (2000) for a comparison of one-factor versus two- and three-factor model fits.

In multi-factor models several, say *k*, observed or unobserved (risk) factors govern the movement of the term structure. The univariate diffusion process of the short rate is substituted by a multivariate diffusion process. Duffie and Kan (hereafter DK, 1996) establish the conditions that have to be fulfilled to still produce affine yield expressions to preserve the tractability of the models in the multidimensional case. The DK-framework has the advantage that it nests most of the existing term structure models. Among them are multi-factor versions of Vasicek (1977) and CIR (1985), as well as Longstaff and Schwartz (1992), Langetieg (1980) and Balduzzi et al. (1996 and 1998).[164] As in the one-factor case these models specify the stochastic process of the factors and derive the bond prices (or yields) as affine functions of the factors and the time to maturity. Since zero coupon bond prices and zero coupon yields are unambiguously tied together, yields (and thus the short rate) are also affine functions of the factors. Their dynamics are driven by the dynamics of the underlying risk factors.

The main (statistical) idea of affine term structure models, i.e., to explain the dynamics of the term structure of interest rates on the basis of few factors, is equal to the *modus operandi* of (purely statistical) factor models, such as the principal component analysis of yield changes that describe the covariance matrix of yield changes in terms of few factors that describe their common movement. For example, on the basis of a factor analysis Bühler and Zimmermann (1996) show that the dynamics of the German interest rate could well be described, i.e. about 90 percent of the variation, by three factors. Litterman and Scheinkman (1991) established the same result for the U.S. term structure within a principal component analysis.[165] The latter authors proposed the interpretation of this components in terms of 'level', 'slope' and 'curvature'. The major drawback of these analyses is that they are purely statistical and do not have any economic content. Affine term structure models start from the strong assumption of the absence of arbitrage and, thus, have an explicit economic content that puts restrictions on the cross-section and time series behavior of bond prices, respectively interest rates.

[164] See Dai and Singleton (2000) for a categorization of affine term structure models. These authors also extensively discuss the restrictions that have to be fulfilled in the parameterization of the models in order be theoretically admissible and econometrically identified.

[165] Canabarro (1995) reports similar results for the US.

6.2.2 *The Implications of the Absence of Arbitrage*

The absence of arbitrage has crucial implications for the dynamics of any asset and, thus, for the term structure of interest rates. Harrison and Kreps (1979) and Harrison and Pliska (1981) prove that the assumption of the absence of arbitrage opportunities within a particular market is equivalent to the existence of a so-called pricing kernel (or stochastic discount factor). They also prove that the absence of arbitrage guarantees the existence of a risk-neutral probability measure, such that the price of any asset in time t that pays no dividend in time $t+1$ equals its time-t-expected discounted value in $t+1$, where the discount factor is the risk-free rate and the expectations are formed under the risk-neutral measure. The risk-free probability can be converted to the data-generating measure (or physical measure) by the *Radon-Nikodym* derivative. The dynamics of the *Radon-Nikodym* derivative are driven by the dynamics of the market price of risk characterized above. The two concepts of the pricing kernel and the risk-neutral probability measure are mathematically equivalent and are jointly referred to as the "Fundamental Theorem of Asset Pricing".[166]

The discrete-time model presented in this section relies on the pricing kernel formulation. This essentially means that in the absence of arbitrage the price of any financial asset corresponds to the present value of its expected future cash flow with the present value being obtained by applying the positive stochastic discount factor (the pricing kernel). In the case of zero coupon bonds whose future cash flows only correspond to their price in the next period, we can establish the following pricing equation:

$$(6.1) \qquad P_{n,t} = E_t\left[M_{t+1}P_{n-1,t+1}\right],$$

where the expectations are taken under the physical probability measure. P represents the price of the zero coupon bond with n denoting its time to maturity. M is the stochastic discount factor which is also known as the price generator, since prices grow from it. In any arbitrage-free environment, there exists a unique positive random variable that satisfies expression (6.1).[167] Arbitrage opportunities are ruled out by applying the same discount factor to all bonds. An arbitrage opportunity is any zero-net-investment strategy that guarantees a positive payoff in some future state of the world with no possibility of a negative payoff in all other future states of the world.[168] Solving forward the

---

[166] See Maes (2004, p. 11 ff) on the exact nature of this equivalence in continuous-time models and Backus et al. (1998a) for the discrete-time models.

[167] See Harrison and Kreps (1979) and Harrison and Pliska (1981) for this fundamental result.

[168] Intuitively, the equivalence of the existence of a unique positive pricing kernel and the absence of arbitrage opportunities can be explained as follows. An arbitrage project would be

basic pricing equation (6.1) by the *law of iterated expectations* and noting that the bond pays exactly one unit at maturity ($P_{0,t+n}$=1) yields:

$$(6.2) \qquad P_{n,t} = E_t[M_{t+1} \ldots M_{t+n}] = E_t\left[\prod_{i=1}^{n} M_{t+i}\right],$$

so that a model of bond prices could also be expressed as a model of the evolution of the pricing kernel. It follows that we can model $P_{n,t}$ (and, thus, associated bond yields) by modeling the stochastic process of M_{t+i}. The bond prices (and, thus, bond yields) are a function of those state variables that are relevant for forecasting the process of the pricing kernel.

In consumption-based equilibrium models, the pricing kernel represents the marginal rate of substitution between present and next period's consumption, i.e. the discounted ratio of marginal utilities of consumption, of a particular representative agent valued at her optimal consumption rate.[169] Since the purpose of financial assets is to allow agents to shift consumption across time and different states, it should come at no surprise that a measure for the market-

---

a trading strategy that satisfies the following condition: $V_t^{\psi} < 0$ and $V_{t+1}^{\psi} \geq 0$, with ψ *being a vector* representing the units held of each asset in a portfolio between time t and $t+1$. This relation basically means that the portfolio has a negative initial value (so that the investor receives money when initiating the strategy in time t), while its value (payoff) in time $t+1$ is non-negative no matter how the world evolves between the two dates. Any rational investor would want to invest in this strategy. Applying (6.1) to this portfolio yields: $V_t^{\psi} = E_t[M_{t+1} V_{t+1}^{\psi}]$.

If the pricing kernel is positive and V_{t+1}^{ψ} is strictly positive, it must be that V_t^{ψ} has to be strictly positive, too. Consequently, if a positive pricing kernel exist, arbitrage as defined above is ruled out.

169 This can be shown by considering the intertemporal choice of an investor who maximizes the expectation of a time-separable utility function:

$$U_t = E_t\left[\sum_{j=0}^{\infty} \Gamma^j u(c_{t+j})\right],$$

which leads to the optimal consumption plan:

$$u'(c_t) = \Gamma \cdot E_t[(1+i_t) \cdot u'(c_{t+1})] = \Gamma \cdot E_t[(P_{n-1,t+1}/P_{n,t}) \cdot u'(c_{t+1})],$$

where i_t is the return of an asset that the investor can freely trade and the second equality comes from the bond considered above, since we have as its gross return: ($P_{n-1,t+1}/P_{n,t}$) = ($1+i_t$). Comparing this to (6.1) it follows that the pricing kernel is $M_{t+1} = \Gamma \cdot u'(c_{t+1}) / u'(c_t)$. Note that this also means that the pricing kernel is always positive since marginal utilities are always positive.

wide pricing information can be captured by the marginal rate of substitution in consumption. Furthermore, the pricing kernel is unique in the case financial markets are complete. A market is complete if all relevant risks can be hedged by forming portfolios of the traded financial assets.[170]

Arbitrage free models can also be considered as equilibrium models, i.e. only equilibrium prices of financial assets are determined. A market is said to be in an equilibrium if it clears in the sense that demand equals supply, and every investor has picked a trading strategy in the financial asset under consideration that serves his preferences and budget constraint. An arbitrage is a trading strategy that generates a riskless profit. If an investor has the opportunity to invest in an arbitrage project, he will surely do so, and hence will change his original trading strategy. In other words, a market that allows for arbitrage is not in an equilibrium. For our purpose this means, when searching for equilibrium prices we can exploit no-arbitrage conditions.

We can also employ the fundamental pricing equation (6.1) to characterize the compensation for risk that an investor demands for holding a risky bond. If we denote the nominal gross return of an asset ($P_{n-1,t+1}/P_{n,t}$) as ($1+i_t$) we can rewrite (6.1) and get:[171]

$$(6.3) \qquad 1 = E_t\left[\frac{P_{n-1,t+1}}{P_{n,t}} M_{t+1}\right] = E_t\left[(1+i_t)M_{t+1}\right] = E_t\left[(1+i_t)\right]E_t\left[M_{t+1}\right] + Cov_t\left[i_t, M_{t+1}\right].$$

It follows that:

$$(6.4) \qquad E_t\left[(1+i_t)\right] = \frac{1}{E_t\left[M_{t+1}\right]}\left(1 - Cov_t\left[i_t, M_{t+1}\right]\right).$$

Since the covariance term has to be zero for a risk-free asset, its rate of return has to satisfy

$$(6.5) \qquad 1 + i_t^f = \frac{1}{E_t\left[M_{t+1}\right]}.$$

The risk free rate is often referred to as the short rate. However, this means that it is only 'instantaneously riskless' because future levels are not known. The short rate is strictly speaking a zero maturity interest rate, i.e. the interest rate of

[170] This essentially means, for example, that options can be artificially created by a suitable buy and sell strategy in the underlying asset.
[171] See Campbell et al. (1997, p. 294).

a bond that matures in the next instant. Since the shortest maturity considered in the empirical exercise is one month, it is convenient the one-month rate as the risk-free short rate. Combining (6.4) and (6.5) we get an expression for the excess return of any risky asset over the risk-free rate, in other words, its risk premium:

$$(6.6) \qquad E_t[i_t]-i_t^f=-(1+i_t^f)Cov_t[i_t,M_{t+1}].$$

The previous equation basically demonstrates that risk premia originate from the co-variation of its return with the pricing kernel. When the return dynamics of an asset covary negatively with the pricing kernel dynamics, the risk premium is positive, and *vice versa*. The minus sign in (6.6) means that investors are willing to accept an expected rate of return below the risk free rate on such securities that tend to have high payoffs when the pricing kernel is higher. This is best understood if we rely on the interpretation of the pricing kernel as the ratio of marginal utilities of consumption. An investor will demand a higher compensation for an asset that behaves cyclically than for an asset that behaves countercyclically, since the former bears higher risk in terms of consumption variability, whereas the latter can be considered as an insurance against consumption risk.[172]

6.3 A General Affine Term Structure Model in Discrete Time

As already mentioned, Duffie and Kan (1996) present a framework that formally preserves the affine property of term structure models. Most existing models can thus be interpreted as a particular parameterization of this framework. Originally the DK-framework was formulated in continuous time. This way of formulation has proven to be very elegant by using well-known results of differential stochastic calculus. However, affine term structure models can also be formulated in discrete time.[173] Since this chapter focuses on econometric testing of the model and its empirical implications, it also relies on a model in discrete

[172] When consumption growth is high the marginal utility of consumption (and thus the pricing kernel) is low. If returns are negatively correlated with the pricing kernel, high returns are associated with states of high consumption. A risk premium has to be paid for such assets because they provide more wealth when it is less needed, respectively they provide less wealth when it is most needed.

[173] See Backus et al. (1998a) for an extensive exposition. Sun (1992) explores the relation between discrete-time and continuous-time models more generally.

time. This might be less elegant but avoids the pitfalls of estimating a continuous-time model with discrete-time data.[174]

The DK model has been reformulated by Backus et al. (1998a/b) into discrete time and is based on the fundamental result of the existence of a unique pricing kernel characterized above. Equation (6.1) demonstrates that in an arbitrage-free environment a model that is intended to explain the development of asset prices consists of a description of the development of the pricing kernel which, in turn, is driven by the process of the underlying risk factors. In particular, the k-dimensional vector of risk factors, Z, satisfies the following stochastic process:[175]

$$(6.7) \qquad Z_{t+1} = (I - \Phi)\cdot\theta + \Phi\cdot Z_t + V(Z_t)^{1/2}\varepsilon_{t+1},$$

where I is an identity matrix and the matrix Φ has positive diagonal elements between zero and one in order to ensure that the factors are stationary. θ is the long-run mean of the risk factors. Thus, the risk factors are governed by a discrete-time *Ornstein-Uhlenbeck* process. The independent shock term is normally distributed with $\varepsilon_t \sim N(0, I)$. Finally, $V(Z_t)$ is the variance-covariance matrix of the random shocks and is defined as a diagonal matrix with the elements $v_j(Z_t) = \alpha_j + \beta_j' Z_t$, where β_j has nonnegative elements.[176] Thus, the factors have an affine volatility structure, which is a generalization of the square-root structure of the CIR model. Moreover, the factors are allowed to be correlated. The square-root process of the risk factor requires that the volatility function $v_j(Z)$ has to be positive, which places particular restrictions on the parameters.[177]

To derive an affine yield model, the distribution of the stochastic discount factor is assumed to be conditionally log-normal. In addition to providing model tractability, this assumption keeps the discount factor positive and unique. Following Backus et al. (1998a), the negative of the log of the pricing kernel ($m_{t+1} \equiv \log[M_{t+1}]$) takes the form:

[174] See Aït-Sahalia (1996). He points out that the approximation of a continuous time process by discretization methods is hard to justify even for daily data.

[175] The following model is covered in greater detail in Cassola and Luis (2003), who also take the DK-framework as the benchmark for their model.

[176] In the subsequent notation the subscripts j generally indicate a particular element within the respective matrix which has no subscript attached. Throughout the paper the subscript j = 1 ... k indicates the number of risk factors, and thus, determines the size of the matrices and vectors.

[177] In a continuous-time framework the dynamics of the risk factors are generally expressed as an Ito diffusion process. Expression (6.7) is its counterpart in discrete time. Formally, (6.7) can be derived via a *Euler discretization* (see Bolder, 2001, p. 51).

$$-m_{t+1} = \delta + \gamma' \cdot Z_t + \xi_{t+1},$$

where δ is a constant and γ is a parameter vector. The innovations to the risk factors and the pricing kernel may be correlated. To capture this we write:

$$\xi_{t+1} = \lambda' \cdot V(Z_t)^{1/2} \varepsilon_{t+1} + \eta_{t+1}.$$

The presence of an uncorrelated shock η_{t+1} will only affect the average level of the term structure and not its average slope nor its time-series behavior. In order to simplify notation it is common to drop it (Campbell et al. 1997), so that we have:

$$(6.8) \qquad -m_{t+1} = \delta + \gamma' \cdot Z_t + \lambda' \cdot V(Z_t)^{1/2} \varepsilon_{t+1},$$

where λ is the vector that governs the correlation between innovations in the risk factors (state variables) and the pricing kernel: risk, in other words.

According to the affine formulation of bond prices it is assumed that bond prices are exponential affine functions of the risk factors:[178]

$$(6.9) \qquad P_{n,t} = \exp(-A_n - B_n' \cdot Z_t),$$

where, again, the second subscript *n* denotes the time to maturity at time *t*. The parameter A_n and the vector of parameters B_n are to be estimated in order to determine bond prices. Both are 'time to maturity-related' constants. The latter is commonly referred to as the vector of factor loadings because it measures the impact of a shock to the risk factors on the bond prices. In case of zero coupon bonds the values A_0 and B_0 have to be equal to zero, because at the time of their maturity ($n = 0$) they pay by definition exactly the face value of one unit. Thus, the log of the price of a maturing bond (denoted by a lower case *p*) has to be zero. The general form of the relation is:

$$(6.10) \qquad -p_{n,t} = A_n + B_n' \cdot Z_t.$$

Since nominal yields and prices of zero coupon bonds are unambiguously linked, nominal yields of zero coupon bonds can be easily computed as

[178] This particular formulation ensures the property that log bond prices, and hence bond yields, are linear (affine) in the state variables. This ensures the desired joint log-normality of bond prices with the stochastic discount factor.

$$(6.11)\qquad i_{n,t} = -\frac{p_{n,t}}{n} = \frac{A_n}{n} + \frac{B_n'}{n} Z_t$$

Equation (3.5) states that we can model the dynamics of the whole term structure if we are able to estimate the parameters A_n and the vector B_n for all values of n. In order to solve for their dynamics, we need to employ a well-known statistical result for the distribution of a log value of any variable X. This result states that if $\log X \sim N(\mu,\sigma^2)$ then $\log E(X) = \mu + \frac{\sigma^2}{2}$.

Applying this to the fundamental pricing relation in (6.1) expressed in logs together with eqs. (6.7), (6.8), (6.10), the known (zero) values A_0 and B_0, and the assumption of the independence of shocks the values of A_n and B_n will follow the subsequent recursive restrictions:[179]

$$(6.12)\qquad A_{n+1} = A_n + \delta + B_n'(I - \Phi)\theta - \frac{1}{2}\sum_{j=1}^{k}\left(\lambda_j + B_{j,n}\right)^2 \cdot \alpha_j$$

and

$$(6.13)\qquad B_{n+1}' = \left(\gamma' + B_n'\Phi\right) - \frac{1}{2}\sum_{j=1}^{k}\left(\lambda_j + B_{j,n}\right)^2 \cdot \beta_j',$$

where k is the number of risk factors that are modeled.

From (6.11) through (6.13) we can obtain the following expression for the one-period interest rate (short rate):

$$(6.14)\qquad \begin{aligned} i_{1,t} &= \delta - \frac{1}{2}\sum_{j=1}^{k}\lambda_j^2 \cdot \alpha_j + \left(\gamma' - \frac{1}{2}\sum_{j=1}^{k}\lambda_j^2 \cdot \beta_j'\right)\cdot Z_t \\ &= \delta + \gamma' \cdot Z_t - \frac{1}{2}\lambda' V(Z_t)\lambda, \end{aligned}$$

where the second equality stems from the fact that the variance-covariance matrix is defined as a diagonal matrix.[180]

[179] See Appendix F for the detailed derivation as well as Campbell, Lo and MacKinlay (1997, ch. 11) for the solution technique.

[180] This expression for the short rate is entirely consistent with the fundamental relationship between the risk-free rate and the pricing kernel in (6.5), once we take the one-period interest rate as the risk-free rate. Expressing (6.5) in logs and employing the usual approximation for

One can also calculate the term premia as the difference between the 'holding period return' and the one-period interest rate (see Appendix G):

$$\Lambda_{n,t} = E_t p_{n,t+1} - p_{n+1,t} - i_{1,t}$$

$$= -\sum_{j=1}^{k}\left(\lambda_j B_{j,n} + \frac{B_{j,n}^2}{2}\right)\cdot \alpha_j - \sum_{j=1}^{k}\left(\lambda_j B_{j,n} + \frac{B_{j,n}^2}{2}\right)\cdot \beta_j' \cdot Z_t .$$

Given the structure of the variance-covariance matrix this is equivalent to:

$$(6.15) \qquad \Lambda_{n,t} = -\lambda' \cdot V(Z_t) \cdot B_n - \frac{B_n' \cdot V(Z_t) \cdot B_n}{2}.$$

This relation basically says that the expected excess log return is the sum of a risk premium term and a *Jensen's Inequality* term in the own variance because of working in logs. The term premium is governed by the vector λ. A negative (positive) sign leads to a positive (negative) bond risk premium. This can be reasoned as follows. Consider a positive shock ε_{t+1} which increases the state variable. According to (6.10) this lowers all bond prices and drives down bond returns. When λ is positive, the shock also drives down the log value of the pricing kernel, which means that bond returns are positively correlated with the pricing kernel. As explained above, this correlation has a hedge value, so that risk premia on bonds are negative. The same reason applies to the case when λ has negative sign, which leads to positive risk premia. λ is usually known as the vector of market prices of risk. In order to facilitate a normally (i.e., positively) sloped yield curve, at least one parameter in the vector λ has to be sufficiently negative.

---

the logarithmic form of the gross rate, $\log(1+i) \cong i$, we have: $\log E_t\left[M_{t+1}\right] = -i_{1,t}$. Given the above stated statistical result of the log-value of an expectation of a log-normal distributed variable, the assumption of the determination of the pricing kernel in (6.8) together with (6.14) yields the above stated expression for the log of the expectation of the pricing kernel, meaning that the general formulation of the model is consistent with the basic pricing relation in an arbitrage free environment discussed in section 6.2.

6.4 A Gaussian Model for the German Term Structure of Interest Rates

This section proposes a particular parameterization of the general model sketched out above. The parameter choice is driven by the following trade-off. On the one hand, the model has to be sufficiently flexible to be able to characterize the dynamics of the German term structure of interest rates. This might call for a fully fledged model with a high number of parameters to be estimated. On the other hand, the interest lies in keeping the number of parameters as low as possible, in order to keep the model empirically tractable and also to assign specific economic interpretation to the estimated parameters. In order to resolve this trade-off, this chapter draws on the study of Cassola and Luis (2003). These authors recently demonstrated that the dynamics of the German term structure of interest rates can be well explained within a constant volatility (or Gaussian) two-factor affine term structure model. Close to their parameterization my choice of parameters is:

$$\theta_j = 0$$

$$\Phi = diag(\varphi_1 \ldots \varphi_k)$$

(6.16) $$\alpha_j = \sigma_j^2$$

$$\beta_j = 0$$

$$\delta = \bar{\delta} + \frac{1}{2}\sum_{j=1}^{k}\lambda_j^2\sigma_j^2 .$$

The long-run mean of the risk factors is set equal to zero because of my particular identification assumption of the risk factors that follows below.[181] The matrix of the mean reversion parameters is assumed to be diagonal so that the dynamics of a particular risk factor only depend on its own current value relative to its long-run mean. The third and fourth definition in (6.16) constitute a

[181] There is another technical justification for this as well. Backus et al. (1998a) show for the single-factor case of the constant volatility model the parameters δ and θ cannot be identified separately, so that one of them could effectively be dropped. Setting either δ or θ to zero implies identical asset prices. However, in the general setup of the model this is not the case.

Gaussian model with constant volatility of the risk factors.[182] The last definition in (6.16) is intended to yield a particular formulation for the short-rate equation.[183] In contrast to Cassola and Luis (2003) the number of restrictions put on the parameters is limited and admits the parameter vector γ to be determined by the data.

The parameterization yields the following equation for the dynamics of the pricing kernel:

$$(6.17)\quad \begin{aligned} -m_{t+1} &= \bar{\delta} + \frac{1}{2}\lambda'\sigma\sigma'\lambda + \gamma' \cdot Z_t + \lambda'\sigma\varepsilon_{t+1} \\ &= \bar{\delta} + \sum_{j=1}^{k}\left(\frac{\lambda_j^2}{2}\sigma_j^2 + \gamma_j z_{j,t} + \lambda_j\sigma_j\varepsilon_{j,t+1}\right) \end{aligned}$$

The vector of risk factors follows a first-order autoregressive process:

$$Z_{t+1} = \Phi \cdot Z_t + \sigma\varepsilon_{t+1},$$

or for individual risk factors j:

$$(6.18)\quad z_{j,t+1} = \varphi_j z_{j,t} + \sigma_j\varepsilon_{j,t+1}.$$

My particular parameterization yields the following recursive restrictions for the factor loadings (see again Appendix F for the derivation):

---

[182] Note that the constant volatility implies that the term premia in (6.15) only depend on the time to maturity but not on time anymore. Due to the constant volatility formulation Backus et al. (1998a, p. 23) redefine the market prices of risk as $\tilde{\lambda}_j \equiv \lambda_j\sigma_j$. This is in line with Duffie and Kan (1996) who also generally assume that the market prices of risk for factor j is proportional to its standard deviation. In equation (6.8) we would than substitute: $\tilde{\lambda}' \equiv \lambda' V(Z_t)^{1/2}$. Rather than following this approach the formulation in this chapter does not make this redefinition. This has the advantage to estimate both parameters and their standard errors independently. Cassola and Luis (2003) also do not redefine the prices of risk in writing down their model, but only provide estimates of $\lambda_j\sigma_j$, which they interpret as the market prices of risk. However, following this would not change my results, since the value $\lambda_j\sigma_j$ can also be calculated from the independent estimates.

[183] In particular, this variance term only arises because the model is working in logs (*Jensen's Inequality*). The normalization lets us get rid of this term.

(6.19) $$A_{n+1} = A_n + \overline{\delta} + \frac{1}{2}\sum_{j=1}^{k}\left[\lambda_j^2\sigma_j^2 - \left(\lambda_j\sigma_j + B_{j,n}\sigma_j\right)^2\right]$$

(6.20) $$B_{j,n+1} = \left(\gamma_j + B_{j,n}\varphi_j\right).$$

From the recursive restrictions (6.19) and (6.20) together with (6.11), and the fact that $A_0 = B_0 = 0$, we can get an expression for the one-period interest rate:

(6.21) $$i_{1,t} = \overline{\delta} + \sum_{j=1}^{k}\gamma_j z_{j,t}\ .$$

The one-period (or short-term) interest rate is determined by a constant and the sum of time-varying risk factors multiplied by related (constant) coefficients. Examining (6.21) and interpreting the one-period interest rate as the policy rate of a central bank, one immediately realizes its equivalence to the popular monetary policy rules, in which the risk factors and their associated coefficients would have very specific economic meanings. In particular, the constant would be the equilibrium level of the nominal short-term interest rate, the γ_j's would resemble the reaction coefficients of the central bank and the risk factors would display macroeconomic variables upon which the central bank reacts. From an empirical point of view equation (4.6) potentially allows us to jointly estimate a monetary policy reaction function together with the arbitrage-free dynamics of the term structure of interest rates. However, the crucial point for this exercise is the (empirical) identification of the risk factors.[184] This is the aim of the subsequent section 6.5.

6.5 Combining Monetary Policy Rules with the Term Structure Dynamics

It has been extensively discussed throughout previous chapters that it has become common practice to model monetary policy as a simple feedback or instrument rule. Taylor-type rules link the short term policy rate to measures of the output gap and the inflation gap, which is repeated here for convenience:

(6.22) $$i_{1,t} = \pi_t + \overline{r} + \gamma_\pi(\pi_t - \pi^*) + \gamma_y(y_t - \overline{y}_t),$$

184 Cassola and Luis (2003) parameterise the model such that the one-period rate is just the sum of risk factors. In the two-factor case they notice that this equals the *Fisher equation*, where the nominal interest rate is the sum of the real interest rate plus expected inflation.

where i_1 is the policy rate, π is inflation with the (*) indicating its target value. The equilibrium real interest rate is $\bar{r}$ and y is an output measure with the upper bar indicating its equilibrium level. The coefficients γ_π and γ_y measure the strength of the reaction to the inflation gap, respectively, the output gap. A comparison of (6.22) and (6.21) reveals the same expression once the sum of the equilibrium real rate and the actual inflation rate reflect the $\bar{\delta}$ and the (two) risk factors are interpreted as the inflation and the output gap.

The empirical chapters 3 and 5 demonstrate that such rules describe the behavior of the Bundesbank and the European Central Bank quite well, once we generalize the formulation in (6.22) to the class of explicitly forward-looking instrument rules and, furthermore, allow for the effect that central banks smooth their changes in the policy rate, so that the actual rate adjusts only partially to its target rate. The empirical representation of the reaction function from chapter 3 is:[185]

(6.23) $$i_t = (1-\rho)\left(\bar{i} + \gamma_\pi E_t(\pi_{t+k} - \pi_t^{norm}) + \gamma_y E_t(y_{t+q} - y_{t+q}{}^*)\right) + \rho i_{t-1} + \upsilon_t$$

where ρ represents the smoothing parameter, E is the (conditional) expectation operator given the information set I_t, q and k are the horizons of the forward-looking behavior. Comparing (6.23) and (6.21) would then relate two risk factors with the expected inflation gap, the expected output gap as well as a third risk factor that comprises the effect of interest rate smoothing behavior and other (stochastic) shocks to the interest rate.

In order to explicitly combine the forward-looking monetary policy rule in representation (6.23) with the arbitrage-free model of the term structure for the following joint estimation, the dynamics of the inflation and the output process have to be characterized. In particular, it is assumed that the inflation gap and the output gap both follow an AR(1) process:

(6.24) $$\tilde{\pi}_{t+1} = \chi_\pi \cdot \tilde{\pi}_t + u_{t+1},$$

(6.25) $$\tilde{y}_{t+1} = \chi_y \cdot \tilde{y}_t + \upsilon_{t+1},$$

where the $\tilde{x}$-notation reflects the gap of the respective variable.[186] Forward iteration of (6.24) yields:

---

[185] This formulation coincides with equation (3.3) from section 3.3, but expressed in a different notation for the reaction coefficients which is more convenient in this chapter and with a time varying inflation target as it was already introduced in equation (3.7).

[186] This processes might seem too simplistic, but the reader is referred to the empirical part, where this assumption turns out to produce quite reasonable results. In addition, since the

$$\tilde{\pi}_{t+q} = \chi_\pi^q \cdot \tilde{\pi}_t + \sum_{i=1}^{q} \chi^{q-i} u_{t+i}. \tag{6.26}$$

If we match one of the risk factors in time t with the expected inflation gap $t+q$ periods ahead

$$z_{\pi,t} = E\left[\tilde{\pi}_{t+q}\right] = \chi_\pi^q \cdot \tilde{\pi}_t, \tag{6.27}$$

the law of motion of this (inflation) risk factor becomes

$$z_{\pi,t+1} = E\left[\tilde{\pi}_{t+q+1}\right] = \chi_\pi \cdot \tilde{\pi}_{t+q} = \chi_\pi \left(\chi_\pi^q \cdot \tilde{\pi}_t\right) + \chi_\pi \left(\sum_{i=1}^{q} \chi^{q-i} u_{t+i}\right). \tag{6.28}$$

Combining (6.27) and (6.28) with the law of motion for the risk factors from the affine term structure model in (6.18) it follows for the identification of parameters that:

$$\begin{aligned} \varphi_\pi &= \chi_\pi \\ \sigma_\pi \varepsilon_{t+1} &= \chi_\pi \cdot \sum_{i=1}^{q} \chi_\pi^{q-i} u_{t+i}. \end{aligned} \tag{6.29}$$

From (6.27) it follows that the actual inflation gap and the actual (inflation) risk factor are connected as follows:

$$\tilde{\pi}_t = \frac{1}{(\varphi_\pi)^q} \cdot z_{\pi,t}. \tag{6.30}$$

By the same token the relationship between the actual output gap and the (output) risk factor is:

$$\tilde{y}_t = \frac{1}{(\varphi_y)^l} \cdot z_{y,t}. \tag{6.31}$$

Equations (6.30) and (6.31) follow from the generalized monetary policy rule in (6.23) and display the general identification of two risk factors with observable macroeconomic variables given the assumption of an AR(1) behavior of the

study links the risk factors whose dynamics are modeled through equation (6.18) to the macroeconomic factors, consistency requires to assume the same autoregressive process.

latter.[187] Equations (6.30) and (6.31) when combined with (6.11) provide us with the possibility to jointly estimate the yields and the two macroeconomic factors as functions of the risk factors.

6.6 Estimation Procedure and Results

In this chapter focuses on the Bundesbank regime because the ECB period is to short for the employed Kalman filter approach. The data are the same as for the previous empirical chapters. As before the data are monthly and cover the period from 1:1979 to 12:1998. The estimates of the German yield curve are gain based on the parameters of the Svensson (1994) smoothing technique. The data set comprises monthly averages of nine daily spot rates for the following maturities (in month): 1, 3, 12, 24, 36, 48, 60, 84 and 120. Because of the somewhat erratic behavior the 'Svensson estimates' of the one month and three months interest rates are substituted by the observed German interbank rates.[188] Figure 6.1 presents the time series properties of the yields (in panel (a)) and the average yield curve over the sample period (panel (b)), while Table 1 presents the summary statistics.

Table 6.1 reveals that yields are highly persistent with monthly autocorrelations above 0.96 for all maturities. The volatility drops with increasing maturity. Also yields are highly correlated along the yield curve but the correlations are not equal to one. This suggests that non-parallel shifts of the yield curve are an important feature. Indeed, the yield curve frequently changed its slope, shape and curvature and even periods of inverse yield curves can be identified. Therefore, a one-factor model is insufficient for explaining the dynamics of the German term structure of interest rates.

[187] The Taylor rule in (6.22) is the special case with $q = l = 0$, so that: $\tilde{\pi}_t = z_{\pi,t}$ and $\tilde{y}_t = z_{y,t}$. In this particular case the risk factors and the two observable macroeconomic variables match on a one to one basis and we need no explicit assumption about the dynamics of the macroeconomic variables.

[188] The study considers the money market rates as a good proxy, because the default risk on loans in the German money market can be considered to be quite low. In general, money market rates apply for unsecured loans between financial institutions and hence reflect a default risk which lead money market rates to be higher than similar bond market rates. Furthermore, in the term structure estimation the one month rate is the shortest maturity and it will be interpreted as the policy rate. The correlation between the overnight money market rate and one month rate in the data set is 0.9951.

Figure 6.1: Term Structure Dynamics 1979 - 1998

Panel (a)

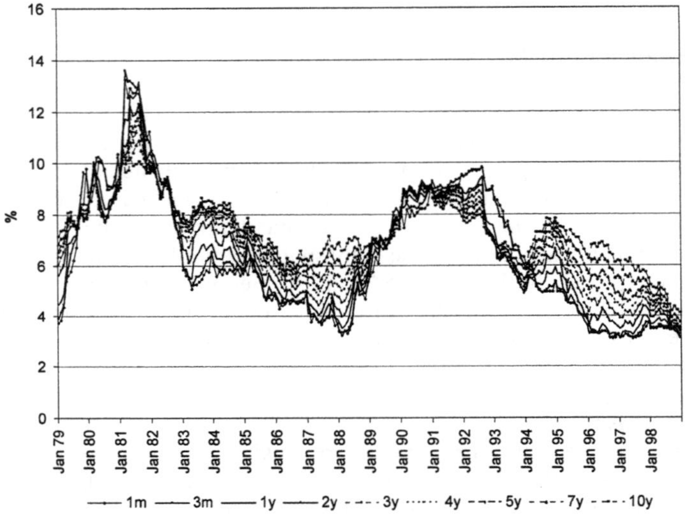

Panel (b)

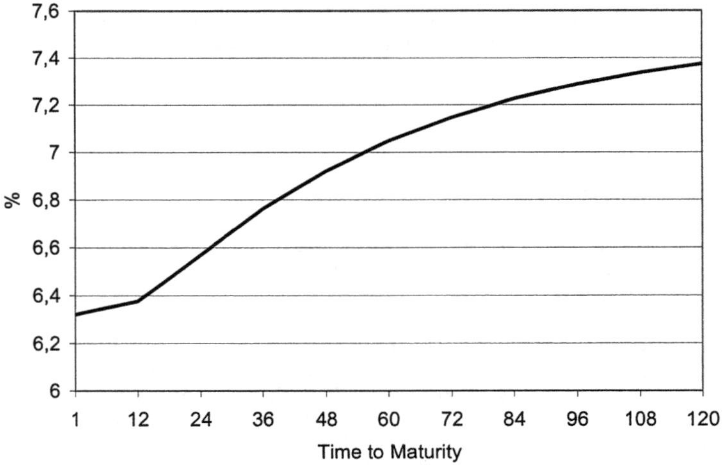

Table 6.1: Statistical Properties of German Government Bond Yields 1979-1998

Statistics Maturity:	1m	3m	12m	24m	36m	48m	60m	84m	120m
Mean	6.321	6.343	6.376	6.569	6.762	6.921	7.048	7.226	7.376
St.Dev	2.499	2.539	2.30	2.078	1.899	1.746	1.616	1.416	1.215
Skewness	0.604	0.599	0.544	0.379	0.316	0.287	0.259	0.167	0.031
Kurtosis	2.487	2.537	2.636	2.408	2.398	2.472	2.571	2.755	2.955
Autocorr.	0.982	0.984	0.982	0.980	0.978	0.976	0.973	0.968	0.960
Correlation Matrix Maturity :	1m	3m	12m	24m	36m	48m	60m	84m	120m
1m	1.0000	0.9967	0.9724	0.9399	0.9132	0.8914	0.8715	0.8319	0.7678
3m		1.0000	0.9826	0.9543	0.9294	0.9084	0.8890	0.8500	0.7870
12m			1.0000	0.9902	0.9755	0.9606	0.9453	0.9119	0.8552
24m				1.0000	0.9959	0.9872	0.9760	0.9489	0.9009
36m					1.0000	0.9974	0.9909	0.9708	0.9307
48m						1.0000	0.9980	0.9850	0.9525
60m							1.0000	0.9938	0.9689
84m								1.0000	0.9899
120m									1.0000

The data on the inflation gap is constructed using the difference of the consumer price index and the price norm that has been announced by the Bundesbank on a yearly basis as already introduced in section 3.3.[189] The output gap is based on the monthly index of industrial production. Although being aware that industrial output is more volatile than, GDP, this chapter again follow the usual practice and opt for this variable in order to obtain monthly figures. The output gap is again constructed on the basis of a linear trend. In order to avoid starting point and end point problems, the trend is computed between the longer period from 1970 through 2003.

[189] See Table 3.3 in section 3.3.

The estimation relies on a Kalman-filter-based maximum likelihood estimator.[190] This approach allows us to estimate the parameters of the model without directly observing the risk factors. However, it is suspected from the theoretical consideration of the monetary policy rules that two of the factors are connected to an inflation and an output measure through equations (6.30) and (6.31). In order to apply a Kalman filter we first have to write the model in the linear state-space form, with the measurement equation resulting from the recursive restrictions and the identification of the factors, and the transition equation resulting from the assumed dynamics of the risk factors.

In particular, in the '3-factor partly-identified' case, where two factors are linked to the inflation gap and the output gap, and the third factor is unobservable, the measurement equation is:

$$(6.32)\qquad \begin{bmatrix} i_{1,t} \\ i_{3,t} \\ \vdots \\ i_{120,t} \\ \tilde{\pi}_t \\ \tilde{y}_t \end{bmatrix} = \begin{bmatrix} a_1 \\ a_3 \\ \vdots \\ a_{120} \\ 0 \\ 0 \end{bmatrix} + \begin{bmatrix} b_{1,1} & b_{1,2} & b_{1,3} \\ b_{3,1} & b_{3,2} & b_{3,3} \\ \vdots & \vdots & \vdots \\ b_{120,1} & b_{120,2} & b_{120,3} \\ 1/(\varphi_\pi)^q & 0 & 0 \\ 0 & 1/(\varphi_y)^l & 0 \end{bmatrix} \cdot \begin{bmatrix} z_{\pi,t} \\ z_{y,t} \\ z_{3,t} \end{bmatrix} + \begin{bmatrix} v_{1,t} \\ v_{3,t} \\ \vdots \\ v_{120,t} \\ v_{\pi,t} \\ v_{y,t} \end{bmatrix},$$

with $a_i = A_i / i$ and $b_{i,j} = B_{i,j} / i$, where the index i represents the number of months to maturity (i = 1, 3, 12, 24, 36, 48, 60, 84, 120) and j the index of the (up to three) risk factors. Expression (6.32) shows that a system of equations is estimated, i.e. a panel for different yields to maturity, with the additional interpretation that the first equation is the monetary policy reaction function of the central bank. Or, from a different angle, we can interpret the present exercise as estimating a monetary policy rule with the additional restriction of the absence of arbitrage in financial markets. In shorter notation we might write the measurement system as:

$$(6.33)\qquad Y_t = A + B \cdot Z_t + v_t .$$

The corresponding transition equation is represented by:

[190] The Kalman filter approach has gained popularity in the affine term structure literature. See, for example, Duan and Simonato (1995), Lund (1997), Gong and Remolona (1997), Geyer und Pichler (1998), Babbs and Nowman (1999), De Jong (2000), Bolder (2001) and Cassola and Luis (2003).

$$(6.34)\qquad \begin{bmatrix} z_{\pi,t+1} \\ z_{y,t+1} \\ z_{3,t+1} \end{bmatrix} = \begin{bmatrix} \varphi_\pi & 0 & 0 \\ 0 & \varphi_y & 0 \\ 0 & 0 & \varphi_3 \end{bmatrix} \cdot \begin{bmatrix} z_{\pi,t} \\ z_{y,t} \\ z_{3,t} \end{bmatrix} + \begin{bmatrix} \sigma_\pi & 0 & 0 \\ 0 & \sigma_y & 0 \\ 0 & 0 & \sigma_3 \end{bmatrix} \cdot \begin{bmatrix} \varepsilon_{\pi,t+1} \\ \varepsilon_{y,t+1} \\ \varepsilon_{3,t+1} \end{bmatrix}$$

or, in short:

$$(6.35)\qquad Z_{t+1} = F \cdot Z_t + u_{t+1}.$$

In standard linear state-space models, no restrictions link the measurement and the transition equation. In this particular setup, however, the measurement equation comes from the transition equation and the no-arbitrage condition, that together yield the recursive restrictions on the factor loadings. Together with our identification of two risk factors the latter constitutes the measurement equation.

In the '2-factor identified' case, the state-space system is written without the third factor leaving the identification for the two remaining factors unchanged. Additionally, a '2-factor non-identified' case that resembles a traditional affine term structure model with only unobserved factors is estimated. The exact Kalman filter algorithm used in the paper is described in Appendix H.[191]

Table 6.2 presents the results of the three specifications. The first specification is the '2-factor non-identified' case. The second is the 2-factor model with both factors being identified with the expected inflation and output gap respectively ('2-factor identified'). Since the '2-factor identified' specification might be very restrictive, also the '3-factor partly-identified' specification is estimated in which two factors are identified as in the previous case and the third factor being unobserved. Both identified specifications set q = 12 and l = 3 as this was already the case in the benchmark estimation of the forward-looking specification of the monetary policy rule.[192]

[191] The algorithm was performed by numerical optimization using Matlab codes. The starting values that are needed for the optimization were obtained by minimizing the sum of squared residuals between the estimated mean yields and the mean observed yields setting the value of the factors to zero (which also reflects their long-run mean by definition).

[192] Versions with no forward looking behavior (i.e. $q = l = 0$) were also estimated, but the fit was not as good as for the forward-looking specifications.

Table 6.2: Parameter Estimates of the Gaussian Term Structure Model

	2F_non_ident	2F_ident	3F_ident
$\varphi_1(\varphi_y)$	0.87 (0.0025)	0.82 (0.0047)	0.98 (0.001)
$\varphi_2(\varphi_\pi)$	0.99 (0.0004)	0.98 (0.0003)	0.99 (0.002)
φ_3	–	–	0.89 (0.0058)
$\sigma_1(\sigma_y)$	0.006 (0.0001)	0.0158 (0.0002)	0.00406 (0.0001)
$\sigma_2(\sigma_\pi)$	0.0016 (0.0001)	0.0007 (0.00001)	0.00045 (0.0001)
σ_3	–	–	0.00286 (0.0001)
$\lambda_1(\lambda_y)$	-1.364 (0.2456)	7.19 (0.2317)	1.743 (1.55)
$\lambda_2(\lambda_\pi)$	-52.16 (0.6664)	-113.89 (0.8467)	- 139.39 (4.69)
λ_3	–	–	-3.688 (4.81)
δ	0.0038 (0.0001)	0.0043 (0.0001)	0.0043 (0.0001)
$\gamma_1(\gamma_y)$	1.363 (0.0287)	0.092 (0.0027)	0.088 (0.0153)
$\gamma_2(\gamma_\pi)$	0.934 (0.0240)	2.374 (0.0369)	1.764 (0.0469)
γ_3	–	–	2.566 (0.116)

Standard errors in parentheses

Especially in the '3-factor partly-identified' specification, the reaction coefficients are close to the levels that were obtained in the estimation of the forward-looking monetary policy rule for the Bundesbank in section 3.3. In particular, the result has to be compared to Regression X from Table 3.4. This regression resulted in reaction coefficients for the inflation gap of 1.68 and for the output gap of 0.09, which are both very close to the ones obtained with the Kalman filter in Table 6.2 (1.764 and 0.088). This indicates that the estimated policy rule is consistent with the absence of arbitrage opportunities in financial markets. The reaction coefficient, the volatility and the coefficient of mean reversion of the third unobserved factor are also significant but its associated market price of risk is not.[193] This suggests that the risk premia in the German term structure of interest rates mainly stems from the inflation and the output risk. Note that only the inflation risk price is negative while the output risk price is positive.

Figure 6.2: Estimated Term Structure Dynamics

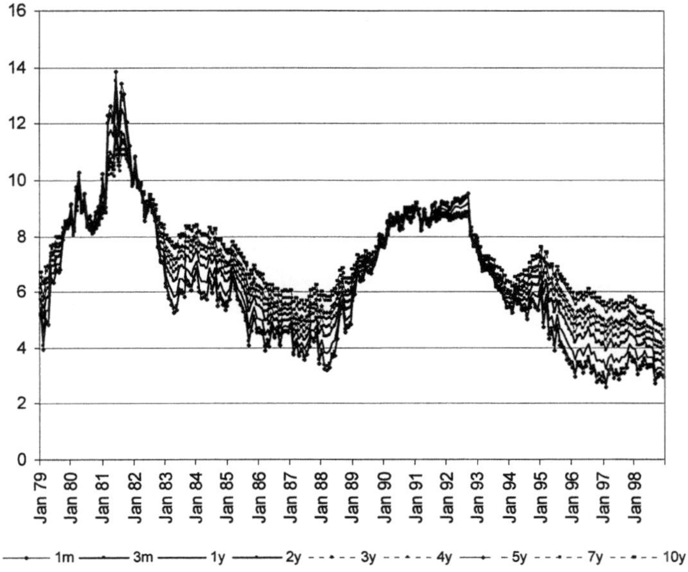

[193] If the third factor includes the smoothing behavior, this result seems quite natural because there is little risk associated with this factor.

The mean-reversion coefficients of inflation and output are quite high but close to the coefficients that can be obtained in a pure AR(1) regression of both. These values for the sample are 0.97 (0.91) for the inflation gap (output gap) with a R^2 of 0.93 (0.83). This suggests that my identification based on a simple AR(1) process is not too far from reality and seems consistent with the data.

Figure 6.2 (on the previous page) shows the estimated dynamics of the term structure for the preferred '3-factor partly-identified' case. It reveals that the model captures the overall movement in the term structure that is shown in Figure 6.1(a) very well.

Figure 6.3 (on the next page) shows the estimated and observed yields for three particular maturities that represent the short end, the middle range and the long end of the yield curve. It shows that the model especially has a good fit at the middle range and the short end. This might not surprise since time-constant (i.e. only maturity dependent) risk premia are modeled.

Figure 6.3: Observed and Estimated Yields for Particular Maturities

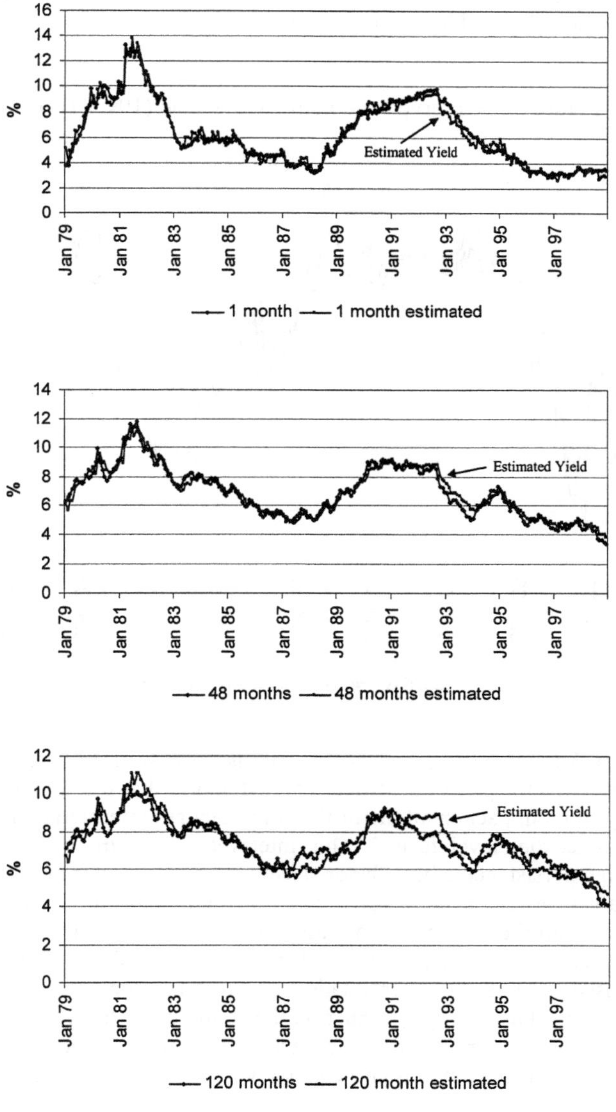

Figure 6.4 answers the question whether the model is able to capture the periods of an inverse term structure of interest rates. It shows the observed and the estimated spread defined as the yield of 10-year bonds minus the yield of one-month bonds. Again the overall fit is good.

Figure 6.4: Observed and Estimated Spread (10y – 1m)

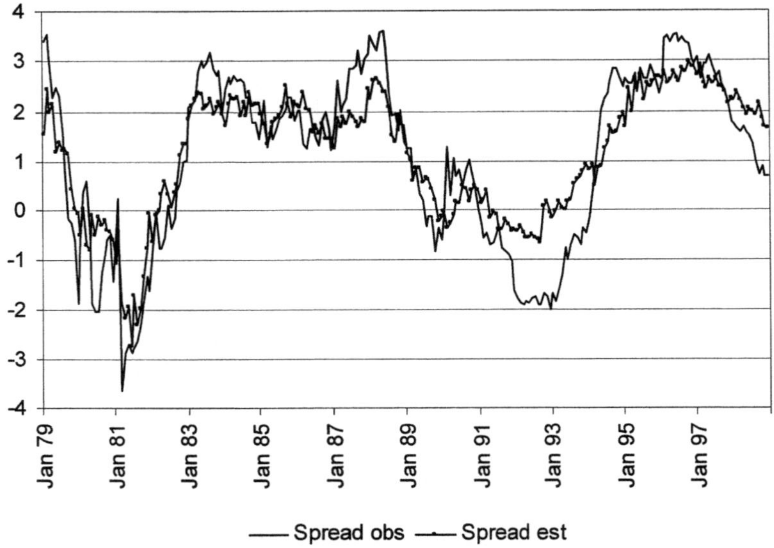

Figure 6.5 (next page) presents the loadings that are associated with each factor in the '3-factor partly-identified' case. It shows that the 'inflation factor' has a nearly equal impact on all maturities. In a standard interpretation we would consider this as the 'level factor'. This interpretation seems quite reasonable given the high persistence of this factor as well as the fact that it incorporates the inflation target of the central bank, and thus the long-run expectations of inflation. Through the Fisher relation, this results in a long-run level of interest rates. The impact of the 'output factor' declines stronger along the yield curve. This is consistent with the interpretation as the 'curvature factor'. The third unobserved factor has its major impact on the short end of the yield curve. This is in line with the third 'smoothing factor' in monetary policy rules that incorporate interest rate smoothing behavior which has its mean impact on the

short end of the yield curve. Independent of its precise interpretation, the third factor can be considered as the 'slope factor'. [194]

Figure 6.5: The Factor Loadings

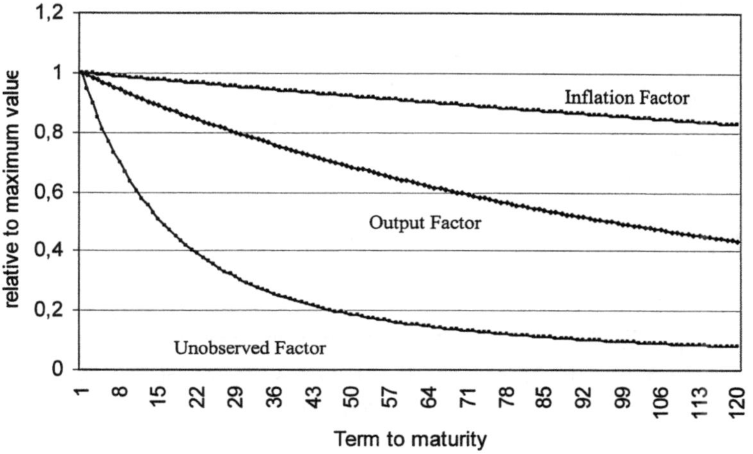

From (6.20) we see that the monetary policy reaction coefficients also influence the factor loadings. However, they do not influence the relative impact of a shock to the particular risk factor along the yield curve as indicated in Figure 5. The strength of the policy reaction to a given shock rather determines the absolute impact of a shock on the yield curve. For instance, a stronger output response *ceteris paribus* leads to greater importance of the 'curvature factor' relative to the other factors, meaning that it is more likely that the yield curve changes its curvature. In this sense, monetary policy reaction determines to what extent given shocks alter the yield curve. Figure 6 shows the change in interest rates along the yield curve due to a shock to the output factor of the size of one standard deviation. The stronger the policy reaction to this given shock is, the greater is the absolute difference between the short rate and the long rate change, thus, the higher the effect on the curvature of the yield curve.

[194] We could also interpret this factor as capturing the forecast error that emerges in the error term of the forward looking specification of the rule.

Figure 6.6: The Influence of the Policy Reaction

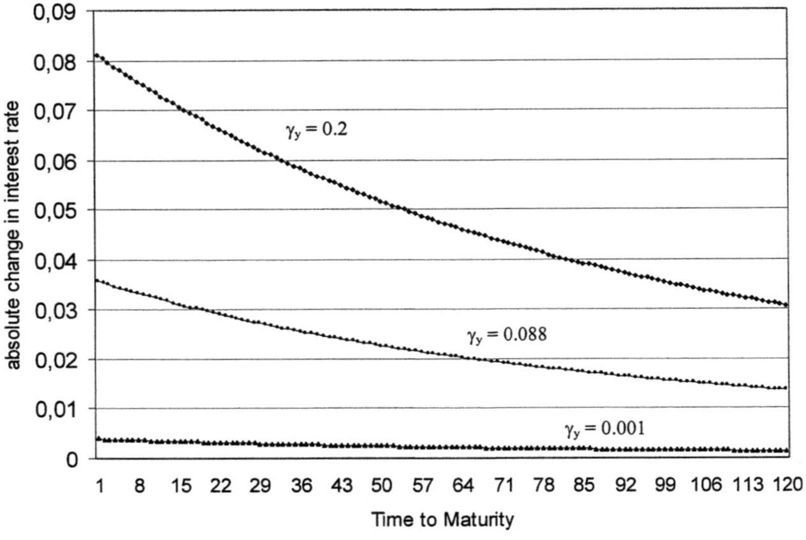

In sum, the analysis in this chapter shows that it is possible to estimate monetary policy reaction functions which are compatible with the absence of arbitrage. With this kind of estimation, the information of the whole term structure is included. A comparison with the results from the GMM estimations in chapters 3 and 5 indicates that the observed reaction coefficients are of about the same size.

Appendix F

Derivation of the Recursive Restrictions

The derivation starts with writing the expression (6.1) in logs (for convenience I let the bond in time t mature in n+1 periods):

(F.1) $$p_{n+1,t} = \log\left(E\left[M_{t+1}P_{n,t+1}\right]\right).$$

With the assumption of joint log-normality of bond prices and the nominal pricing kernel and using the statistical principle that if $\log X \sim N(\mu,\sigma^2)$ then $\log E(X) = \mu + \frac{\sigma^2}{2}$, it follows that:

(F.2) $$p_{n+1,t} = E_t\left[m_{t+1} + p_{n,t+1}\right] + \frac{1}{2}Var_t\left[m_{t+1} + p_{n,t+1}\right].$$

From (6.8) and (6.10) we get

(F.3) $$m_{t+1} + p_{n,t+1} = -\left(\delta + \gamma' Z_t + \lambda V(Z_t)^{1/2}\varepsilon_{t+1}\right) - A_n - B_n' Z_{t+1}.$$

We can substitute for Z_{t+1} from equation (6.7) and after sorting terms we arrive at the following expression:

(F.4) $$m_{t+1} + p_{n,t+1} = -(A_n) + \delta + B_n'(1-\Phi)\cdot\theta - \left(\gamma' + B_n'\Phi\right)\cdot Z_t$$
$$-\left(\lambda' + B_n'\right)\cdot V(Z_t)^{1/2}\varepsilon_{t+1},$$

so that

(F.5) $$E_t\left[m_{t+1} + p_{n,t+1}\right] = -(A_n) + \delta + B_n'(1-\Phi)\cdot\theta - \left(\gamma' + B_n'\Phi\right)\cdot Z_t,$$

(F.6) $$Var_t\left[m_{t+1} + p_{n,t+1}\right] = \left(\lambda' + B_n'\right)^2\cdot V(Z_t).$$

Substituting these moments into (F.2) and recognizing the typical diagonal elements in the variance-covariance matrix we have after sorting the terms:

(F.7)
$$-p_{n+1,t} = A_n + \delta + B_n'(1-\Phi)\cdot\theta - \frac{1}{2}\left(\sum_{j=1}^{k}\left(\lambda_j + B_{j,n}\right)^2 \cdot \alpha_j\right) + \left[\gamma' + B_n'\Phi - \frac{1}{2}\sum_{j=1}^{k}\left(\lambda_j + B_{j,n}\right)^2 \cdot \beta_j'\right]\cdot Z_t.$$

Matching the variables in order to verify that

(F.8)
$$-p_{n+1,t} = A_{n+1} + B_{n+1}' \cdot Z_t$$

it must be that

(F.9)
$$A_{n+1} = A_n + \delta + B_n'(I-\Phi)\cdot\theta - \frac{1}{2}\sum_{j=1}^{k}\left(\lambda_j + B_{j,n}\right)^2 \cdot \alpha_j$$

(F.10)
$$B_{n+1}' = \left(\gamma' + B_n'\Phi\right) - \frac{1}{2}\sum_{j=1}^{k}\left(\lambda_j + B_{j,n}\right)^2 \cdot \beta_j'.$$

The last two expressions correspond to the recursive restrictions stated in the text. The recursive restrictions of the Gaussian version in section 6.4 of the paper follow by the same steps, or can be directly obtained by substituting the parameter restrictions (6.16) into the just derived general restrictions.

Appendix G

Derivation of the Term Premia

The term premia is defined as the difference between the 'holding period return' and the one-period interest rate:

(G.1) $$\Lambda_{n,t} = E_t p_{n,t+1} - p_{n+1,t} - i_{1,t} .$$

The individual elements of (G.1) are:

(G.2) $$E_t p_{n,t+1} = -A_n - B_n' \cdot E_t[Z_{t+1}] = -A_n - B_n'(I - \Phi) \cdot \theta - B_n' \Phi \cdot Z_t$$

(G.3) $$-p_{n+1,t} = A_{n+1} + B_{n+1}' \cdot Z_t$$

and

(6.14)/(G.4) $$i_{1,t} = \delta - \frac{1}{2}\sum_{j=1}^{k} \lambda_j^2 \cdot \alpha_j + \left(\gamma' - \frac{1}{2}\sum_{j=1}^{k} \lambda_j^2 \cdot \beta_j'\right) \cdot Z_t .$$

Substituting the recursive restrictions (6.12) and (6.13) into (G.3) and combining the elements according to the definition (G.1) yields after rearranging:

$$\Lambda_{n,t} = -\frac{1}{2}\sum_{j=1}^{k}(\lambda_j + B_{j,n})^2 \cdot \alpha_j - \left[\frac{1}{2}\sum_{j=1}^{k}(\lambda_j + B_{j,n})^2 \cdot \beta_j'\right] \cdot Z_t + \frac{1}{2}\sum_{j=1}^{k}\lambda_j^2 \alpha_j + \dots$$
$$\dots + \left[\frac{1}{2}\sum_{j=1}^{k}\lambda_j^2 \beta_j'\right] \cdot Z_t$$

Solving the binomials and sorting terms leads to the expression of the term premia in the text:

(G.5) $$\Lambda_{n,t} = -\sum_{j=1}^{k}\left(\lambda_j B_{j,n} + \frac{B_{j,n}^2}{2}\right) \cdot \alpha_j - \sum_{j=1}^{k}\left(\lambda_j B_{j,n} + \frac{B_{j,n}^2}{2}\right) \cdot \beta_j' \cdot Z_t ,$$

which is equivalent to (6.15) in the text given the particular structure of the variance-covariance matrix.

Appendix H

The Kalman Filter

The Kalman Filter recursively computes the optimal estimate of a state variable at the moment t based on the information available up to period t-1. Unknown parameters are usually estimated by a maximum likelihood procedure. This appendix describes how the Kalman Filter is used in the paper.[195] In order to perform the Kalman Filter the model has to be written in state space form, as in equations (6.2) and (6.4). The first equation that builds on the recursive restrictions is the observation or measurement equation that has the following general form:

(H.1) $$Y_t = A + B \cdot Z_t + v_t,$$

where $v_t \sim N(0,R)$.

The state or transition equation has the following form:

(H.2) $$Z_{t+1} = C + F \cdot Z_t + u_{t+1},$$

where $u_{t+1} \sim N(0,Q)$.

The Kalman Filter procedure generally consists of five steps, that are described next:

1. Initializing the state vector

The first step of the Kalman Filter is the initializing of the state vector Z_t at t=1 to start the recursion. $\hat{Z}_0$ can be seen as a guess concerning the value of Z using all information up to t=0. P_0 is the uncertainty about the prior guess. Using $\hat{Z}_0$ and P_0 in (H.2), the optimal estimator for Z_1 is given by:

(H.3) $$\hat{S}_{1|0} = C + F \cdot \hat{S}_0.$$

---

[195] The Kalman Filter and the maximum likelihood estimations were carried out using Matlab codes. Details on the Kalman Filter can be found in Hamilton (1994, ch. 13).

The associated mean squared error (MSE) matrix is

$$\text{(H.4)} \qquad \begin{aligned} P_{1|0} &\equiv E\left[(Z_1 - \hat{Z}_{1|0})(Z_1 - \hat{Z}_{1|0})'\right] \\ &= FP_{1|0}F' + Q. \end{aligned}$$

If the eigenvalues of F are all inside the unit circle, the process for Z_t in (H.2) is covariance-stationary. In this case the Kalman Filter iteration can be started with $\hat{Z}_{1|0} = 0$ and $P_{1|0}$ whose elements expressed as a column vector are (Hamilton, 1994, p. 378):

$$vec(P_{1|0}) = \left[I_{k^2} - (F \otimes F)\right]^{-1} \cdot vec(Q),$$

with k being the number of unobservable factors.

2. Forecasting the measurement vector Y_t

Given the starting values $\hat{Z}_{1|0}$ and $P_{1|0}$ the next step is to calculate the respective values for the following dates. Generalizing the equations (H.3) and (H.4), we have the following prediction equations:

$$\text{(H.5)} \qquad \hat{Z}_{t|t-1} = C + F \cdot \hat{Z}_{t-1} \qquad \text{and}$$

$$\text{(H.6)} \qquad P_{t|t-1} = FP_{t|t-1}F' + Q.$$

The forecast of Y_t can, thus, directly be obtained from (H.1):

$$\text{(H.7)} \qquad \hat{Y}_{t|t-1} = A + B \cdot \hat{Z}_{t|t-1},$$

with the following forecast MSE:

$$\text{(H.8)} \qquad E\left[(Y_t - \hat{Y}_{t|t-1})(Y_t - \hat{Y}_{t|t-1})'\right] = BP_{t|t-1}B' + R.$$

3. Updating the inference about the state vector

Since Z_t and Y_t are related by the measurement equation, the knowledge of the value Y_t can be used to update $\hat{Z}_{t|t-1}$. In order to perform this, we need to characterize the joint distribution of the observation and the state vector. Therefore, we need to compute the conditional covariance between the two forecast errors:

(H.9) $$E\left[(Y_t - \hat{Y}_{t|t-1})(Z_t - \hat{Z}_{t|t-1})'\right] = BP_{t|t-1}.$$

Using equations (H.7), (H.8) and (H.9), the conditional distribution of the vector (Y_t, Z_t) given the information I_{t-1} is:

(H.10) $$\begin{bmatrix} Y_t | I_{t-1} \\ Z_t | I_{t-1} \end{bmatrix} \sim N\left(\begin{bmatrix} A + B\hat{Z}_{t|t-1} \\ \hat{Z}_{t|t-1} \end{bmatrix}, \begin{bmatrix} BP_{t|t-1}B' + R & BP_{t|t-1} \\ P_{t|t-1}B' & P_{t|t-1} \end{bmatrix} \right).$$

From (H. 10) we obtain the following updating equations:[196]

(H.11) $$\hat{Z}_{t|t} = \hat{Z}_{t|t-1} + P_{t|t-1}B'(BP_{t|t-1}B' + R)^{-1}\left[Y_t - (A + B\hat{Z}_{t|t-1})\right]$$

and

(H.12) $$P_{t|t} = P_{t|t-1} - P_{t|t-1}B'(BP_{t|t-1}B' + R)^{-1}BP_{t|t-1}.$$

4. Forecasting the state vector

After estimating $\hat{Z}_{t|t}$ and $P_{t|t}$, we can proceed with the estimation of $\hat{Z}_{t|t+1}$ and $P_{t|t+1}$. Using equations (H.5) and (H.6), we get:

(H.13) $$\hat{Z}_{t+1|t} = C + F\hat{Z}_{t|t} \quad \text{and}$$

[196] I made use of the following general rule: if two variables X_1 and X_2 have a joint normal conditional distribution given by $\begin{bmatrix} X_1 \\ X_2 \end{bmatrix} \sim N\left(\begin{bmatrix} \mu_1 \\ \mu_2 \end{bmatrix}, \begin{bmatrix} \Delta_{11} & \Delta_{12} \\ \Delta_{21} & \Delta_{22} \end{bmatrix} \right)$, then the distribution of $X_2 | X_1$ is $N \sim (m, \Sigma)$, with $m = \mu_2 + \Delta_{21}\Delta_{11}^{-1}(X_1 - \mu_1)$ and $\Sigma = \Delta_{22} - \Delta_{21}\Delta_{11}^{-1}\Delta_{12}$.

(H.14) $$P_{t+1|t} = FP_{t|t}F' + Q.$$

5. Maximum likelihood estimation of parameters

The log-likelihood function is built up recursively

(H.15) $$\log L(\widetilde{Y}_T) = \sum_{t=1}^{T} \log f(Y_t | I_{t-1}),$$

with

$$f(Y_t | I_{t-1}) = (2\pi)^{-n/2} \left| BP_{t|t-1}B' + R \right|^{-1/2} \cdot \ldots$$

$$\ldots \cdot \exp\left\{ -\frac{1}{2}(Y_t - A - B\hat{Z}_{t|t-1})'(BP_{t|t-1}B' + R)^{-1}(Y_t - A - B\hat{Z}_{t|t-1}) \right\}$$

where n is here the dimension of the vector Y. The parameters of the measurement and the state equations can then be obtained by a numerical maximization of the likelihood function. The outlined steps of the Kalman filter are presented graphically in Figure H.1 on the next page. Finally, the standard errors can be numerically computed on estimates of the inverse of the Hessian matrix at the convergence point. See Judd (1998) for the so-called 'finite difference method'.

Figure H.1: The Kalman Filter: An Overview

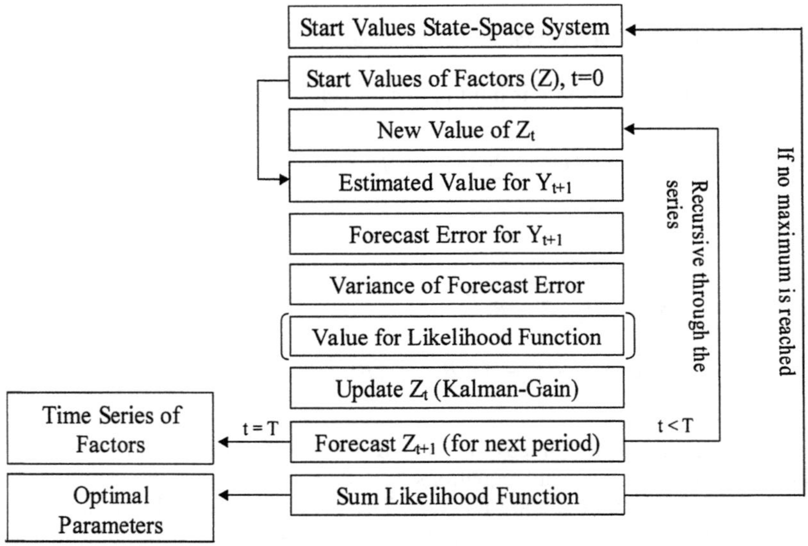

References

Altig, D, Christiano, L. J., Eichenbaum, M. and J. Linde (2002), Technology shocks and aggregate fluctuations, mimeograph, Northwestern University, Chicago.

Andolfatto, D. (1996), Business cycles and labor-market search, *American Economic Review*, Vol. 86, 112-132.

Ang, A. and M. Piazessi (2003), A no-arbitrage vector autoregression of term structure dynamics with macroeconomic and latent variables, *Journal of Monetary Economics* Vol. 50, 745-787.

Aït-Sahalia, Y. (1996), Testing continuous time models of the spot interest rate, *Review of Financial Studies*, Vol. 9, 385-426.

Arnold, L.G. (2002), Business Cycle Theory, Oxford University Press, Oxford.

Babbs, S. H. and K. B. Nowman (1999), Kalman Filtering of Generalized Vasicek Term Structure Models, *Journal of Financial and Quantitative Analysis*, 34, 115-130.

Backus, D., Foresi, S. and C. Telmer (1998a), Discrete Models of Bond Pricing, NBER Working Paper No. 6736, Cambridge/MA.

Backus, D., Foresi, S. and C. Telmer (1998b), Affine Models of Currency Pricing: Accounting for the Forward Premium Anomaly, mimeo, Stern School of Business.

Balduzzi, P., Das, S. and S. Foresi (1998), The central tendency: A second factor in bond yields, *Review of Economics and Statistics*, Vol. 80, 60-72.

Balduzzi, P., Das, S. and S. Foresi (1996), A simple approach to three-factor affine term structure models, *Journal of Fixed Income*, Vol. 6, 43-53.

Ball, L. (1999), Efficient Rules for Monetary Policy, *International Finance*, Vol. 2, 63-83.

Barro, R. J. and D. Gordon (1983), A Positive Theory of Monetary Policy in a Natural Rate Model, *Journal of Political Economy*, Vol. 91, 589-610.

Basu, S., J. Fernald and M. Kimball (2004), Are Technology Improvements Contractionary?, Working Paper 2004-20, Federal Reserve Bank of Chicago.

Batini, N. and A. G. Haldane (1999), Forward-Looking Rules for Monetary Policy, in Taylor, J. B. (ed.), *Monetary Policy Rules*, University of Chicago Press, Chicago, 157-92.

Bayoumi, T. (2004), GEM: A New International Macroeconomic Model, Occasional Paper No. 239, International Monetary Fund, Washington/DC.

Beetsma, R. and H. Jensen (2002), Monetary and fiscal policy interaction in a micro-founded model of a monetary union, *ECB Working Paper*, no. 166, European Central Bank, Frankfurt.

Bernanke, B. S., Reinhart, V. R. and B. Sack (2004), Monetary Policy Alternatives at the Zero Bound: An Empirical Assessment, *Brookings Papers on Economic Activity*, 2/2004, 1-100.

Bernard, H. and S. Gerlach, (1996), Does the Term Structure Predict Recessions? The International Evidence, Bank of International Settlements Working paper No. 37, Basle.

Black, F. and M. Scholes (1973), The Pricing of Options and Corporate Liabilities, *Journal of Political Economy*, Vol. 81, 637-654.

Blanchard, O. (1997), Comment on Goodfriend and King, *NBER Macroeconomics Annual 1997*, 289-293.

Blanchard, O. and N. Kiyotaki (1987), Monopolistic competition and the effects of aggregate demand, *American Economic Review*, Vol. 77, 647-666.

Bolder, D. J. (2001), Affine Term-Structure Models: Theory and Implementation, Bank of Canada Working Paper 2001-15, Ottawa.

Bomfim, A. N. (2001), Measuring Equilibrium Real Interest Rates: What Can we Learn from Yields on Indexed Bonds?, Working Paper, Board of Governors of the Federal Reserve System, Washington/DC.

Bühler, A. and H. Zimmermann, A Statistical Analysis of the Term Structure of Interest Rates in Switzerland and Germany, *Journal of Fixed Income*, Vol. 6, 55-67.

Brainard, W. (1967), Uncertainty and the Effectiveness of Policy, *American Economic Review*, Vol. 57, 411-425.

Buiter, W. and N. Panigirtzoglou, (1999), Liquidity Traps: How to Avoid Them and How to Escape Them, NBER Working Paper No. 7245, Cambridge/MA.

Bullard, J. and K. Mitra (2000), Determinacy, learnability, and monetary policy inertia, Working Paper no. 2000-030, Federal Reserve Bank of St. Louis.

Bullard, J. and K. Mitra (2002), Learning About Monetary Policy Rules, *Journal of Monetary Economics*, Vol. 49, 1105-1129.

Calvo, G. (1983), Staggered prices in a utility-maximizing framework, *Journal of Monetary Economics*, Vol. 12, 383-398.

Campbell, J. Y. (1995), Some Lessons from the Yield Curve, Journal of Economic Perspectives, Vol. 9, 129-52.

Campbell, J. Y., Lo, A. W. and A. C. MacKinlay (1997), The Econometrics of Financial Markets, Princeton University Press, Princeton/NJ.

Canabarro, E. (1995), Where Do One-Factor Interest Rate Models Fail?, *The Journal of Fixed Income*, Vol. 6, 31-52.

Canzoneri, M.B., Cumby, R. E. and B.T. Diba (2002a), Recent developments in the macroeconomic stabilization literature: is price stability a good stabilization strategy?, mimeograph, Georgetown University, Washington.

Canzoneri, M. B., Cumby, R. E. and B. T. Diba, (2002b), The need for international policy coordination: what's old, what's new, what's yet to come?, *NBER Working Paper*, no. 8765, Cambridge/MA, forthcoming *Journal of International Economics*.

Canzoneri, M. B., Cumby, R. E. and B. T. Diba (2005), How Do Monetary and Fiscal Policy Interact in the European Union?, *NBER Working Paper*, no. 11055, Cambridge/MA.

Cassola, N. and J. B. Luis (2003), A Two-factor Model of the German Term Structure of Interest Rates, *Applied Financial Economics*, Vol. 13, 783-806.

Chan, K.-C., Karolyi, G., Longstaff, F. and A. Sanders (1992), An Empirical Comparison of Alternative Models of the Short-Term Interest Rate, *Journal of Finance*, Vol. 47, 1209-1227.

Chari, V. V., Kehoe, P. J. and E. McGrattan, (2000), Sticky price models of the business cycle: can the contract multiplier solve the persistence problem?, *Econometrica*, Vol. 68, 1151-1179.

Christiano, L. J., Eichenbaum, M. and C.L. Evans (1997), Sticky price and limited participation models: a comparison, *European Economic Review*, Vol. 41, 1201-1249.

Christiano, L., Eichenbaum, M. and C. Evans (1999), Monetary Policy Shocks: What Have We Learned and to What End?, in: Woodford, M. and J. B. Taylor (eds.), *Handbook of Macroeconomics*, North Holland.

Christiano, L.J., Eichenbaum, M. and C.L. Evans (2001), Nominal Rigidities and the Dynamic Effects of a Shock to Monetary Policy, *NBER Working Paper, no.* 8403, Cambridge/MA.

Christiano, L. and M. Rostagno, (2001), Money Growth Monitoring and the Taylor Rule, NBER Working Paper 8539, Cambridge/MA.

Christiano, L.J., Vigfusson, R. and M. Eichenbaum (2004), The response of hours to a technology shock: evidence based on direct measures of technology, *Journal of the European Economic Association*, Vol. 2, 381-395.

Clarida, R., Galí, J. and M. Gertler (1998), Monetary policy rules in practice: Some international evidence, *European Economic Review*, Vol. 42, 1033-1067.

Clarida, R., Galí, J. and M. Gertler (1999), The science of monetary policy: a new Keynesian perspective, *Journal of Economic Literature*, Vol. 37, 1661-1707.

Clarida, R., Galí, J. and M. Gertler (2000), Macroeconomic Policy Rules and Macroeconomic Stability: Evidence and Some Theory, *Quarterly Journal of Economics*, Vol. 115, 147–180.

Clarida, R. J., Galí, J. and M. Gertler (2001), Optimal monetary policy in open versus closed economies: an integrated approach, *American Economic Review* (Papers and Proceedings), Vol. 79, 248-252.

Clarida, R., Galí, J. and M. Gertler (2002), A simple framework for international monetary policy analysis, *Journal of Monetary Economics*, Vol. 49, 879-904.

Cook, T. and T. Hahn, (1989), The Effect of Changes in the Federal Funds Rate Target on Market Interest Rates in the 1970s, *Journal of Monetary Economics*, Vol. 24, 331-51.

Cooley, T. F. (1995), Frontiers in Business Cycle Research, Princeton University Press, Princeton.

Cooley, T. F. and G. D. Hansen (1989), The inflation tax in a real business cycle model, *American Economic Review*, Vol. 79, 733-746.

Cox, J., Ingersoll, J. and S. Ross (1985), A Theory of the Term Structure of Interest Rates, *Econometrica*, Vol. 53, 385-407.

Culbertson, J. M. (1957), The Term Structure of Interest Rates, *Quarterly Journal of Economics*, Vol. 71, 485-517.

Dai, Q. and K. Singleton (2000), Specification Analysis of Affine Term Structure Models, *Journal of Finance*, Vol. 55, 1943-1978.

De Jong, F. (2000), Time Series and Cross-section Information in Affine Term-Structure Models, *Journal of Business & Economic Statistics*, Vol. 18, 300-314.

Deutsche Bundesbank (1999), Taylor Interest Rate and Monetary Conditions Index, Monthly Report April 1999, 47-63.

Dewachter, H., and K. Maes (2000), Fitting Correlations Within and Between Bond Markets, Working Paper, KU Leuven CES DP 00.05.

Diebold, F. X., Piazzesi, M. and G. D. Rudebusch (2005), Modeling Bond Yields in Finance and Macroeconomics, NBER Workings Paper No. 11089, Cambridge/MA.

Duan, J. C. and J. G. Simonato (1995), Estimating and Testing Exponential-Affine Term Structure Models by Kalman Filter, working paper, Centre Universitaire de Decherche et analyze des Organizations (CIRANO).

Duffee, G. R. (2002), Term Premia and Interest Rate Forecasts in Affine Models, *Journal of Finance*, Vol. 57, 405-443.

Duffie, D. and R. Kan (1996), A yield factor model of interest rates, *Mathematical Finance*, Vol. 6, 379-406.

Eggertsson, G. B. (2003), How to Fight Deflation in a Liquidity Trap: Committing to Being Irresponsible, IMF Working Paper, WP/03/64, Washington/DC.

Ehrmann, M. and F. Smets, (2001), Uncertain Potential Output: Implications for Monetary Policy, European Central Bank Working Paper, Frankfurt.

Eijffinger, S., Schaling, E. and Verhagen, W. (2000), The Term Structure of Interest Rates and Inflation Forecast Targeting, CEPR Discussion Paper No. 2375, London.

Erceg, C., Henderson, D. and A. Levin (2000), Optimal monetary policy with staggered wage and price setting, *Journal of Monetary Economics*, Vol. 46, 281-313.

Estrella, A. and J. C. Fuhrer (1999), Are 'deep' Parameters Stable? The Lucas Critique as an Empirical Hypothesis, Working Paper no. 99-4, Federal Reserve Bank of Boston.

Estrella, A. and J. C. Fuhrer (2002), Dynamic Inconsistencies: Counterfactual Implications of a Class of Rational Expectations Models, *American Economic Review*, Vol. 92, 1013-28.

Estrella, A. and F. S. Mishkin, (1995), The Term Structure of interest Rate and its Role in Monetary Policy for the European Central Bank, NBER Working Paper 5279, Cambridge/MA.

European Central Bank (2001), Issues Related to Monetary Policy Rules, Monthly Bulletin, October, 37-50.

European Central (Bank 2003), The Outcome of the ECB's Evaluation of its Monetary Policy Strategy, Monthly Bulletin, June, 79-92.

European Central Bank (2004), Monetary Analysis in Real Time, Monthly Bulletin, October, 43-66.

Fukao, M. (2003), Financial Strains and the Zero Lower Bound: the Japanese Experience, mimeo, Keio University.

Faust, J., Rogers, J. H., and Wright, J. H. (2001), An empirical Comparison of the Bundesbank and the ECB Monetary Policy Rules, International Finance Discussion Papers, No. 690.

Fendel, R. (2004a), New Directions in Stabilization Policies, *Banca Nazionale del Lavoro Quarterly Review*, no. 231 (December 2004), 365-394.

Fendel, R. (2004b), Grenzen und Perspektiven der Verwendung geldpolitischer Regeln, *Perspektiven der Wirtschaftspolitik*, Vol. 5, 169-192.

Fendel, R. and M. Frenkel, (2004), Deflation and the Zero Lower Bound on Nominal Interest Rates, *Financial Markets and Portfolio Management*, Vol. 18, 160-180.

Fendel, R. and M. Frenkel, (2005a), Five Years of European Single Monetary Policy: Is the ECB Rule-Based?, under resubmission *Contemporary Economic Policy*.

Fendel, R. and M. Frenkel, M. (2005b), Taking the European Central Bank to the Data, Zeitschrift für Wirtschaftspolitik, Vol. 54, 101-114.

Fourçans, A. and R. Vranceanu, (2004), The ECB interest rate rule under the Duisenberg presidency, *European Journal of Political Economy*, Vol. 20, 579-595.

Francis, N. and V. Ramey (2001), Is the technology-driven real business cycle hypothesis dead? Shocks and aggregate fluctuations revisited, mimeograph, University of California at San Diego, San Diego.

Friedman, B. (2003), The LM curve: a not-so-fond farewell, NBER Working Paper, no. 10123, Cambridge/MA.

Fuhrer, J. C. (1997), The (un)importance of forward looking behavior in price setting, *Journal of Money, Credit and Banking*, Vol. 29, 338-350.

Fuhrer, J. C. and G. R. Moore (1995), Inflation persistence, *Quarterly Journal of Economics*, Vol. 110, 127-160.

Galí, J. (1999), Technology, employment, and the business cycle: do technology shocks explain aggregate fluctuations", *American Economic Review*, Vol. 89, 249-271.

Galí, J. (2002), New perspectives on monetary policy, inflation and business cycle, in: M. Dewatripont, Hansen, L. and S. Turnovsky (eds.) *Advances in*

Economic Theory – Vol. III, Cambridge University Press, Cambridge, 51-197.

Galí, J. (2004), On the role of technology shocks as a source of business cycles: some new evidence, *Journal of the European Economic Association*, Vol. 2, 372-380.

Galí. J. and M. Gertler (1999), Inflation dynamics: a structural econometric analysis, *Journal of Monetary Economics*, Vol. 44, 195-222.

Galí, J., Gertler, M. and D. López-Salido (2001), European inflation dynamics, *European Economic Review*, Vol. 45, 1237-1270.

Gerberding, C., Worms, A. and F. Seitz (2004), How the Bundesbank really conducted monetary policy: A analysis based on real-time data, Deutsche Bundesbank Discussion Paper No 25/2004, Frankfurt am Main.

Gerdesmeier, D. and B. Roffia, (2003), Empirical Estimates of Reaction Functions for the Euro Area, Working Paper No. 206, European Central Bank, Frankfurt.

Gerdesmeier, D. and B. Roffia, (2004), Taylor rules for the euro area: the issue of real-time data, Deutsche Bundesbank Discussion Paper, No. 37/2004, Frankfurt.

Gerlach-Kirsten, P. (2003), Interest Rate Reaction Functions and the Taylor Rule in the Euro Area, ECB Working Paper No. 258, Frankfurt.

Gerlach, S. and G. Schnabel, G. (1999), The Taylor Rule and Interest Rates in the EMU Area: A Note, BIS Working Paper No. 73, Basle.

Gertler, M., Gilchrist, S. and F. M. Natalucci (2001), External constraints on monetary policy and the financial accelerator, mimeo.

Geyer, A. L. and S. Pichler (1998), A State-Space Approach to Estimate and Test Multifactor Cox-Ingersoll-Ross Models of the Term Structure of Interest Rates, working paper, Department of Operations Research, University of Economics Vienna.

Giannoni, M. P. (2002), Does Model Uncertainty Justify Caution? Robust Optimal Monetary Policy in a Forward-Looking Model, *Macroeconomic Dynamics*, Vol. 6, 111-144.

Gong, F. F. and E. M. Romolona (1997), Two factors along the yield curve, *The Manchester School*, Vol. 65 (Supplement), 1-31.

Goodfriend, M. (1993), Interest Rate Policy and the Inflation Scare Problem: 1979-1992, Federal Reserve Bank of Richmond Economic Quarterly, Vol. 79, 1-24.

Goodfriend, M. (1998), Using the Term Structure of Interest Rates for Monetary Policy, Federal Reverse Bank of Richmond Economic Quarterly, Vol. 84, 13-30.

Goodfriend, M. (2000), Overcoming the zero bound on interest rate policy, *Journal of Money, Credit and Banking*, Vol. 32, 1007-1035.

Goodfriend, M. (2002), Monetary policy in the new neoclassical synthesis: a primer, *International Finance*, Vol. 5, 165-191.

Goodfriend, M. and R. King (1997), The new neoclassical synthesis and the role of monetary policy, *NBER Macroeconomics Annual 1997*, 231-283.

Goodhart, C. (1997), Why Do Monetary Authorities Smooth Interest Rates?, in: Collignon, S. (ed.), *European Monetary Policy*, 119-78.

Goodhart, C. (1999), Central Bankers and Uncertainty, *Bank of England Quarterly Bulletin*, Vol. 39, 102-114.

Hall, R. E. (1978), Stochastic implications of the life cyle-permanent income hypothesis: theory and evidence, *Journal of Political Economy*, Vol. 86, 971-987.

Hamalainen, N. (2004), A Survey of Taylor-Type Monetary policy Rules, Canadian Department of Finance, Working paper 2004-02.

Hamilton, A. C. (1994), Time Series Analysis, Princeton University Press, Princeton/NJ.

Hansen, L. (1982), Large sample properties of generalized method of moments estimators, Econometrica, Vol. 55, 1029-1054.

Harrison, M. and D. Kreps (1979), Martingales and Arbitrage in Multiperiod Security Markets, *Journal of Economic Theory*, Vol. 20, 381-408.

Harrison, M. and S. Pliska (1981), Martingales and Stochastic Integrals in the Theory of Continuous Trading, *Stochastic Processes and Their Application*, Vol. 11, 215-260.

Hayo, B and B. Hofmann, B. (2003), Monetary Policy Reaction Functions: ECB versus Bundesbank, ZEI Working Paper, Bonn.

Henderson, D. and W. J. McKibbin, (1993), A Comparison of Some Basic Monetary Policy Regimes for Open economies: Implications of Different Degrees of Instrument Adjustment and Wage Persistence, *Carnegie Rochester Conference Series on Public Policy*, Vol. 39, 221-318.

Hördahl, P., Tristani, O and D. Vestin (2003), A joint econometric model of macroeconomic and term structure dynamics, mimeo, European Central Bank.

Ireland, P. N. (2002), Endogenous money or sticky Prices, NBER Working Paper, no. 9390, Cambridge/MA.

Johnston, J. and J. DiNardo, (1997), Econometric methods, 4th edition, McGraw-Hill, New York.

Judd, K. L. (1998), Numerical Methods in Economics, MIT Press, Cambridge/MA.

Kimball, M. (1995), The quantitative analytics of the basic neomonetarist model, *Journal of Money, Credit, and Banking*, Vol. 27, 1241-1277.

King, R. G. (2000), The new IS-LM model: language, logic, and limits, *Federal Reserve Bank of Richmond Economic Quarterly*, Vol. 86, 45-103.

King, R. G. and A. Wolman (1996), Inflation targeting in a St. Louis model of the 21st century, *Federal Reserve Bank of St. Louis Review*, Vol. 78, 83-107.

Kydland, F. E. and E. C. Prescott (1977), Rules Rather Than Discretion, *Journal of Political Economy*, Vol. 85, 473-492.

Langetieg, T. (1980), A Multivariate Model of the Term Structure, *The Journal of Finance* 35, 71-97.

Lansing, K. J. and B. Trehan, B. (2003), Forward-looking Behaviour and the Optimal Discretionary Monetary Policy, Working Paper, Federal Reserve Bank of San Francisco.

LaSalle, J. P. (1986), The Stability and Control of Discrete Processes, Applied Mathematical Sciences No. 62, Springer, New York.

Laubach, T. and J. C. Williams (2001), Measuring the Natural Rate of Interest, Working Paper, Board of Governors of the Federal Reserve System, Washington/DC.

Levin, A., Wieland, V. and J. C. Williams (1999), Robustness of Simple Monetary Policy Rules under Model Uncertainty, in: Taylor, J. B. (ed.), *Monetary Policy Rules*, University of Chicago Press, Chicago, 263-299.

Linnemann, L. A. and A. Schabert (2003), Fiscal policy in the new neoclassical synthesis", *Journal of Money, Credit, and Banking*, Vol. 35, 911-929.

Litterman, R. and J. Scheinkman (1991), Common Factors Affecting Bond Return, *Journal of Fixed Income*, Vol. 1, 54-61.

Longstaff, F. and E. Schwartz (1992), Interest Rate Volatility and the Term Structure: A Two-Factor General Equilibrium Model, *The Journal of Finance*, Vol. 47, 1259-1282.

Lucas, R. E. (1973), Some international evidence on output-inflation tradeoffs, *American Economic Review*, Vol. 63, 326-334.

Lund, J. (1997), Econometric Analysis of Continuous-Time Arbitrage-Free Models of the Term Structure of Interest Rates, manuscript, Department of Finance, The Aarhus School of Business.

Maes, K. (2004), Modeling the Term Structure of Interest Rates: Where Do We Stand?, National Bank of Belgium Working Paper, No. 42, Brussels.

Mankiw, N. G. and R. Reis (2002), Sticky information versus sticky prices: a proposal to replace the new Keynesian Phillips curve, *Quarterly Journal of Economics*, Vol. 117, 1295-1328.

McCallum, B. T. (1981), Price Level Determinacy with an Interest-Rate Policy Rule and Rational Expectations, *Journal of Monetary Economics*, Vol. 8, 319-329.

McCallum, B. T. (1988), Robustness properties of a rule for monetary policy, *Carnegie-Rochester Conference Series on Public Policy*, Vol. 29, 173-204.

McCallum, B. T. (1999), Issues in the design of monetary policy rules, in: J.B. Taylor and M. Woodford (eds.) Handbook of Macroeconomics, Amsterdam.

McCallum, B. T. (2001), Inflation Targeting and the Liquidity Trap, in: Loayza, N. and R. Soto, (eds), Inflation Targeting: Design Performance, Challenges, Central Bank of Chile, 395 – 437.

McCallum, B. T. (2005), A Monetary Policy Rule for Automatic Prevention of a Liquidity Trap, NBER Working Paper, No. 11056, Cambridge/MA.

McCallum, B. T. and E. Nelson (1999a), An optimizing IS-LM spezification for monetary policy and business cycle analysis, *Journal of Money, Credit, and Banking*, Vol. 31, 296-316.

McCallum, B. T. and E. Nelson (1999b), Nominal income targeting in an open economy optimizing model, *Journal of Monetary Economics*, Vol. 43, 553-578.

McGrattan, E. R. (1994), The macroeconomic effects of distortionary taxation, *Journal of Monetary Economics*, Vol. 33, 573 – 601.

Merz, M. (1995), Search in the labor market and the real business cycle, *Journal of Monetary Economics*, Vol. 36, 269-300.

Meyer, L. H. (2001), Does Money Matter?, *Federal Reserve Bank of St. Louis Review*, Vol. 83, 1-15.

Modigliani, F. and R. Sutch (1966), Innovations in Interest Rate Policy, *American Economic Review* (Papers and Proceedings), Vol. 56, 178-97.

Modigliani, F. and R. Sutch, (1967), Debt Management and the Term Structure of Interest Rates: An Empirical Analysis of Recent Experience, *Journal of Political Economy*, Vol. 75, 568-89.

Neumann, M. J. M. and J. von Hagen (1993), Germany (chapter 9), in: Fratianni, M. und D. Salvatore (eds.), *Monetary Policy in Developed Economies, Studies in Comparative Economic Policies, Vol. 3*, North-Holland.

Neumann, M. J. M. and J. von Hagen (2002), Does Inflation Targeting Matter?, *Federal Reserve Bank of St. Louis Review*, Vol. 84, 127-148.

Newey, W. and K. West (1987), A simple, positive definite, heteroskedasticity and autocorrelation consistent covariance matrix, *Econometrica*, Vol. 55, 703-708.

Orphanides, A. (1998), Monetary Policy Evaluation with Noisy Information, *Finance and Economics Discussion Series Working Paper*, No. 1998-50, Board of Governors of the Federal Reserve System.

Orphanides, A. (1999), The quest for prosperity without inflation, mimeo. Board of Governors of the Federal Reserve System.

Orphanides, A. (2001), Monetary policy rules based on real-time data, *American Economic Review*, Vol. 91, 964-985.

Orphanides, A., Porter, R., Reifschneider, D., Tetlow, R. and F. Finan (2000), Errors in the measurement of the output gap and the design of monetary policy, *Journal of Economics and Business*, Vol. 52, 117-141.

Orphanides, A. and V. Wieland (1998), Price stability and monetary policy effectiveness when nominal interest rates are bound at zero, Finance and Economics Discussion Papers No. 98-35, Board of Governors of the Federal Reserve System, Washington, DC.

Piazzesi, M. (2003), Affine Term Structure Models, forthcoming *Handbook of Financial Econometrics*.

Robinson, T. and A. Stone (2005), Monetary Policy, Asset-Price Bubble and the Zero Lower Bound, NBER Working Paper No. 11105, Cambridge/MA.

Rotemberg, J. J. and M. Woodford (1997), An Optimization-Based Econometric Framework for the Evaluation of Monetary Policy, in Bernanke, B. and J. Rotemberg (eds.): *NBER Macroeconomics Annual 1997*, 297-346.

Rotemberg, J. J. and M. Woodford (1999), The cyclical behavior of prices and costs, chapter 16, in: J. B. Taylor and M. Woodford eds, *Handbook of Macroeconomics*, Elsevier Publisher, New York et al., pp. 1051-1135.

Rudebusch, G. D. (1995), Federal Reserve Interest Rate Targeting, Rational Expectations, and the Term Structure, *Journal of Monetary Economics*, Vol. 30, 245-74.

Rudebusch, G. D. (2001), Is the Fed too Timid? Monetary Policy in an Uncertain World, *Review of Economics and Statistics*, Vol. 83, 203-217.

Rudebusch, G. D. (2002), Term structure evidence on interest-rate smoothing and monetary policy inertia, *Journal of Monetary Economics*, Vol. 49, 1161-1187.

Rudebusch G. D. and Svensson, L. E. O. (1999), Policy Rules for Inflation Targeting, in: Taylor, J. B. (eds.), *Monetary Policy Rules*, University of Chicago Press, Chicago, 203-246.

Rudebusch. G. D. and T. Wu (2003), A Macro-Finance Model of the Term Structure, Monetary Policy, and the Economy, Federal Reserve Bank of San Francisco Working Paper No. 2003-17.

Sargent, T. J. and N. Wallace (1975), Rational Expectations, the Optimal Monetary Instrument, and the Optimal Money Supply Rule, *Journal of Political Economy*, Vol. 83, 241-254.

Schich, S. T. (1996), Alternative Specification of the German Term Structure and its Information Content Regarding Inflation, Discussion Paper 8/96, Deutsche Bundesbank, Frankfurt.

Shapiro, M. D. and M. Watson (1988), Sources of business cycle fluctuations", *NBER Macroeconomics Annual 1988*, 111-148.

Shea, J. (1998), What do technology shocks do?, *NBER Macroeconomics Annual 1998*, 275 - 310.

Shiller, R. J. (1990), The Term Structure of Interest Rates, in: Friedman, B. M. and F. H. Hahn (eds.), *Handbook of Monetary Economics*, Vol. 1 , Amsterdam, 627-722.

Smets, F. (2002), Output gap uncertainty: Does it matter for the Taylor rule?, *Empirical Economics*, Vol. 27, 113-129.

Smets, F. and R. Wouters (2002), An estimated stochastic dynamic general equilibrium model of the Euro area, ECB Working Paper, no. 171, European Central Bank, Frankfurt.

Söderlind, P. (1999), Solution and Estimation of RE Macromodels with Optimal Policy, *European Economic Review*, Vol. 43, 813-823.

Söderström, U. (2002), Monetary Policy with Uncertain Parameters, *Scandinavian Journal of Economics*, Vol. 104, 125-145.

Sun, T. (1992), Real and nominal Interest Rates: A Discrete-Time Model and Its Continuous-Time Limit, *Review of Financial Studies*, Vol. 5, 581-611.

Surico, P. (2003a), How Does the ECB Target Inflation? ECB Working Paper, no. 229, Frankfurt am Main.

Surico, P (2003b), Asymmetric Reaction Functions for the Euro Era, *Oxford Review of Economic Policy*, Vol. 19, 44-57.

Svensson, L. E. O. (1994), Estimating and Interpreting Forward Interest Rates: Sweden 1992- 94, IMF Working Paper 94/114, International Monetary Fund, Washington/DC.

Svensson, L. E. O. (1997), Inflation Forecast Targeting: Implementing and Monitoring Inflation Targets, *European Economic Review*, Vol. 41, 1111 – 1146.

Svensson, L. E. O. (1999), Inflation Targeting: Some Extensions, *Scandinavian Journal of Economics*, Vol. 101, 337-361.

Svensson, L. E. O. (2000), Open-economy inflation targeting, *Journal of International Economics*, Vol. 50, 155-183.

Svensson, L. E. O. (2001), The Zero Bound in an Open-Economy: A Foolproof Way of Escaping from a Liquidity Trap, *Monetary and Economic Studies*, Vol. 19, Bank of Japan, 277-312.

Svensson, L.E.O. (2003), Escaping from a Liquidity Trap and Deflation: The Foolproof Way and Others, *Journal of Economic Perspectives*, Vol. 17, 145-166.

Staiger, D., Stock, J. and M. Watson (1996), How precise are estimates of the natural rate of unemployment, in: Romer, D und Romer, C. (eds.), *Reducing Inflation: Motivation and Strategy*, University of Chicago Press.

Sylos Labini, P. (1988), The great debates on the laws of returns and the value of capital: when will economists finally accept their own logic?, *Banca Nazionale Del Lavoro Quarterly Review*, Vol. 41, 263-291.

Taylor, J. B. (1980), Aggregate dynamics and staggered contracts, *Journal of Political Economy*, Vol. 88, 1-23.

Taylor, J. B. (1993), Discretion versus policy rules in practice, *Carnegie-Rochester Conference Series on Public Policy*, Vol. 39, 195-214.

Taylor, J. B. (1999a), Staggered price and wage setting in macroeconomics, chapter 15, in: J. B. Taylor and M. Woodford (eds.), *Handbook of Macroeconomics*, Elsevier Publisher, New York et al.,1009-1050.

Taylor, J. B. (ed.,1999b), *Monetary Policy Rules*, University of Chicago Press, Chicago.

Taylor, J. B. (1999c), A historical analysis of monetary policy rules, in: J. B. Taylor (ed.) Monetary Policy Rules, Chicago 1999, 319-341.

Taylor, J. B. (1999d), The robustness and efficiency of monetary policy rules as guidelines for interest rate setting by the European central bank, *Journal of Monetary Economics*, Vol. 43, 655-679.

Tetlow, R. J. and P. von zur Muehlen (2001), Robust Monetary Policy with Misspecified Models: Does Uncertainty Always Call for Attenuated Policy, *Journal of Economic Dynamics and Control*, Vol. 25, 911-949.

Uhlig, H. (2004), Do technology shocks lead to a fall in total hours worked?, *Journal of the European Economic Association*, Vol. 2, 361-371.

Vasicek, O. (1977), An Equilibrium Characterization of the Term Structure, *Journal of Financial Economics*, Vol. 5, 177-188.

Von Hagen, J. (1988), Alternative Operating Regimes for Money Stock Control in West Germany: An Empirical Evaluation, *Weltwirtschaftliches Archiv*, Vol. 124, 89-107.

Von Hagen, J. (1990), Operating Targets and Information Variables in Monetary Control, *Weltwirtschaftliches Archiv*, Vol. 126, 643-661.

Walsh, C. E. (2003), Monetary Theory and Policy, 2nd edition, MIT Press, Cambridge/MA.

Wicksell, K. (1898), Interest and Prices, English translation by R. F. Kahn for the Royal Economic Society, Macmillan, London 1936. Reprinted Augustus M Kelley, New York 1962.

Wieland, V. (1998), Monetary Policy and Uncertainty About the Natural Unemployment Rate, Finance and Economics Discussion Papers No. 98-22, Board of Governors of the Federal Reserve System, Washington, DC.

Woodford, M. (1999), Optimal Monetary Policy Inertia, NBER Working Paper, No. 7261, Cambridge/MA.

Woodford, M. (2001a), The Taylor rule and optimal monetary policy, *American Economic Review* (Papers and Proceedings), Vol. 91, 232-237.

Woodford, M. (2001b), Inflation Stabilization and Welfare, NBER Working Paper, No. 8071, Cambridge/MA.

Woodford, M. (2003), Interest and Prices: Foundations of a Theory of Monetary Policy, Princeton University Press.

Woodford, M. (2004), Inflation Targeting and Optimal Monetary Policy, *Federal Reserve Bank of St. Louis Review*, Vol. 86, 15-41.

Yates, T. (2004), Monetary Policy and the Zero Lower Bound to Interest Rates: A Review, *Journal of Economic Surveys*, Vol. 18, 427-480.

Yun, T. (1996), Nominal price rigidity, money supply endogeneity, and business cycles, *Journal of Monetary Economics*, Vol. 37, 345-370.

Studien zu Internationalen Wirtschaftsbeziehungen

Herausgegeben von Prof. Dr. Michael Frenkel

Band 1 Christiane Nickel: Insider und Outsider bei der Osterweiterung der Europäischen Währungsunion. 2002.

Band 2 Georg Stadtmann: Noise-Trader auf Devisenmärkten. Viel Lärm um Nichts? 2002.

Band 3 Wolf-Heimo Grieben: Trade and Technology as Competing Explanations for Rising Inequality. An Endogenous Growth Perspective. 2003.

Band 4 Alexander Mende: Order Flow Analyses and Foreign Exchange Dealing. 2005.

Band 5 Torsten Wezel: Determinants of Foreign Direct Investment in Emerging Markets. An Empirical Study of FDI Flows from Germany and its Banking Sector. 2005.

Band 6 Steffen Kern: The Behaviour of Interest Groups in Trade and Industry Towards Monetary Policy and Central Banks. Theory and Evidence on Germany and the Euro Area. 2006.

Band 7 Holger Michaelis: Kapitalbilanzliberalisierung in der Volksrepublik China und ihre Einbettung in den volkswirtschaftlichen Reformprozess. 2006.

Band 8 Ralf Fendel: Monetary Policy, Interest Rate Rules, and the Term Structure of Interest Rates. Theoretical Considerations and Empirical Implications. 2007.

www.peterlang.de

Peter Lang · Europäischer Verlag der Wissenschaften

Marc Peter Radke

Explaining Financial Crises

A Cyclical Approach

Frankfurt am Main, Berlin, Bern, Bruxelles, New York, Oxford, Wien, 2005.
XX, 410 pp., 33 fig., 17 tab.
Hohenheimer volkswirtschaftliche Schriften.
Editor in charge: Harald Hagemann. Vol. 53
ISBN 3-631-54350-6 / US-ISBN 0-8204-7777-X · pb. € 68.50*

This book develops a new theoretical approach to the explanation of systemic financial crises in industrial and emerging market countries. In contrast to standard models, the present *cyclical* approach is consistent with the following three stylized facts. Firstly, systemic financial crises are a recurrent phenomenon generally accompanied by excessive boom-bust cycles. Secondly, the frequency of financial crisis cycles is very irregular. Thirdly, most financial crisis cycles are initiated by positive shocks to profit expectations which induce an unsustainable build-up of financial fragility driven by *irrational exuberance*. The present approach is based on a sophisticated balancesheet structure with many assets, as well as on an expectation formation scheme which combines the rational expectations hypothesis with Keynes' *Beauty Contest Theory*.

Contents: Financial Crises and Financial Instability: Definitions and Principles · Stylized Facts and Standard Theory of Financial Crises · A Model of Financial Crises and Endogenous Fluctuations in Industrial Countries · A Model of Financial Crises and Endogenous Fluctuations in Emerging Market Countries · A Calibration Model of Financial Crises in Emerging Markets